Studies in Musical Genesis and Structure

General Editor: Lewis Lockwood, Harvard University

Studies in Musical Genesis and Structure

Anna Bolena and the Artistic Maturity of Gaetano Donizetti
Philip Gossett

Beethoven's Diabelli Variations
William Kinderman

Robert Schumann and the Study of Orchestral Composition
The Genesis of the First Symphony Op. 38
Jon W. Finson

Euryanthe and Carl Maria von Weber's Dramaturgy of German
Opera
Michael C. Tusa

Beethoven's 'Appassionata' Sonata
Martha Frohlich

Richard Strauss's *Elektra*
Bryan Gilliam

Wagner's
Das Rheingold

WARREN DARCY

CLARENDON PRESS · OXFORD

Oxford University Press, Walton Street, Oxford OX2 6DP

Oxford New York
Athens Auckland Bangkok Bombay
Calcutta Cape Town Dar es Salaam Delhi
Florence Hong Kong Istanbul Karachi
Kuala Lumpur Madras Madrid Melbourne
Mexico City Nairobi Paris Singapore
Taipei Tokyo Toronto

and associated companies in
Berlin Ibadan

Oxford is a trade mark of Oxford University Press

Published in the United States by
Oxford University Press Inc., New York

First published 1993
New as paperback 1996

British Library Cataloguing in Publication Data
Data available

Library of Congress Cataloging in Publication Data
Darcy, Warren.
Wagner's Das Rheingold / Warren Darcy.
(Studies in musical genesis and structure)
Includes bibliographical references and index.
1. Wagner, Richard, 1813–1883. Ring des Nibelungen. Rheingold.
I. Title. II. Title: Rheingold. III. Series.
MT100.W26D33 1993 782.1—dc20 93-20275
ISBN 0–19–816603–6 (pbk.)

Printed in Great Britain
on acid-free paper by
Biddles Ltd, Guildford and King's Lynn

For
Marsha

Editor's Preface

THIS series provides a number of monographs, each dealing with a single work by an important composer. The main focus of each book is on the compositional process by which the work developed from antecedent stages, so far as these can be determined from the sources. In each case the genesis of the work is connected to an analytical overview of the final version. Each monograph is written by a specialist, and, apart from the general theme of the series, no artificial uniformity is imposed. The individual character of both work and evidence, as well as the author's special critical viewpoint, dictates differences in emphasis and treatment. Thus some studies may stress a combination of sketch evidence and analysis, while others may shift the emphasis to the position of the work within its genre and context. Although no such series could possibly aim at being comprehensive, it will deal with a representative body of important works by composers of stature across the centuries.

Although the fundamental importance of *Das Rheingold* in Wagner's artistic development has long been clear, intensive studies of it as an individual work, apart from its function as Prelude to the *Ring* as a whole, have been few and far between. Perhaps this is owing in part to its relative obscurity when compared to the other monumental parts of the *Ring* cycle. Even for convinced Wagnerians this work presents problems of comprehension not only for its dramatic material but for the complexity of its musical language, which adheres more closely than that of any later Wagner work to the precepts for a new kind of symphonic drama that he had laid down in *Opera and Drama*.

Now Warren Darcy proposes a new and solidly detailed study of the whole of *Das Rheingold*, based on close study of the surviving textual and musical sources and providing an analytical overview of each major unit of the work and of the entire opera. His approach goes some distance towards countering a recent and widely influential view of Wagner, namely, that he abandoned all concern with architectural musical form in structuring his larger works. The result is a carefully wrought interpretation, which both analyses the work and elucidates its compositional history. It should deepen and extend the reader's understanding of *Das Rheingold* not only as a monumental musical structure but as a complex drama whose every word and gesture were conceived by Wagner as being co-ordinated with his musical ideas and with the larger complex patterns into which both text and music are developed. All this is reason enough to welcome his work to this series.

Lewis Lockwood
Harvard University

Author's Preface

IT has become almost *de rigueur* to begin a book on Wagner by apologizing for having written it, or at least rationalizing adding to the already voluminous Wagner bibliography. Be that as it may, the author of a new Wagner study cannot but feel keenly aware of the great debt he owes his predecessors; names such as Otto Strobel, Curt von Westernhagen, Carl Dahlhaus, Robert Bailey, Deryck Cooke, and John Deathridge loom large in this respect. Without the ground-breaking work of these and many other scholars, this book would never have been written.

I am greatly indebted to numerous individuals and institutions as well. Oberlin College supported my work through several grants: a Curriculum Development Fellowship to prepare a course on the *Ring*; a Research Status Appointment which enabled me to carry out several months of archival work in Bayreuth; a Grant-in-Aid that underwrote a visit to the Scheide Library at Princeton University; and another grant that offset the cost of preparing the musical examples. Dr Manfred Eger, Director of the National Archiv der Richard-Wagner-Stiftung, granted me unlimited access to Wagner's textual and musical manuscripts, while his assistant, Herr Günther Fischer, could not have been more helpful nor more gracious. Mr William A. Scheide allowed me to examine his portion of the *Partiturerstschrift* on two separate occasions, during which I was assisted by his librarians Ms Janet Ing and Mr William Stoneman.

I owe a special debt of gratitude to my editor Lewis Lockwood, whose suggestions greatly improved the book's readability, and who convinced me of the wisdom of incorporating frequent cross-references to the Schirmer vocal score. I would also like to thank Bruce Phillips, who encouraged and supported this project from its inception, as well as the anonymous Oxford readers, whose perceptive criticism influenced the study in many subtle ways.

Other individuals who contributed in one way or another to the genesis of this book include Jim Hepokoski, who read and commented upon initial drafts of Chapters 4 and 5; Walter Frisch, who edited the version of Chapter 6 that appeared in *19th Century Music*; Allen Cadwallader, who is probably unaware of the extent to which the analytical portions of this book were influenced by our lunchtime discussions about Schenker; Speight Jenkins, who commissioned several articles on the *Ring* for the Seattle Opera's programme booklets, thereby allowing me to try out several ideas which found their way into Chapter 3; Barry Millington and Stewart Spencer, who gave me the opportunity to publish some of my work on the *Ring* manuscripts, a process that enriched Chapter 2; and Robert Bailey and David Lewin, who wrote grant recommendations for me. In addition, this study was enhanced in a myriad of ways by conversations with past and present colleagues at Oberlin, including Walter Aschaffenburg, Peter Spycher, and Sylvan Suskin.

Mention should also be made of the hospitality shown my wife and myself during our five-month sojourn in Bayreuth. Those who made us feel at home in a foreign country include our landlady, Frau Gschwilm; our neighbours, Frau Fleissner and her daughter Martha, who also placed their apartment at our disposal on a return visit; and our friends Hilary and Klaus Maier.

I conclude by thanking the four people without whose love, support, and encouragement this project would never have been conceived, let alone brought to fruition: my parents, Gerald and Melodia Darcy; my sister, Virginia Ludwig; and above all my wife Marsha, to whom I owe more than words can express.

W.J.D.
Oberlin, Ohio
May 1992

Contents

Abbreviations   xiii

Structural Outline of *Das Rheingold*   xiv

1 Preliminaries   1

2 The Documentary Sources   6

3 The Forging of the Text   25

4 Analytical Positions   45

5 The Opera as a Whole   59

6 *Creatio ex Nihilo*: The Prelude   62

7 Scene One   87

8 First Transformation and Scene Two   127

9 Second Transformation and Scene Three   161

10 Third Transformation and Scene Four   181

11 Summary and Conclusion   215

Appendix: Transcriptions from Wagner's Complete Draft   220

Works Cited   248

Index   255

Abbreviations

Full bibliographical details are given in *Works Cited*.

GS   *Gesammelte Schriften und Dichtungen von Richard Wagner*

RWPW   *Richard Wagner's Prose Works*, trans. Ellis

SB   *Richard Wagner, Sämtliche Briefe*

WWV   *Wagner Werk-Verzeichnis (WWV): Verzeichnis der musika-
        lischen Werke Richard Wagners und ihrer Quellen*

Structural Outline of Das Rheingold

Section/Dramatic content	Key(s)	Location
SCENE 1		
PRELUDE The depths of the Rhine.	E♭ major	1/1/1 (m. 1)
EPISODE 1 Alberich woos the Rhinedaughters.	E♭ major	5/4/1 (m. 137)
TRANSITION Alberich chases the Rhinedaughters.	modulatory	28/1/1 (m. 448)
EPISODE 2 Alberich renounces love and steals the gold.	C major → C minor	31/1/3 (m. 514)
POSTLUDE Darkness in the depths.	V/C minor	52/1/2 (m. 716)
FIRST TRANSFORMATION	modulatory	53/4/3 (m. 744)
SCENE 2		
EPISODE 3 Wotan hails the fortress.	D♭ major	55/1/1 (m. 769)
EPISODE 4 Wotan and Fricka argue.	D minor	58/1/4 (m. 826)
EPISODE 5 Freia flees the giants.	E minor	63/3/1 (m. 914)
EPISODE 6 The giants demand their wages.	F major/minor → D major	68/1/1 (m. 984)
EPISODE 7 Donner and Froh arrive.	D major	75/3/1 (m. 1134)
EPISODE 8 Loge finally appears.	F♯ major/minor	77/4/2 (m. 1184)
EPISODE 9 Loge's tale of the ring.	D major	84/4/4 (m. 1321)

Section/Dramatic content	Key(s)	Location
EPISODE 10 The giants carry off Freia.	F major/minor	98/1/1 (m. 1587)
EPISODE 11 The premature twilight.	E minor	103/1/1 (m. 1669)
SECOND TRANSFORMATION	modulatory	110/2/3 (m. 1803)
SCENE 3		
EPISODE 12 Alberich's tyranny and Mime's woe.	B♭ minor	114/1/1 (m. 1878)
EPISODE 13 Alberich's downfall.	A major	134/5/1 (m. 2320)
THIRD TRANSFORMATION The ascent from Nibelheim.	modulatory	155/2/1 (m. 2752)
SCENE 4		
EPISODE 14 Alberich loses all and curses the ring.	B♭ minor → B minor	160/1/1 (m. 2857)
EPISODE 15 The giants bring back Freia.	C major	178/5/6 (m. 3208)
EPISODE 16 The gods ransom Freia.	E♭ major → C minor	181/4/3 (m. 3264)
EPISODE 17 Erda's warning.	C♯ minor	192/3/1 (m. 3456)
EPISODE 18 Wotan yields the ring; the curse begins to work.	E♭ major/minor	195/2/4 (m. 3527)
EPISODE 19 Donner summons the storm.	B♭ major	203/2/2 (m. 3666)
EPISODE 20 Entrance of the gods into Valhalla.	D♭ major	208/3/1 (m. 3713)

Note: The main entry in the 'Location' column refers to the Schirmer vocal score of *Das Rheingold* (page/system/measure number); the parenthetical entry gives the measure number as counted from the beginning of the opera.

1 Preliminaries

Mark well my new poem—it contains the beginning and end of
the world!

(Wagner to Franz Liszt, 11 February 1853)

Opera-goers settling into their seats for a performance of Richard
Wagner's *Das Rheingold* often feel, as the house lights dim and the
double basses begin their familiar drone, as if they are embarking
upon a long journey—an odyssey through time and space that will
encompass, as Wagner himself put it, 'the beginning and end of the
world'. A book about this opera may itself be viewed as an extended
journey through Wagner's extraordinary dramatic–musical universe.
Before setting forth, however, it may be worthwhile to establish both
the purpose and itinerary of such a trip.

Let us begin with a question: Why is *Das Rheingold* a suitable
subject for scholarly investigation? How—when the existing Wagner
literature bulks so large—can such a study be justified?

When Wagner began the music of *Das Rheingold* on 1 November
1853, it marked his return to operatic composition after a hiatus of
almost five years. During this interval, he had written little music but
a great deal of argumentative prose, as well as the poem of the *Ring*.
Das Rheingold signified his definitive break with the operatic conventions whose presence can still be felt even in such a progressive
work as *Lohengrin*, and the change from the *Endreim* of his earlier
librettos to the *Stabreim* of the *Ring* poem exerted considerable
influence upon his musical phraseology. In addition, the whole question of dramatic–musical form, and the role of tonality in articulating
this form, had to be reconsidered. Because *Das Rheingold* is such a
watershed in Wagner's compositional output—and in the history of
music in general—it may seem rather astonishing that the opera has
not already undergone close musicological scrutiny. Yet such indeed
is the case.

Wagner scholarship has taken enormous strides over the past few
decades, both in the United States and Europe. Nevertheless, monographs which treat complete operas are still few in number, fewer still
if one is seeking sophisticated musical analysis.[1] Even in the realm of

---

[1] A recent exception is Patrick McCreless's *Wagner's 'Siegfried': Its Drama, History, and*

sketch study (in which the analytical element is often secondary or non-existent), extended discussions of the *Ring* operas are surprisingly scarce.[2] Although the recently published *Wagner-Werk-Verzeichnis* (*WWV*) has finally established Wagner sketch study on a firm basis, few scholars to date have taken full advantage of this magnificent tome.[3]

Because no extended study of *Das Rheingold* exists—let alone one which incorporates recent developments in Music Theory and Wagner scholarship—the need for a book such as this should be apparent. What methodology—or combination of methodologies—might best serve its purpose?

The availability of Wagner's sketches and drafts suggests that a careful study of the opera might well be founded upon an examination of these documents. Yet sketch study can be employed for various ends: to establish chronology, to verify biographical facts, or to elucidate compositional process. Because Wagner carefully preserved and dated his sketches, chronology is seldom an issue. As regards biography, some scholars have made almost a fetish out of using the manuscripts to disprove certain statements in Wagner's autobiography *Mein Leben*.[4] This can be an amusing and by no means unproductive pastime, but its relentless scepticism eventually wears rather thin. Far more promising is the use of sketches to elucidate compositional process. On the one hand, knowledge of how a master composer like Wagner actually went about putting notes on paper is fascinating in its own right; on the other, such knowledge might well serve as an aid to interpretation and analysis.

Whatever theoretical stance we ultimately adopt, it seems reasonable to assume that our analytical endeavours can be guided (and at times even corrected) by a study of compositional process. At the same time, a grasp of the opera's formal/tonal structure cannot but inform our study of the manuscripts. Exactly *how* sketch study relates

Music (Ann Arbor, Mich., 1982). There remains, of course, Alfred Lorenz's monumental four-volume study *Das Geheimnis der Form bei Richard Wagner* (Berlin, 1924–33; repr. Tutzing, 1966). Both books are discussed in Ch. 4.

[2] Among the important shorter studies that have appeared are two classic articles by Robert Bailey: 'Wagner's Musical Sketches for *Siegfrieds Tod*', in *Studies in Music History: Essays for Oliver Strunk*, ed. Harold Powers (Princeton, NJ, 1968), 459–94; and 'The Structure of the *Ring* and its Evolution', *19th Century Music*, 1 (1977), 48–61. Also worthy of mention is Reinhold Brinkmann's '"Drei der Fragen stell' ich mir frei": Zur Wanderer-Szene im I. Akt von Wagners *Siegfried*', in *Jahrbuch des Staatlichen Instituts für Musik-Forschung Preussischer Kulturbesitz* (Berlin, 1972), 120–62.

[3] *Verzeichnis der musikalischen Werke Richard Wagners und ihrer Quellen* (hereafter *WWV*), ed. John Deathridge, Martin Geck, and Egon Voss (Mainz, 1986).

[4] See, for example, John Deathridge, 'Cataloguing Wagner', in *The Richard Wagner Centenary in Australia*, ed. Peter Dennison (Adelaide, 1985), 185–99. Chapter 6 of the present study challenges one of Deathridge's 'demystifications'—that of the infamous La Spezia 'vision'.

to analysis (or even *if* the two can be properly related) has of course formed the subject of much recent controversy. The interrelationship of the two is admittedly very difficult—perhaps impossible—to define in the abstract, but it *can* be demonstrated, and this I have attempted in Chapters 6 to 10.

The purpose of this book then is twofold: (1) to trace the genesis of *Das Rheingold* through the various textual and musical sketches and drafts to the final score, and (2) to develop a theoretical framework within which the opera can be meaningfully analysed.

These two purposes are already interrelated. Wagner's sketches and drafts display a 'layering' effect, in which the work gradually increases in complexity: the basic dramatic idea outlined in the prose sketch is expanded in the prose draft and versified in the verse draft; the text is then set in the complete musical draft, whose sparse texture is fleshed out and orchestrated in the instrumentation draft. In Schenkerian terms, the manuscripts as a whole show a gradual 'composing-out' of the work from 'background' to 'foreground'.

It may be well to alert the reader about various sidepaths our investigation will *not* explore. This book contains no detailed exegesis of the dramatic function, emotional affect, and melodic interdependence of the so-called 'leitmotifs'; no extensive examination of Wagner's literary sources; and no thoroughgoing interpretation of the 'symbolic meaning' of the opera. These topics have been discussed at length by many scholars,[5] and little purpose would be served by rehashing them yet again. In addition, the present study does not attempt to trace the growth of the work through Wagner's correspondence (except where a given letter is critical to understanding some crucial point), nor does it discuss the opera's reception history. By avoiding such well-trodden territory, it is hoped that the reader will discover either new facts, or new interpretations of old ones, on almost every page.

Before proceeding further, certain advance preparations are necessary. Chapter 2 offers a chronological overview of the evolution of the *Ring* poem and the musical composition of *Das Rheingold*, and describes the relevant manuscript sources. Chapter 3 offers a more detailed discussion of the evolution of the *Rheingold* text, outlines the dramatic parallelisms between *Siegfried's Tod* and *Das Rheingold*,

[5] Notably by Robert Donington in *Wagner's 'Ring' and its Symbols* (London, 1963, 1969, 1974) and Deryck Cooke in *I Saw the World End* (London, 1979). For a more recent study of the *Ring*'s literary sources, see Elizabeth Magee, *Richard Wagner and the Nibelungs* (Oxford, 1990). Because Magee was able to consult the loan journals of the Sächsische Landesbibliothek at Dresden, her bibliographical research is more reliable than Cooke's. Nevertheless, Cooke's interpretation of Wagner's manipulation of his sources has yet to be surpassed.

and explains how various elements from *Siegfried's Tod*, *Der junge Siegfried*, and *Die Walküre* found their way into *Das Rheingold*. Chapter 4 summarizes the more important analytical trends in Wagner scholarship, as a context for the ensuing discussion. Chapter 5 offers a preliminary structural overview of the entire opera, and sets forth the analytical assumptions upon which this study is based.

Our journey proper begins with Chapter 6, an account of the compositional genesis, musical structure, and metaphorical meaning of the drama's famous Prelude. Chapters 7 to 10 discuss each of the opera's twenty main divisions or 'episodes', in most cases tracing the unit's textual and musical genesis before proceeding to a consideration of its formal/tonal design. Chapter 11 summarizes the results of the investigation and offers a final structural overview of the work. The Appendix contains transcriptions of selected portions of Wagner's complete draft (*Gesamtentwurf*), while *Works Cited* lists the manuscripts and other sources upon which the study is based.

Such a book must necessarily make some demands upon the reader. It presupposes not only a certain familiarity with the *Ring* in general and its 'Preliminary Evening' in particular, but a willingness to consult the score frequently. In fact, continual reference to either an orchestral or a piano–vocal score is a virtual necessity for the full comprehension of Chapters 6 to 10. Unfortunately, this necessitates

TABLE 1.1 Guide to measure-numbering

Page	Measure	Page	Measure	Page	Measure
1	1	75	1127	150	2653
5	125	80	1226	155	2748
10	201	85	1323	160	2857
15	264	90	1427	165	2932
20	347	95	1525	170	3022
25	420	100	1619	175	3119
30	493	105	1707	180	3233
35	549	110	1799	185	3333
40	585	115	1894	190	3416
45	643	120	1984	195	3522
50	690	125	2099	200	3608
55	769	130	2217	205	3683
60	853	135	2326	210	3734
65	937	140	2427	215	3813
70	1022	145	2544	220	3865

Note: Page numbers refer to the Schirmer vocal score of *Das Rheingold*. The first measure of each page is given.

numbering the measures in advance, an admittedly tedious labour which I have attempted to lighten through numerous textual cues, as well as frequent cross-references to the widely available Schirmer vocal score (Table 1.1 is offered as a guide to the measure-numbering process). In addition, some familiarity with the precepts and graphing techniques of Schenkerian analysis is assumed; however, the reader lacking such background should still be able to navigate the analytical chapters without undue difficulty.

2 *The Documentary Sources*

> Great plans for Siegfried: three dramas, with a three-act prelude.
> —When all the German theatres collapse in ruins, I shall run up
> a new one on the Rhine, summon people together, and perform
> the whole thing in the space of a week.
>
> (Wagner to Theodor Uhlig, October 1851)

I. COMPOSITIONAL HISTORY

The compositional genesis of *Das Rheingold* is, of course, intimately
bound up with that of the *Ring* as a whole. This is especially true of
the text, whose evolution is traced in Chapter 3. The story of how
Wagner wrote the *Ring* has been retold many times, and there would
be little point in rehearsing it all here. The purpose of the present
chapter is to acquaint the reader with the autograph sources upon
which this study is based and to present a general outline of Wagner's
compositional methods.

We first turn to the text. Wagner's usual procedure for constructing
an operatic libretto involved four distinct steps: a brief, succinct prose
sketch (*Prosaskizze*), a more elaborate prose draft (*Prosaentwurf*),
a verse draft (*Erstschrift des Textbuches*), and a fair copy of the poem
(*Reinschrift des Textbuches*).[1] Sometimes, for one reason or another,
he made more than one fair copy of the poem (in which case the first
copy may be called the *Zweitschrift*, the second the *Drittschrift*, etc).
The chronology in Table 2.1 shows how this four-step procedure
generated each of the dramas in the tetralogy.

To say that Wagner conceived the text of the *Ring* 'backwards'
is thus to oversimplify and distort an extremely complex process.
As Table 2.1 shows, the *Ring* poem evolved through several clearly demarcated phases, the first of which comprised the writing of
Siegfried's Tod.[2] In the case of this drama, the usual prose sketch was

---

[1] The German terminology used to describe the manuscripts is that employed by *WWV*.
Where possible, I have used English equivalents (not literal translations) of these terms.
Sometimes manuscripts are cited by their *WWV* catalogue numbers; for example, the complete
draft (*Gesamtentwurf*) of *Das Rheingold* is listed in *WWV* as 'WWV 86A Musik II'. See *Works
Cited* for a complete list of manuscripts and other sources cited in the present study.

[2] Although the apostrophe was dropped from the title in the 1871 *Gesammelte Schriften* (*GS*)
version of the poem, it appears in all the textual manuscripts as well as the 1853 private imprint.
I have therefore retained Wagner's original spelling.

TABLE 2.1 Rough chronology of *Ring* poem and musical composition of *Das Rheingold*

1848	Oct.	First Nibelung 'scenario': draft and fair copy
		Siegfried's Tod: prose draft
	Nov.	verse draft
	[Dec.]	first fair copy of poem
		first revision and second fair copy of poem
1850	[May]	third fair copy of poem
	[Aug.]	music begun and abandoned
1851	[May]	*Der junge Siegfried*: prose sketches
	May	prose draft
	June	verse draft
	[July]	first fair copy of poem
	[Aug.]	second fair copy of poem
		music begun and abandoned
	[Oct.]	*Das Rheingold*: prose sketch
	[Nov.]	*Die Walküre*: prose sketch
1852	[Winter]	*Das Rheingold/Die Walküre*: supplementary prose sketches (in pocket notebook)
	March	*Das Rheingold*: prose draft
	May	*Die Walküre*: prose draft
	June	*Die Walküre*: verse draft
	Sept.–Nov.	*Das Rheingold*: verse draft
	[Nov.–Dec.]	*Der junge Siegfried*: first revision
		Siegfried's Tod: second revision
		Das Rheingold/Die Walküre: fair copies of poems
		Siegfried's Tod: fourth fair copy of poem
1853	[Feb.]	Private printing of *Ring* poem (fifty copies)
	Sept.	La Spezia 'vision'
	Nov.–	*Das Rheingold*: complete (musical) draft
1854	Jan.	
	Feb.–May	draft of full score
	Feb.–Sept.	fair copy of full score (lost)
	Summer	anonymous copy of Prelude
1854–5		copy of full score by Friedrich Wölfel

Note: Brackets indicate that the manuscript lacks a date. The 1848 textual autographs are written in German script, the rest in Latin script. Terms used to designate the manuscripts are English equivalents of the German terminology employed in *WWV*.

replaced by a lengthy 'scenario', in which Wagner outlined his entire reconstruction of the Nibelung myth. The draft of this scenario, which bears the title *Die Nibelungensage (Mythus)*, was completed on 4 October 1848, and was followed four days later by a fair copy entitled *Die Sage von den Nibelungen*. The text was published for the first time in Wagner's *Gesammelte Schriften und Dichtungen (GS)*;[3] because the latter contains minor variants not present in the original draft, scholars have naturally assumed that the *GS* version was based upon Wagner's fair copy. However, a perusal of the latter reveals that it too diverges from the *GS* text; in fact, the fair copy contains variants not carried over into the *GS* version, while the *GS* version exhibits variants not present in the fair copy! This mystery was solved by the present author's discovery (in early 1987) of a hitherto unknown copy of the 1848 scenario. This ink copy, found in a metal box in the Bayreuth Archives, is written in an unknown hand, and follows the wording of the original draft (not the fair copy); it contains pencil corrections in Wagner's hand, and clearly served as *Stichvorlage* for the *GS* printing. The title is changed to *Der Nibelungen Mythus. Als Entwurf zu einem Drama*, the names 'Wodan' and 'Brünhild' are altered throughout to 'Wotan' and 'Brünnhild', and there are various changes in punctuation and paragraph division which agree with the *GS* printing.[4]

Because much of this 'scenario' was devoted to the story of Siegfried's downfall, it replaced Wagner's customary prose sketch. By 20 October, he had finished a prose draft entitled *Siegfried's Tod (Oper in drei Akten)*. In late October or early November he drafted a Prologue, intended to give the audience a bit more information about the drama's prehistory as well as introduce them to Siegfried and Brünnhilde. Then, between 12 and 28 November, he drafted the poem of *Siegfried's Tod*, which had now become 'eine grosse Heldenoper in drei Akten'. Although the manuscript of this verse draft is now in an inaccessible private collection, a photocopy is available in the Bayreuth Archives.

In early December(?) 1848 Wagner prepared a fair copy (now in the Stadtbibliothek Winterthur, Switzerland), in which he altered some scenic directions, but left the verses largely unchanged. Perhaps almost immediately he revised the drama, entering revisions in both manuscripts. Years later, Friedrich Nietzsche prepared a copy to serve as *Druckvorlage* for the *GS* printing;[5] he worked from Wagner's fair copy, in which the author had restored (in pencil) the original wording. The *GS* version of *Siegfried's Tod* thus represents the pre-revision (first version) wording of the fair copy, which, as noted, does differ in some details from the original draft.

Wagner next made a second fair copy of the poem, reflecting the

[3] 10 vols., Leipzig, 1871–83. See vol. ii (1871), 201–14.

[4] I am grateful to Herr Günther Fischer, *Diplombibliothekar* of the Nationalarchiv der Richard-Wagner-Stiftung in Bayreuth, for drawing my attention to this anonymous copy of the 1848 scenario, which is not mentioned in *WWV*. It was presumably made in 1871.

[5] *GS* ii. 215–300.

changes of the first revision (one of which was the addition of the 'Hagen's Watch' episode to Act I); he now classified the work as 'eine Heldenoper in drei Akten'. This undated manuscript is also unavailable, but a facsimile of the final page shows that, like the preceding documents, it is written in German script.[6] This suggests that it predates 18 December 1848, the day Wagner began to use Latin script, which would contradict Otto Strobel's suggested dating of early 1849. Two marginal additions (discussed in Chapter 3) are also written in German script, and although the verses in the right margin are usually assigned a much earlier date than those in the left, both marginalia might well pre-date 18 December 1848.

In May 1850, the hope of publication prompted Wagner to make yet a third fair copy of the poem, which he now called merely 'eine Tragödie'; this manuscript (presently in the Bayreuth Archives) thus represents the second copy of the first revision. It is written in Latin script, and presumably follows the wording of the second fair copy; however, because it was later used for the second (1852) revision of *Siegfried's Tod*, some of the original pages were discarded and are now lost. The final pages are among those missing, so it is impossible to tell whether any of the marginal verses on the last page of the second fair copy were incorporated into Brünnhilde's final speech.

Sometime that summer (probably during August), Wagner began and abandoned some musical sketches for *Siegfried's Tod*;[7] he then threw his energy into writing *Oper und Drama*. The next spring (presumably early May 1851) he jotted down some prose sketches for *Der junge Siegfried*, and between 24 May and 1 June he completed a lengthy prose draft of this 'comic counterpart' to *Siegfried's Tod*. The verse draft, dated 3–24 June, was soon followed by a fair copy; because this copy differed in places from the original, the latter was corrected by Theodor Uhlig to make the two manuscripts agree. Wagner then made another fair copy for Franz Liszt, and this second stage in the evolution of the *Ring* text terminated, like the first, in an abortive attempt at composing the music, followed by yet another long essay (*Eine Mittheilung an meine Freunde*). Although William Ashton Ellis hypothesized a second reworking of *Siegfried's Tod* during the summer of 1851, the autographs contain no evidence of such a revision.

The remaining two dramas were conceived more or less simultaneously, the prose sketch and prose draft of *Das Rheingold* preced-

---

[6] See Otto Strobel, *Richard Wagner: Skizzen und Entwürfe zur Ring-Dichtung: Mit der Dichtung 'Der junge Siegfried'* (Munich, 1930), facing p. 58.

[7] For a discussion of these sketches, see Bailey, 'Wagner's Musical Sketches'. See also Ch. 6.

ing their respective counterparts for *Die Walküre* (in these two instances, then, the text was written in 'normal' order). Wagner jotted down the brief prose sketches for *Das Rheingold* and *Die Walküre* during the autumn of 1851; sometime during the following winter he made supplementary prose sketches (in pencil) for both dramas in a pocket notebook. Between 23 and 31 March he wrote out a prose draft which he originally entitled *Der Raub: Vorspiel*; he later changed this to *Der Raub des Rheingoldes; Vorspiel*, to which he still later appended the remark 'oder: *Das Rheingold*?' The prose draft of *Die Walküre* soon followed (17–26 May). Wagner then began the task of versifying these two dramas, beginning with the second. On the title page of the verse draft of *Die Walküre* (1 June–1 July 1852) Wagner wrote out what he had decided upon as the tetralogy's collective title: *Das Gold des Nibelungen*. In a letter to August Röckel of 12 September 1852, Wagner referred to the whole as *Der Reif des Nibelungen*,[8] but on 14 October he wrote to Uhlig that he had decided upon *Der Ring des Nibelungen*.[9] Wagner then completed the third stage in the evolution of the *Ring* text by drafting the poem of his 'Preliminary Evening' (15 September–3 November), which he originally entitled *Der Raub des Rheingoldes*, but which by 14 October (as demonstrated by the same letter to Uhlig) he had decided to call *Das Rheingold*.

The fourth and final stage in the evolution of the *Ring* text began with a thoroughgoing revision of *Der junge Siegfried*, and continued with an equally far-reaching second revision of *Siegfried's Tod*. Wagner entered the changes to *Der junge Siegfried* into the first fair copy, and those to *Siegfried's Tod* into the third, in both cases replacing some pages with newly written ones.[10] Then followed fair copies of *Das Rheingold* and *Die Walküre*, and a fourth fair copy of *Siegfried's Tod*; for some reason, Wagner never made another fair copy of the extensively revised *Der junge Siegfried*. The entire process was completed by 15 December 1852, as shown by the date at the end of the fourth fair copy of *Siegfried's Tod*.

Wagner had fifty copies of the *Ring* poem privately printed at his own expense, an action he was later to regret. By February 1853, these copies were ready for distribution to some of his close friends;

[8] *Richard Wagner, Sämtliche Briefe*, ed. Gertrude Strobel, Werner Wolf, Hans-Joachim Bauer, and Johannes Forner (Leipzig, 1967–) (hereafter *SB*), iv. 470.

[9] *Richard Wagner Briefe an Theodor Uhlig, Wilhelm Fischer, Ferdinand Heine* (Leipzig, 1888), 236.

[10] The principal changes to *Siegfried's Tod* involved the Norns scene in the Prologue, the Waltraute scene in Act I, and Brünnhilde's final speech. The first two changes required both prose and verse drafts, the third only a verse draft; the fair copies of these passages were added to the manuscript on separate sheets.

he sent a number of them to Liszt, along with a cover letter in which he exhorted his future father-in-law to 'mark well my new poem—it contains the beginning and end of the world!'[11] However, this 1853 imprint does not represent the final version of the text. As we shall see, Wagner often altered the *Ring* text while setting it to music, and he entered these changes into his personal copy of the 1853 printing. Some but *not all* of these alterations were incorporated into the 1863 public printing and the 1872 *GS* version. The latter therefore inhabits a rather nebulous 'no man's land' somewhere between the 1853 printing and the version found in the musical score. It is unclear why Wagner did not take more pains to make the *GS* imprint[12] (upon which all subsequent *GS* editions are based) conform more closely to the final version of the text as found in the score, but his carelessness in this regard has proven disastrous for translators, analysts, and stage directors alike. In any case, the scholar who attempts to trace the genesis of the *Ring*, and who is interested in how word might have inspired tone, cannot work from the *GS* text; he must consult the 1853 imprint, of which a small number of copies survive.

Before beginning the first complete draft of an opera, Wagner customarily made some preliminary musical sketches. Three sets of such sketches for *Das Rheingold* survive; one set was entered in the verse draft, one in Wagner's copy of the 1853 printing, and the third was made on an undated sheet of music paper. These sketches will be described later, but it should be emphasized that Wagner may have made many more such jottings which have not come down to us. As Robert Bailey has pointed out, the more free of alterations and errors a passage of the complete draft is, the stronger the likelihood that it was preceded by preliminary sketching.[13]

The circumstances surrounding the beginning of the complete musical draft of *Das Rheingold* (including the infamous La Spezia 'vision') are well known, and will be dealt with in Chapter 6. Wagner began this complete draft (*Gesamtentwurf*) on 1 November 1853 and finished it two and a half months later, on 14 January 1854. He then almost immediately (1 February) began a full ink score; however, this *Partiturerstschrift* (draft of the score) soon turned into a pencil sketch of the instrumentation. On 15 February he began a fair copy of the score (*Reinschrift der Partitur*), and for a while he worked back and forth between these two manuscripts, working out a passage in

---

[11] 'Beachte wohl meine neue Dichtung—sie enthält der Welt Anfang und Untergang!' *Franz Liszt–Richard Wagner Briefwechsel*, ed. Hanjo Kesting (Frankfurt, 1988), 267.

[12] *GS* v. 257–352 (*Das Rheingold*) and vi. 1–364.

[13] 'The Method of Composition', in *The Wagner Companion*, ed. Peter Burbidge and Richard Sutton (London, 1979), 293.

the former, then entering it into the latter. Wagner completed the *Partiturerstschrift* on 28 May, and almost immediately began the composition of *Die Walküre*. He worked on and off at the fair copy of the score, finishing it on 25 September.

At some point during the Summer of 1854 Wagner hired a copyist to make an ink score of the opera; the copyist completed the Prelude (using Wagner's fair copy as a model), after which he was dismissed. Although Wagner apparently hoped to spare himself the trouble of completing his *Reinschrift*, the copyist's appalling errors (such as bringing in horn 3 a measure too late, putting it in unison with horn 2!) soon disabused him of this notion. After completing his *Reinschrift*, Wagner sent it to the Dresden copyist Friedrich Wölfel, who on 11 November 1855 finished a beautiful ink copy. Because Wagner's fair copy has disappeared, and because Wölfel's copy is extremely accurate (as shown by a comparison with facsimiles of two pages of the *Reinschrift*), the latter is an extremely important document; in fact, it served as *Stichvorlage* for the first printing of the opera (Mainz: B. Schott's Söhne, 1873).

The genesis of the *Ring* continues with the composition of *Die Walküre*, but our account necessarily ends with the completion of *Das Rheingold*. The next section describes more fully those manuscripts which bear most directly on its evolution.

II. THE MANUSCRIPTS

1. Textual Manuscripts

The brief prose sketch to *Das Rheingold* (WWV 86A Text Ia) is written on the recto side of a single sheet of paper watermarked 'Bath'. It is entitled *Das Rheingold. (Vorspiel)*, and contains two brief paragraphs followed by a third and longer one, each prefaced by a Roman numeral.[14] The first two paragraphs outline the events of Scenes 1 and 2 of the completed opera, while the third covers those of Scenes 3 and 4; evidently, Wagner originally planned this work in three main divisions.

Although the sheet is undated, it is not difficult to situate it approximately. First, the three numbered paragraphs correspond to Wagner's remark (quoted at the beginning of this chapter) in a letter to Uhlig written between 7 and 11 October 1851 from Albisbrunn,

---

[14] Upside down in the top margin are scribbled some thoughts on Goethe's *Faust*: 'Göthe. (Mann und Weib—Faust und Gretchen, | die kindesmörderin: darauf Faust bei Hufe | u.s.w.) pfui!!'

where he was taking a water cure: 'Great plans for Siegfried: three dramas, with a three-act prelude.'[15] Furthermore, a letter to Uhlig of 12 November outlines the action of this 'prelude' to a degree which suggests that the prose sketch had already been written.[16] We may conclude, therefore, that the latter was written sometime between early October and early November 1851.

The verso side of this sheet contains the prose sketch of *Die Walküre* Act I and the first part of Act II; the conclusion of Act II is written on the recto of a separate sheet, whose verso exhibits the sentence which begins the final paragraph of *Oper und Drama*. No prose sketch for Act III is extant, although it may have been written upon another sheet which has disappeared; the *Oper und Drama* sentence might have dissuaded Wagner from using the verso of sheet 2 for this purpose. In any case, the fact that the prose sketch of *Die Walküre* continues onto a second sheet strongly suggests that the *Rheingold* sketch had already been written on the reverse side of the first sheet. Thus the prose sketch of *Das Rheingold* preceded that of *Die Walküre*; the latter was probably written sometime in November.

During the winter of 1851–2, Wagner jotted down supplementary prose sketches to both *Das Rheingold* and *Die Walküre* in a small oblong notebook. Wagner apparently carried this notebook about in his pocket, entering both prose and musical sketches as they occured to him, most in pencil but a few in ink. The order in which the entries occur does not necessarily correspond to the order in which they were made.[17]

In addition to the prose sketch and the entries in the pocket notebook, one other document should be added to these early plans for *Das Rheingold*: Wagner's letter to Liszt of 20 November 1851, which describes the scenic action in much more detail than the prose sketch.[18]

As mentioned above, Wagner originally entitled the prose draft (WWV 86A Text II) *Der Raub: Vorspiel*; he later added the words *des Rheingoldes* after *Der Raub*, and still later appended the remark '(oder: *das Rheingold*)?' This closely written ink draft outlines the

---

[15] 'Mit dem Siegfried noch grosse Rosinen im kopfe: drei Dramen, mit einem dreiaktigen Vorspiel.' *SB* iv. 131–2.

[16] *SB* iv. 175.

[17] The light green pages have been numbered by an unknown hand from 1 to 108. Page 8 contains an entry headed *Walküre II act*, which expands upon Wotan's relationship to Erda. Pages 9–12 contain notations for *Das Rheingold*, entitled *Der Raub*; they deal primarily with events of the first two scenes (WWV 86A Text Ib). Pages 13–14 contain two paragraphs headed *Walküre I*, while pp. 15–17 expand upon the history of Siegmund and Sieglinde in a section entitled *Geschichte der Wälsungen*.

[18] *SB* iv. 188.

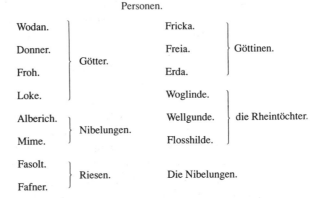

Personen.

Wodan.		Fricka.		
Donner.	Götter.	Freia.	Göttinen.	
Froh.		Erda.		
Loke.		Woglinde.		
Alberich.	Nibelungen.	Wellgunde.	die Rheintöchter.	
Mime.		Flosshilde.		
Fasolt.	Riesen.	Die Nibelungen.		
Fafner.				

FIG. 2.1 Cast page of Wagner's verse draft

action of the opera with remarkable clarity, and often anticipates the spoken dialogue; it will be cited frequently in the following chapters.[19]

The verse draft (WWV 86A Text III) was written on gathered bifolios which have been bound together.[20] Pages 4 and 6 contain the first set of preliminary musical sketches mentioned earlier; these are discussed below. Four unnumbered pages (one bifolio) were added to the manuscript later; the first and third of these are title-pages,[21] the second is blank, and the fourth contains a cast of characters. The cast page is given in Fig. 2.1. Even at this rather late stage in the evolution of the libretto, Loge is still named 'Loke', as he is in the earlier prose sketches and draft; not until Wagner revised the Norns scene of *Siegfried's Tod* did he change this to 'Loge' (see Chapter 3). On the other hand, Wotan remained 'Wodan' all the way through the musical composition of *Das Rheingold* and beyond.

Because Wagner's fair copy of the poem (WWV 86A Text IV)

---

[19] The ten-page prose draft is written on two non-nested bifolios and one folio. The second bifolio and the folio are numbered II and III respectively in the upper left-hand corner; of the individual pages, only 4 to 9 are numbered. Page 1 bears the date '(23 März 52)' in the upper right-hand corner, while p. 10 is dated 'R.W. | 31 März 52' in the lower right.

[20] The pages are written in ink on both sides; the first page of text is unnumbered, the remainder numbered (top centre) from 2 to 43; and the reverse side of p. 43 is blank.

[21] The first title-page, that for the entire tetralogy, originally ran: *Der Ring des Nibelungen* | *Ein Bühnenfestspiel* | *aufzuführen an drei tagen und einem vorabende.* | *Von* | *Richard Wagner.* Later the third line was altered to: *für drei tage und einen vorabend.* The second title-page reads simply: *Vorabend:* | *Das Rheingold.*

The first page of the poem is dated '(15 Sept. 52)' in the upper right-hand corner, although the '15' was originally '14'. The title originally read: *Vorabend:* | *Der Raub des Rheingoldes*, but the second line was later changed to *das Rheingold*. At the end of the poem (p. 43) is written: 'Zürich 3 Nov. 52 | Richard Wagner'.

served as *Druckvorlage* for the 1853 private printing, it is not surprising that these two documents resemble each other in practically every detail. On the other hand, the differences between the verse draft and the fair copy fall into three categories:

1. Differences in capitalization and punctuation: the verse draft uses lower-case letters to begin substantives (Wagner's usual practice at the time), whereas the fair copy bows to tradition in this respect.

2. In those places where the verse draft exhibits two or more versions of the same passage, the fair copy incorporates the final version.

3. In a very few places, the fair copy exhibits a variant not contained in the verse draft.

Because the fair copy contains little that is not present in the verse draft, and because it is virtually identical to the 1853 printing, it is probably the least interesting of all the textual documents. In fact, the scholar with access to a copy of the 1853 printing would have little need to examine the fair copy.[22]

Like the fair copy, the 1853 private printing (WWV 86A Text VI) does not list Wagner's name upon the first title-page. However, facing this title-page is a short preface by Wagner setting forth his reasons for issuing the private imprint. It is interesting to note that in neither the fair copy nor the 1853 printing (nor, for that matter, in the verse draft) are the four scenes of *Das Rheingold* marked as such; rather, a short dividing line separates the end of one scenic division from the beginning of the next.[23]

Only a small number of the original fifty copies have been located. By far the most important of these is Wagner's personal copy, into which he entered both musical sketches and text changes made during composition. Unfortunately for our investigation, the last six pages of *Das Rheingold* (pp. 29–34, containing, among other things, the crucial Erda episode) are lost. Of the remaining pages of *Das Rheingold* (WWV 86A Text Va), pp. 1–20 are at Schott's publishing house in Mainz, while pp. 21–8 are in the Bayreuth archives (along with the remaining pages of this copy). In addition to some textual changes, the extant *Rheingold* pages contain another set of preliminary musical sketches, entered in pencil on pp. 8–11; the missing pages may possibly have contained further sketches.

---

[22] It consists of two title-pages containing instructions for the printer, followed by sixty-two beautifully handwritten pages. The first page of text is headed: *Vorabend:* | *Das Rheingold*, followed by the cast of characters (in which Wotan is still 'Wodan', but Loge is no longer 'Loke') and the initial scenic description.

[23] *Das Rheingold* occupies pp. 1–34, *Die Walküre* 35–73, *Der junge Siegfried* 75–119, and *Siegfried's Tod* 121–59.

One might well question why pp. 1–20 of this document are at Schott's instead of in Bayreuth. The answer is that in 1869, Schott's published the first independent edition of the *Rheingold* poem (WWV 86A Text VIIb). For this printing, Wagner inked over the textual corrections and alterations he had pencilled into his personal copy, and sent these pages (1–34) to Schott's. He included handwritten title and cast pages (crossing out the printed title and cast list at the top of page 1), labelled the four scenes as 'Erste Scene', 'Zweite Scene', etc., and directed the printer (on page 8) to change 'Wodan' to 'Wotan' throughout. Although Schott's retained the title and cast pages, as well as pp. 1–20, they must have returned pp. 21–8 to Wagner, as these pages are in Bayreuth. The further history of the missing pp. 29–34 is unknown.[24]

It should be noted that in the 1863 edition (published in Leipzig by J. J. Weber), the third drama is entitled *Siegfried*, the fourth *Götterdämmerung*, and that Wotan's name is spelled 'Wotan' throughout. The texts of *Das Rheingold*, *Die Walküre*, and the first two acts of *Siegfried* reflect some (but not all!) of the changes made during composition. However, *Siegfried* Act III and *Götterdämmerung* follow the 1853 imprint, as Wagner had not yet set these acts to music. In preparation for the GS printing, some of the text changes made during the composition of *Götterdämmerung* were entered into a copy of the 1863 imprint; otherwise, the GS version follows that of 1863.[25]

Faced with so many conflicting versions of the *Ring* text, which one are we to choose as 'definitive'? Obviously that contained in the musical score, although this does not totally agree with any of the editions cited above. Furthermore, the scholar interested in compositional process, in how word inspired tone as Wagner set the text, must be familiar with the 1853 imprint. Stage directors, on the other hand, must be sure that they follow the version of the poem found in the score, not in one of the earlier editions. This is especially true in the case of the scenic directions, of which one example stands out: Towards the conclusion of *Götterdämmerung*, Gutrune in the original poem turns away from Siegfried and, 'wracked with grief,

---

[24] Still another, interleaved, copy of the 1853 printing was altered and corrected according to the changes Wagner had made in his own copy; this interleaved copy (WWV 86A Text Vb, now in the Pierpont Morgan Library) served as *Druckvorlage* for the 1863 public imprint of the *Ring* (WWV 86A Text VIIa). The 1863 edition, in turn, was used as *Vorlage* for the 1872 GS version (*WWV* 86A Text VIIf).

[25] For the sake of completeness, it may be mentioned that still another extant copy of the 1853 printing (WWV 86A Text Vc) contains changes and corrections entered by Mathilde Wesendonck, plus one pencil correction by Wagner. There are also, of course, other printings of *Das Rheingold* and the *Ring*, but these do not affect the evolution of the text.

Ex. 2.1

bends over Gunther's corpse';[26] in the completed opera, however, she 'bends dying over Gunther's corpse.'[27] In other words, while setting the text to music, Wagner decided that Gutrune should die, and during the 1876 rehearsals he pointed out to Heinrich Porges the exact measure in which the girl expires.[28] Yet how many directors, following an earlier version of the poem, have left Gutrune alive? The point is perhaps academic, as the end of the world is only minutes away, but Gutrune's death does underscore something many interpreters of the *Ring* refuse to deal with: the all-inclusive nature of Wagner's final cataclysm.

2. Musical Manuscripts

Of the three extant sets of preliminary musical sketches for *Das Rheingold*, one (WWV 86A Music Ia) was entered into the verse draft; these two sketches are transcribed in Ex. 2.1. The first (Ex. 2.1a) is written in ink on a hand-drawn staff which runs from top to bottom on the left side of p. 4; it consists of two bars of a wave-like arpeggiated figure. Both clef and key signature are missing, but the most likely candidates are C major (treble clef) or Eb major (bass clef); of the two possibilities, the latter would seem favoured by the fact that Wagner settled rather early upon Eb as the opening key of Scene 1 (see Chapter 6). The second sketch (Ex. 2.1b) occurs at the bottom of p. 6, to the left of Woglinde's 'Lugt, Schwestern!';

---

[26] 'Sie . . . beugt sich im Schmerz ausgelöst über Gunther's Leiche.' See WWV 86D Text XIII, 156.
[27] 'Sie . . . beugt sich nun ersterbend über Gunther's Leiche.'
[28] Heinrich Porges, *Wagner Rehearsing the Ring*, trans. Robert L. Jacobs (Cambridge, 1983), 143.

Ex. 2.2

although obviously a vocal rhythm, it is unclear what words Wagner associated with it. While we cannot date these two ink sketches exactly, we may surmise that they were written sometime between the beginning of the verse draft (15 September 1852) and the printing of the private edition (February 1853); if they had occurred to Wagner after the latter event, he would have entered them into his personal copy of the private imprint.

Wagner entered a second set of musical sketches (also WWV 86A Music Ia) into his copy of the 1853 imprint; that is, into the portion which is now in the Schott Archive in Mainz. These four sketches all pertain to Scene 2; they have faded terribly, and are extremely difficult to decipher. Each was obviously notated after February 1853, and at the latest by the time Wagner reached the corresponding part of the complete draft; yet they all could have been written before the complete draft was begun (1 November 1853). Each represents an early version of a different motif; they are transcribed in Ex. 2.2.[29]

---

[29] These transcriptions were made from photocopies which Schott's kindly furnished the Bayreuth Archives.

Page 5 contains a sketch for the all-important Valhalla motif (Ex. 2.2*a*); this runs from top to bottom in the lower left margin, then from left to right in the bottom left margin. Written in the tenor clef, it seems intended for trombones, the instruments specified in the complete draft (later changed to Wagner tubas); the Db key signature is given, and the metre is clearly 3/4. The two bars in the left margin contain the basic form of the motif (cf. Scene 2, mm. 1–2, repeated in mm. 3–4), while the single bar in the bottom margin contains its fragmentation (cf. Scene 2, m. 5); even the repeated-note fanfare figure is suggested, although it starts a beat later than in the complete draft. This is a good example of how motifs often occurred to Wagner at their 'definitive' pitch levels.

Page 9 contains a sketch of the Freia motif, running from bottom to top in the right margin. As Ex. 2.2*b* indicates, the first portion is indecipherable. The second portion begins with a treble clef and presents the Freia motif in its lyrical D major form, that in which it appears later in Scene 2 when love-struck Fasolt sings about the goddess. Wagner may have conceived this lyrical D major form before the agitated E minor version to which Freia enters; or he could have written it as a variant on the E minor version, after he had entered the latter into the complete draft.

Page 10 contains a sketch of the Giants motif, running from top to bottom in the left margin; it comprises two bars, with the first barline misplaced. Although taken by itself, this sketch (Ex. 2.2*c*) might imply a tonal centre of C major, the score suggests a strident emphasis upon the dominant of F minor. The tempo indications suggest that Wagner sketched this motif when he reached the entrance of the giants in the complete draft.

Page 11 contains a sketch for the triplet bass figure which precedes Donner's 'Fasolt und Fafner, | füllet ihr schon . . .', running from bottom to top in the right margin (Ex. 2.2*d*). This sketch is so faint that it could easily be overlooked.

The third set of preliminary sketches (WWV 86A Music Ib) are notated in ink on an oblong sheet of staff paper. Because these sketches pertain specifically to the Prelude, they are discussed in Chapter 6, and transcribed in Ex. 6.3.

Certainly the most important of the various musical documents pertaining to *Das Rheingold* is the complete draft (*Gesamtentwurf*), a continuous pencil sketch of the entire opera (WWV 86A Musik II). Wagner notated this draft on oblong half-sheets of staff paper, each created by tearing or cutting a larger sheet in half.[30] Wagner's

---

[30] Each half-sheet measures approximately 25 cm. wide by 18 cm. high, and contains fourteen

original pencil notation has been inked over, presumably by Mathilde Wesendonck. The paper has somewhat yellowed with age, but is still in remarkably good condition.

As Robert Bailey pointed out in connection with the *Tristan* manuscripts, Mathilde Wesendonck's inking over is often less than accurate.[31] In addition, certain markings were not inked over at all, and the original pencil has faded, leaving only faint impressions in the paper. Furthermore, Wagner never erased his original thoughts; he either crossed them out (in the case of an immediate alteration) or wrote over them (in the case of a later alteration). Mathilde inked over everything, earlier and later versions alike, with results that are occasionally indecipherable.[32] Also, there is no way of telling exactly *when* the inking over occurred. Bailey suggests that it was done before Wagner began the *Partiturerstschrift* (draft of the full score), on the premiss that he preferred to work from an ink draft.[33] However, it seems unlikely that Wagner would have permitted Mathilde to tinker with such a valuable manuscript before he was finished with it; besides, he made his fair copy of the full score from the pencil *Partiturerstschrift* without having the latter inked over first. Probably Mathilde inked over the draft in order to preserve it for posterity, but only *after* Wagner had sketched the instrumentation. The matter is further complicated by the fact that Wagner made certain entries in the complete draft while scoring, a fact that Curt von Westernhagen, among others, conveniently ignores. Thus, the mere appearance of an instrumentation marking alongside a theme in the complete draft does not necessarily imply that Wagner conceived theme and timbre simultaneously; ironically, only when an instrumental indication *differs* from the final scoring can one logically assume that it was made at the same time as the draft. In any case, since preliminary

staves. Thirty-eight of these sheets are written on both sides, while the thirty-ninth is written on one side only, resulting in seventy-seven written sides. The recto of each sheet has been numbered in the upper left corner. In the upper right corner of fo. 1^r is written '1 Nov:53'; on fo. 29^r, before the measure containing Loge's 'Bist du befriedigt?' (Scene 4), the marking '1 Jan:54' appears; and the lower right side of fo. 39^r is marked '14 Januar 1854 | RW | Und weiter nichts?? | Weiter nichts??'

[31] 'The Genesis of *Tristan und Isolde* and a Study of Wagner's Sketches and Drafts for the First Act', Ph.D. diss. (Princeton University, 1969), 74–5.

[32] These conditions suggest why the serious scholar must consult the original document; microfilms or photocopies will not suffice. Yet apart from a few indecipherable passages, the manuscript poses no insurmountable difficulties in transcription, certainly none which excuse the innumerable errors and faulty readings which riddle Curt von Westernhagen's *The Forging of the 'Ring'* (trans. Arnold and Mary Whittall (Cambridge, 1976), originally published as *Die Entstehung des 'Ring'* (Zurich, 1973)). However, Westernhagen's mistakes are exactly the sort which might occur when working with photocopies, leading one to question whether he actually saw the manuscript itself.

[33] 'The Method of Composition', 293.

sketches (now lost) could have preceded any given passage in the complete draft, statements about the 'simultaneity' of Wagner's musical conceptions are tenuous at best.

Throughout the complete draft, Wagner uses systems of either two or three staves, usually one staff for the vocal line(s) and one (sometimes two) for the instrumental part. Purely instrumental passages, such as the orchestral transitions between scenes, are elaborated on two (sometimes three) staves. The sparse texture of the instrumental staves allows us to see what Wagner considered most important about a given passage; it almost constitutes a sort of a priori musical reduction, and can often be used as a guide to analysis or as a check upon analytical results. It will be cited often in the following pages, especially in connection with the analytical discussion in Chapters 6 to 10. Transcriptions of selected portions may be found in the Appendix.

Had Wagner followed his prior compositional practice, he would have made a second complete draft in ink, fleshing out the rather sparse texture of the pencil draft, and only then have written out the score. However, an elaboration of the instrumental opening (already conceived as a composed-out E♭ triad) would have come so close to being a full score anyway that he decided to go ahead and make one right away (see Chapter 6). Wagner notated the full ink score of the Prelude in brown ink on large bifolios of manuscript paper; the portion which has survived (mm. 1–118) is written on two non-nested bifolios (eight written sides).[34]

When Wagner reached the opening of Scene 1, he found that he could not automatically score his pencil draft. The manuscript (WWV 86A Music III) at this point changes from a full ink score into a pencil sketch of the instrumentation, a document called by Wagner an '*Instrumentationsskizze*' (instrumentation sketch),[35] by Strobel and the editors of *WWV* a '*Partiturerstschrift*' (draft of the full score), and

[34] Each side measures 31 cm. wide by 38 cm. high, and contains thirty staves; the sides are numbered, top middle, from 1 to 8. In the upper left corner of p. 1 is written (in pencil): 'L. Köhler. | Rich. Wagners Handschrift. | von Liszt bekommen.' In the upper right corner is written (in ink): 'Zürich, 1 Feb. 54 | RW.' Page 1 displays the heading *Das Rheingold.* | *Vorspiel* | *und* | *erste Scene.* | *(auf dem Grunde des Rheines)*; however, it lacks the scenic indications found in both the 1853 text and the printed score.

The first eight pages of the *Partiturerstschrift* had fallen into the hands of Louis Köhler of Königsberg, who apparently received them from Liszt. An unpublished letter in the Bayreuth Archives (III B 21-7-1) from Köhler to Cosima Wagner, dated 17 Sept. 1878, contains (p. 2) the following sentence: 'Durch Hr. Glasenapp erfuhr ich, dass eine Sammlung von Rich. Wagner'-schen Handschriften angelegt werden soll; ich sende Ihnen für dieselbe hier die erste Skizze des Anfangs zum "Rheingold", die ich bis jetzt wie ein Heligthum in der Lohengrin-Partitur verwahrt u. mit Fafnerischem Argwohn gehütet habe.'

[35] In a letter to Karl Klindworth of 4 Oct. 1855. Because Hans von Bülow did not have time to make the piano reduction, Wagner gave this job to Klindworth.

by Bailey an 'instrumentation draft'. A missing portion of manuscript (mm. 119–51) makes it impossible to ascertain exactly where Wagner switched to this reduced pencil format, but it probably happened at the entrance of the voices.[36]

As mentioned earlier, Wagner on 15 February 1854 began a *Reinschrift der Partitur*, or fair copy (in ink) of the full score (WWV 86A Musik IV). For a while, he worked back and forth between this and the *Partiturerstschrift*, working out a passage in the latter, then entering it in the former. As he prepared to enter a passage into the fair copy, he calculated page and system divisions by means of various markings written in the margins of the *Partiturerstschrift*. The character of these markings changes as the *Partiturerstschrift* proceeds; together with the peculiar pagination of that draft, they allow us to surmise how Wagner switched back and forth between the two manuscripts.[37] After working out the instrumentation up to m. 250,

---

[36] Wagner also changed to a different paper size, a smaller twenty-stave sheet 25 cm. wide by 32.5 cm. high. He orchestrated mm. 152–358 on these sheets; the sheet containing mm. 240–50 is lost. He then again changed paper, creating a new format by tearing a bifolio of the large thirty-stave paper down the crease, then cutting or tearing each resultant sheet in half, creating 'half-sheets' 31 cm. wide by 19 cm. high. He scored mm. 359–420 on these sheets; the half-sheets containing mm. 368–76 and 387–94 are missing. He worked out the instrumentation for mm. 421–47 (the Rhinedaughters' first concerted song) directly in the complete draft, returning to the half-sheets at m. 448; thus, although *WWV* lists mm. 421–47 of this manuscript as 'missing', they almost certainly never existed. Most of the remainder of the *Partiturerstschrift* is notated on these half-sheets, except for several passages in Scene 4 whose complex instrumental texture required more staves; these sections are written on yet another type of paper, a thirty-stave sheet measuring 27 cm. wide by 35 cm. high (each sheet torn from a bifolio) manufactured by Lard Esnault, 25 Rue Feydeau, Paris.

The initial portion (mm. 1–420) of the *Partiturerstschrift* (WWV 86A Musik III) is in the Bayreuth Archives (A III a 2), except, of course, for the missing portions and one page (mm. 403–12) which somehow found its way into the New York Public Library (JOC 73-24). The bulk of the manuscript (mm. 448–end, plus supplementary harp parts) is housed in the Scheide Collection at Princeton University.

The history of the Scheide portion of the *Partiturerstschrift* is recounted by J. Merrill Knapp in 'The Instrumentation Draft of Wagner's *Das Rheingold*' (*Journal of the American Musicological Society*, 30 (1977), 272–95) a well-intentioned and potentially useful article which unfortunately contains many errors and misleading statements. Those mistakes which concern the Bayreuth portion of the draft are perhaps understandable, as Professor Knapp had access only to photocopies. The misstatements regarding the Scheide portion, to which he had direct access, are more disturbing. For example, Knapp claims that Wagner used the 27 × 35 cm. Esnault paper for *all* of the Scheide draft, cutting most of it into half-sheets. However, the half-sheets measure 31 × 19 cm., and therefore could not possibly have been cut from the Esnault paper; it would require all the magic of the Tarnhelm to expand the width of a sheet of paper from 27 cm. to 31! In fact, only the thirteen full sheets represent the Esnault paper; the half-sheets were cut from the 31 × 38 cm. paper used for the Prelude.

[37] While making the *Partiturerstschrift*, Wagner began his practice of laying two sheets side by side on his desk; he would write on the recto side of each sheet, one after the other, then turn both over at the same time and write on the verso sides. Thus, for example, the recto side of the first sheet in the Scheide Collection is numbered 1, while the verso is numbered 3.

he entered this in the full score; he then did the same with mm. 251–358 and mm. 359–420, then sketched the instrumentation of mm. 421–47 in the complete draft itself and scored it.[38] In the opinion of the present author, he then worked out the instrumentation of the rest of the opera (mm. 448–end, the portion of the *Partiturerstschrift* now in the Scheide Collection at Princeton University) before returning to his work on the fair copy. Unfortunately the *Reinschrift* has disappeared, which makes Friedrich Wölfel's copy all the more important.[39]

The significance of the *Partiturerstschrift* to the scholar is twofold: it provides many fascinating insights into Wagner's method of orchestration; and, perhaps more important, it contains instances of actual recomposition. It thus constitutes a vital link between the complete draft and the full score.

The anonymous copy of the Prelude (WWV 86A Musik Va) corresponds in layout to Wölfel's (which faithfully reproduces Wagner's fair copy); it was therefore almost certainly made from the fair copy, not from the *Partiturerstschrift*, as Bailey implies.[40] It is notated on

---

However, the pagination of the *Partiturerstschrift* is not consecutive throughout the entire manuscript. The eight pages containing the extant portion of the Prelude are numbered (probably by Wagner) from 1 to 8; the eight full sheets of the pencil draft are numbered (not by Wagner) from 1 to 16; the Bayreuth half-sheets are numbered by Wagner beginning with 1 and by someone else beginning with 17; and the Scheide half-sheets are numbered (by Wagner) beginning again with 1. The numbering of the Scheide portion is itself somewhat inconsistent, but runs essentially from 1 to 360.

[38] Folio 3ᵛ of the complete draft contains a sketch of the instrumentation for the Rhinedaughters' first concerted song, written over the original composition draft; because it utilizes the Erda/Norn figurations of the revised Prelude (see Ch. 6), this sketch was clearly entered after the *Partiturerstschrift* had been started. In addition, this folio contains page and system markings which correspond to those in Wölfel's copy of Wagner's *Reinschrift*. Obviously Wagner wanted to spare himself the trouble of writing out a complete sketch of this passage in the *Partiturerstschrift*, perhaps because the Rhinedaughters' song is essentially a reprise of material already scored (the opening of Scene 1).

[39] On 25 Aug. 1865 Wagner sent this manuscript to King Ludwig II of Bavaria as a birthday gift; it subsequently found its way into the *Wittelsbacher Ausgleichsfond* (King Ludwig's family archives). The German Chamber of Industry and Commerce purchased it from the *Ausgleichsfond* and presented it to Adolf Hilter on his fiftieth birthday (20 Apr. 1939). Hilter probably kept it in his bunker beneath the Berlin chancellery, where it was presumably destroyed (along with other Wagner autographs) in April 1945. However, rumours of its survival continue to circulate.

One German scholar whom I met in Bayreuth proposed the following theory: Towards the close of the war, Hitler transferred all his Wagner manuscripts (including the *Rheingold* fair copy) to another location, where they were eventually confiscated by American armed forces. The documents were transported to the United States, where they repose to this day, jealously guarded by the government; the latter refuses to acknowledge their existence for fear of an international dispute over ownership. Of such conspiracy theories are thrillers born.

[40] 'The Method of Composition', 295. However, Wagner presumably expected the copyist to switch over to the *Partiturerstschrift* when he reached the end of the completed portion of the fair copy.

the same type of paper used by Wagner for a small portion of the *Partiturerstschrift*.[41]

Because Wölfel's copy of the opera[42] was used as *Stichvorlage* for the first printing,[43] it contains numerous editorial markings for page and system breaks corresponding to those in the Schott score. The transpositions of the low brass (presumably carried over from Wagner's fair copy) differ from those in the printed score; these differences are discussed in Chapter 6.

For the sake of completeness, one further document should be mentioned: a sketch for the orchestral part to Freia's 'Helft! Helft vor den Harten!' in Scene 2 (WWV 86A Musik Ic). This actually represents a recomposition of the parallel passage in the complete draft. It is written in pencil (inked over) on the bottom of a sheet of music paper whose reverse side contains Wagner's sketch for a concert ending to Gluck's *Iphigénie in Aulis*. The *Rheingold* sketch is transcribed and discussed in Chapter 8, but is cited here because it could easily be overlooked by the scholar: the Bayreuth archivists have filed it with the sketches for *Tristan und Isolde*!

---

[41] That is, on the smaller 'Esnault' paper. This copy of the Prelude (WWV 86A Musik Va) is also housed in the Scheide Collection, and I must extend my gratitude to Mr Scheide for allowing me to examine it.

[42] Wölfel's copy (WWV 86A Musik Vb) is notated in brown ink on both sides of sheets containing a variable number of staves; the text is written in Latin script except for one brief lapse into German. At the top of p. 1 is written *Das Rheingold.* | *Vorspiel und erste Scene.* | *: In der Tiefe des Rheines :* ; the scenic description is again missing, suggesting that Wagner's fair copy also lacked it. A date on the last page indicates that Wölfel completed it on 11 Nov. 1855; the supplementary harp parts are not included.

I am grateful to Dr Manfred Eger, Director of the National Archiv der Richard-Wagner-Stiftung, for retrieving this document for me from Munich, where it was on loan to the editors of the critical edition of *Das Rheingold* (*Richard Wagner, Sämtliche Werke*, ed. Carl Dahlhaus and Egon Voss (Mainz, 1970–), vol. x). One may gauge the accuracy of Wölfel's copy by comparing it with facsimiles of two pages (70 and 265) from Wagner's *Reinschrift* which were published in Strobel's article 'Die Originalpartitur von Richard Wagners *Rheingold*', *Bayreuther Festspielführer* (1928), following p. 48. The facsimiles agree with the corresponding pages of Wölfel's copy in every detail.

[43] WWV 86A Musik IX. The availability of this edition in the 1985 Dover reprint facilitated a comparison with Wölfel's copy.

3 The Forging of the Text

> As for the poem itself, there is nothing more I can or wish to say
> at present . . . But the prospect of setting all this to music now
> attracts me greatly: as regards the form, it is already fully fashioned
> in my head, and I have never been so clear in my own mind
> about the musical execution of a work as I now am in relation to
> this poem.
>
> (Wagner to Franz Liszt, 11 February 1853)

This chapter explores in more detail the evolution of the *Rheingold*
poem. Beginning with a consideration of the original Nibelung scenario, it traces the way in which Wagner's attitude towards his material
gradually changed as he shaped it into an operatic tetralogy. This
leads to a discussion of the many dramatic parallels between *Das
Rheingold* and *Götterdämmerung*, and an interpretation of their
significance. The chapter concludes with a demonstration of how
various elements from *Siegfried's Tod*, *Der junge Siegfried*, and *Die
Walküre* found their way into *Das Rheingold*.

I. THE 1848 SCENARIO

Die Nibelungensage (Mythus)[1] begins with several dense paragraphs
outlining the prehistory of *Siegfried's Tod*—events which ultimately
formed the basis of the first three *Ring* operas. The bulk of the
scenario describes in much greater detail the action of *Siegfried's
Tod*, the only part of the story originally destined for dramatic treatment. Although the tale of Siegfried's downfall is not our primary
concern, it was the generative impulse behind the entire Nibelung
project, and as such warrants attention. The scenario represents
Wagner's first attempt to impose dramatic order upon his mythological material; it begins with Alberich's theft of the Rhinegold
(for which, significantly, no renunciation of love is required), and
concludes with Brünnhilde's self-immolation. Because the story recounted in the 1848 scenario differs in some respects from that
familiar to the *Ring* audience, a brief synopsis may not be out of
place.

---

[1] WWV 86D Text Ia; transcribed in Strobel, *Skizzen und Entwürfe*, 26–33.

Unlike most of the later drafts, this one contains an interpretative commentary which clearly sets forth its moral/ethical framework. The fundamental notion underlying the 1848 scenario is that of Siegfried as the gods' redeemer. Taking advantage of a conflict between Alberich and the race of giants, the gods (not just Wotan) steal the dwarf's hoard and ring, using them as payment for Valhalla. The giants give their booty into the charge of a dragon, while Alberich and the Nibelungs toil fruitlessly in bondage to the ring. As the years pass, the gods attempt to order the world; their goal is moral consciousness, but their rule is flawed, established as it was through force and deceit. Their guilt can be purged only if the ring is stolen from the dragon and returned to the Rhine; this would release the Nibelungs from servitude. Yet the gods themselves cannot undertake such an action without committing yet another sin. Only one who is independent of the gods may perform the beneficent deed of liberation, one who does it of his own free will. This capacity the gods see in mankind, in whom they strive to implant their divinity—realizing, however, that they might ultimately be forced to relinquish their immediate influence to the freedom of human consciousness.

Several generations finally produce the needed hero. Following only his inner dictates, Siegfried kills the dragon and gives the ring to Brünnhilde, who bestows upon him her godly wisdom. Yet Siegfried does not use this gift; he still relies solely upon himself. Disguised as Gunther, he wrests the ring from Brünnhilde, thereby recreating the gods' fatal theft and assuming their guilt. Warned by three mermaids, he refuses to relinquish the ring; he defies the Norns, the gods, and death itself. He thus atones for the gods' guilt through his independence, his fearlessness, and ultimately his downfall. After Hagen murders him, Brünnhilde regains her unused wisdom, which gives her the necessary insight to complete Siegfried's work: returning the ring to the Rhine, she finally liberates Alberich and the Nibelungs. Armed as a Valkyrie, she immolates herself in order to lead Siegfried in triumph to Valhalla. The gods' rule is firmly reestablished, although the implication is that ultimately they will pass away, leaving mankind—now brought to full moral consciousness—to reign supreme.

Within the context of this scenario, Siegfried's actions appear perfectly consistent and unproblematic. His innocence and 'ignorance' are crucial: knowing nothing of any higher scheme of things, he follows only his instincts. Because he must not accept aid from the gods, he cannot even avail himself of Brünnhilde's wisdom. His deeds not only redeem the gods, but ultimately benefit the human race. In fact, Siegfried comes amazingly close to fulfilling Hegel's concept of the world-historical figure, the hero who, heeding only inner necessity, unwittingly assists the dialectical process of history.[2]

As the single projected drama gradually expanded into a tetralogy, Wagner elaborated upon elements of the 1848 scenario, especially those contained in its opening paragraphs. However—and this is crucial—he also began to change his attitude towards the material, with the result that its moral/ethical framework was considerably altered. Yet his subsequent revisions left the character of Siegfried largely untouched, so that the hero's actions grew increasingly dissonant with this changing framework; in effect, Wagner abandoned his hero, leaving him to play out a role whose dramatic *raison d'être* had long since collapsed. Thus, in the context of *Götterdämmerung*, Siegfried's actions often appear inconsistent with premises laid down earlier in the tetralogy. Again, this is not our principal concern, but it is important to the extent that *Das Rheingold* itself developed out of Wagner's changing attitude towards his dramatic material. In fact, our discussion of the genesis of the *Rheingold* poem will be far more meaningful if we first trace the general outlines of this changing attitude.

II. WAGNER'S CHANGING ATTITUDE TOWARDS SIEGFRIED, WOTAN, AND THE *RING*

The prose draft of *Siegfried's Tod*[3] fleshes out the events of the scenario, beginning with Siegfried's arrival at Gibichung Hall. However, this draft naturally lacks not only the drama's extensive pre-history, but also the interpretative commentary which, in the earlier scenario, had established its ethical framework. To remedy this loss, Wagner drafted a two-part prologue.[4] In a scene quite different from that which opens *Götterdämmerung*, the Norns explain the moral significance of Siegfried's mission. The leave-taking scene which follows (almost identical with the one we know) emphasizes Siegfried's dependence upon Brünnhilde, a connection which must be broken if the hero is to fulfil his destiny. This, incidentally, explains the original purpose behind the potion of forgetfulness: it enabled

---

[2] Wagner would have found this notion in the introduction to Hegel's *Vorlesungen über die Philosophie der Weltgeschichte*. In his autobiography, Wagner mentions having read this work in Dresden, and it was apparently the only work by a modern philosopher which found its way into his Dresden library. See Richard Wagner, *My Life*, trans. Andrew Gray, ed. Mary Whittall (Cambridge, 1983), 429–30, and Curt von Westernhagen, *Richard Wagners Dresdener Bibliothek, 1842–1849: Neue Dokumente zur Geschichte seines Schaffens* (Wiesbaden, 1966), 51, 93.

[3] WWV 86D Text IIa; transcribed in Strobel, *Skizzen und Entwürfe*, 38–55.

[4] WWV 86D Text IIb; Strobel, *Skizzen und Entwürfe*, 56–8.

Siegfried to regain his independence. Although Wagner probably drafted the farewell scene with an eye towards its possibilities for heroic love music, the concept of redemptive love as yet played no part in the drama: *Lohengrin* had cooled the composer's enthusiasm for this theme, and his interest in it was not rekindled for some years, perhaps under the influence of Ludwig Feuerbach.

As noted in Chapter 2, the second fair copy of the poem[5] contains two significant marginal alterations to Brünnhilde's closing speech. In the original scenario, the prose draft, and both versions of the poem, Brünnhilde concludes the drama by proclaiming Wotan's continuing rule. However, in the first marginal entry, Brünnhilde announces 'blessed atonement' ('selige Sühnung') for the eternal gods, and urges them to welcome Siegfried into their midst. Wagner here attempted to restore the notion of Siegfried as the gods' redeemer, a concept crucial (as noted above) to the 1848 scenario but somehow missing from both the prose draft and the poem of *Siegfried's Tod*. In the second entry, added later, Brünnhilde admonishes the gods to 'depart powerless' ('machtlos scheidet'), and 'fade away in bliss' ('erbleichet in Wonne') before Siegfried's deed, and she concludes by foretelling their 'blessed redemption in death' ('selige Todeserlösung') from their anxious fear. The notion of the gods' demise, already alluded to in the first scenario, was coming into ever sharper focus, and it crystallized in *Der junge Siegfried*. Wagner now set Wotan himself upon the stage, to be informed by the Wala of his approaching end. Nevertheless, the god genially yields place to Siegfried without a struggle, and the second opera would still have concluded with the temporary re-establishment of Wotan's rule.

The expansion into a tetralogy was motivated by Wagner's desire to dramatize the entire tragedy of Wotan. For it was now Wotan the god, not Siegfried the hero, who fascinated him. At the same time, his reading of Feuerbach had suggested a possible foundation for the entire cycle: the eternal conflict between love and power. While versifying the two new dramas, Wagner decided to destroy the gods by fire, demonstrating how Wotan's original misdeed led ultimately to the collapse of his whole world. Yet he failed to apprise Siegfried of this radical change of plan.

Wagner next revised *Der junge Siegfried*. Because his interest in Siegfried had waned, he primarily altered those scenes involving Wotan: the doomed god now embraces his own annihilation as he wills his spear to be shattered on Siegfried's sword. The new love/power conflict proved difficult to work in, for this third drama had

---

[5] WWV 86D Text V.

always revolved around the concept of fear, not love. Yet Wagner's identification of the fear of death as the source of all lovelessness permitted him to view fearless Siegfried as the man 'who never ceases to love'.[6] In any case, he probably realized that the closing duet could be understood as the long-awaited triumph of love over power, and his eventual musical setting certainly underscores that interpretation.

Finally Wagner revised *Siegfried's Tod*, replacing the liberation of the Nibelungs with the destruction of the gods. Unable to inject a heavy dose of *Liebe* into this drama, he appended to Brünnhilde's closing lines a rather Feuerbachian speech extolling love over worldly possessions. Released from Alberich's curse, love is again free to rule the world: 'Rapture in joy and sorrow comes—from love alone!'[7] The drama had apparently come full circle: just as Alberich once renounced love for the sake of power, Brünnhilde, by restoring the ring to the Rhine, now renounces power for the sake of love.[8] This rather ineffectual attempt to bring *Siegfried's Tod* into line with *Das Rheingold* and *Die Walküre* was not likely to satisfy Wagner for long, especially since he had come to view its concluding catastrophe as the destruction, not only of the gods, but of the world as well.

In the autumn of 1854 Wagner encountered the works of Arthur Schopenhauer, and he claims to have read *Die Welt als Wille und Vorstellung* four times over the course of the following year.[9] Schopenhauer's writings afforded him an almost cosmic vision of the true meaning of his work. Love, he now realized, is not the final remedy; rather, the suffering it causes may vouchsafe an insight into the essential nullity of existence, the reality of human misery, and the necessity for rejecting the phenomenal world as an evil illusion. The only right course is to renounce the Will, as Brünnhilde demonstrates

---

[6] Letter to August Röckel of 25/26 Jan. 1854. See *Selected Letters of Richard Wagner*, trans. and ed. Stewart Spencer and Barry Millington (London, 1987), 307.

[7] 'Selig in Lust und Leid | lässt—die Liebe nur sein!' For a well-reasoned discussion of the possible influence of Hegel and Feuerbach upon the text of the *Ring*, see George C. Windell, 'Hegel, Feuerbach, and Wagner's *Ring*', *Central European History*, 9 (1976), 27–57.

[8] The notion that the *Ring* ends with the release of love from Alberich's *Liebesfluch* is undoubtedly what led Hans von Wolzogen to dub the drama's final musical theme 'Liebeserlösung'—literally, the 'redemption (or release) of love', a meaning which has been obscured by the traditional translation 'redemption through love' (see his *Thematischer Leitfaden durch die Musik zu Richard Wagner's Festspiel 'Der Ring des Nibelungen'* (Leipzig, 1876), 121–2). It should be noted that Wolzogen based his interpretation upon the 1852 ending (on p. 63 he quotes the 'Lust und Leid' lines as 'the moral of the poem'), an ending which Wagner not only discarded but actually repudiated (in a letter to August Röckel of 23 Aug. 1856; see *Selected Letters*, 358). In any case, Wagner himself referred to the concluding theme as 'the glorification of Brünnhilde' ('die Verherrlichung Brünnhildens'), as Cosima reported in an unpublished letter of 6 Sept. 1875 to the chemist Edmund von Lippmann (quoted in 'Reviews', *19th Century Music*, 5 (1981), 84 by John Deathridge, who cites as his source for the letter 'Catalogue 100, *Proszenium, Theater- und Film Fachantiquariat*, Kemnath Stadt (Germany, n.d.)').

[9] *My Life*, 510. Wagner also read *Parerga und Paralipomena*.

by relinquishing both the ring of power and life itself. Consequently Wagner decided to replace his heroine's 'Feuerbachian' lines with a 'Schopenhauerian/Buddhistic' speech; he wrote out a prose sketch for this in 1856, but did not versify it until 1871 or 1872. Although ultimately not set to music, this speech expressed for him the final meaning of the *Ring*; it concludes: 'Deepest suffering of grieving love opened my eyes: I saw the world end.'[10]

Yet where did all this leave poor Siegfried? Stripped of his role as the gods' redeemer, totally uninterested in metaphysical speculation, he doggedly fights on in a world which no longer understands him. In fact, Siegfried's dramatic function had changed drastically. In *Siegfried's Tod* he was the gods' redeemer and the benefactor of humanity. In *Götterdämmerung*, however, his actions may be understood as recreating all the mistakes Wotan made in *Das Rheingold*: embracing power, entangling himself in false treaties, and renouncing true love. Wagner had come to believe that social progress was an illusion, that humanity was fated endlessly to repeat past errors, and that the ideal future he had once envisaged could never be realized. The Act III funeral march serves simultaneously as a commentary upon Wotan's plan for moral regeneration (symbolized by the Sword and Volsung themes) and as a lament for the futility of that idea—an idea which had dominated the 1848 scenario.

That Wagner no longer believed the world worth saving is beyond question. In July 1872 he mentioned to Cosima that Wotan 'has recognized the guilt of existence and atones for the error of creation'.[11] But already in October 1854, in a passage that reads almost like a gloss on the new direction the *Ring* had taken, Wagner wrote to Liszt: 'Let us treat the world only with contempt; for it deserves no better; but let no hope be placed in it, that our hearts be not

---

[10] 'Trauender Liebe | tiefstes Leiden | schloss die Augen mir auf: | enden sah ich die Welt.' The prose draft of Brünnhilde's new speech (WWV 86D Text VIIIb) was written in a pocket notebook, the verse draft and fair copy (WWV 86D Text VIIIc) on p. 159 of Wagner's personal copy of the 1853 printing. The new verses were meant to be inserted before the passage beginning 'Grane, mein Ross, | sei mir gegrüsst!'

Although Wagner ultimately rejected these new lines also, he reprinted them in the 1872 *GS* version of the text, accompanied by his comment that he had excised them because 'their meaning is already expressed with the greatest precision in the effect of the drama-sounding-in-music' ('weil ihr Sinn in der Wirkung des musikalisch ertönenden Drama's bereits mit höchster Bestimmtheit ausgesprochen wird' (*GS* vi. 364)). Most critics have disputed this assertion. For a demonstration that the concluding music of the *Ring* can indeed be interpreted along the lines of the 1856 ending, see my article 'The Pessimism of the *Ring*', *The Opera Quarterly*, 4/2 (1986), 24–48.

[11] *Cosima Wagner's Diaries*, ed. Martin Gregor-Dellin and Dietrich Mack, trans. Geoffrey Skelton (New York, 1978), i. 426.

deluded! It is evil, evil, *fundamentally evil* . . . It belongs to *Alberich*: no one else!! Away with it!'[12]

III. DRAMATIC PARALLELS BETWEEN *DAS RHEINGOLD* AND GÖTTERDÄMMERUNG

The preceding outline suggests that Siegfried's actions in *Götterdämmerung* mean something quite different from what they did in *Siegfried's Tod*: namely, that they recreate Wotan's fatal errors. In effect, Siegfried follows the path Wotan trod in *Das Rheingold*, with equally devastating results. *Götterdämmerung* may in fact be interpreted as a 'replay' of *Das Rheingold*, but in mortal terms: Siegfried functions, in a sense, as the human 'god' whose downfall the final drama chronicles. This suggests that when Wagner worked out the poem of his 'Preliminary Evening', he may have structured it—consciously or unconsciously—so that it dramatically parallels the 'Third Evening'. In fact, the parallels between *Das Rheingold* and *Götterdämmerung* are evident even in their large-scale formal designs, and are underscored by musical means.

The division of the final drama into a prologue and three acts reflects the division of the first drama into an introductory scene (the theft of the gold) followed by three main scenes (the story of the gods).[13] The first scene of *Das Rheingold* features the three Rhinedaughters, while the Prologue to *Götterdämmerung* focuses initially upon the three Norns; as will be demonstrated, Wagner established specific dramatic and musical parallels between the two sets of sisters. Tonally, *Das Rheingold* Scene 1 opens in the key of Eb major and closes in C minor as the three Rhinedaughters witness the theft of their gold; the Prologue to *Götterdämmerung* opens in Eb *minor*, and its first half closes in B (or Cb) minor as the three Norns experience the breaking of their rope. In each case, a tragic event of cosmic significance is underscored by the tonal move of a descending third.

The action of *Das Rheingold* then shifts to the environs of Valhalla, whereas that of *Götterdämmerung* eventually moves to Gibichung Hall; the less-than-honourable machinations of Wotan and the gods are paralleled by the truly despicable actions of Hagen, Gunther, and eventually Siegfried. When the mortal men plot the double wedding

---

[12] *Selected Letters*, 319.
[13] As pointed out in Chapter 2, the prose sketch for *Das Rheingold* suggests that Wagner originally conceived the work in three main divisions; the third division was eventually bisected into the present Scenes 3 and 4. Thus the structural parallelism with *Götterdämmerung* was apparently not part of Wagner's initial conception, but something towards which he worked.

of Brünnhilde and Gutrune, they do it in Gutrune's absence, re-creating the male gods' bartering away of Freia (about which Fricka once complained: 'Slyly you men kept us women away, in order to discuss matters secretly with the giants'). Siegfried's departure (with Gunther) for Brünnhilde's rock reflects Wotan's departure (with Loge) for Nibelheim: Siegfried hopes to win Gutrune by abducting Brünnhilde, just as Wotan hopes to win back Freia by stealing the ring (and abducting Alberich). In the terrible moment when Siegfried brutally wrests the ring from Brünnhilde, he re-creates Wotan's fatal act in stealing it from Alberich, and renders himself vulnerable to the curse.[14]

Strong dramatic parallels may also be observed between the last two acts of *Götterdämmerung* and the last two scenes of *Das Rheingold*. Alberich appears at the opening of *Götterdämmerung* Act II, just as he does at the beginning of *Das Rheingold* Scene 3; the dwarf's lordship over the Nibelungs is reflected by Hagen's leadership of the Gibichung vassals. The altars to Wotan, Fricka, and Donner that brood over Gibichung Hall remind the audience that it is viewing a mortal re-enactment of events that originally involved the gods. The fatal combat between the half-brothers Gunther and Hagen recalls that between the giant brothers Fasolt and Fafner; Erda's interven-tion at the critical moment (preventing Wotan from keeping the ring) is paralleled by Brünnhilde's intervention (preventing Hagen from seizing the ring).

These striking dramatic parallels (and the reader can probably think of others) cannot be purely fortuitous; Wagner must have designed them for some purpose. As Deryck Cooke points out, *Das Rheingold* is an allegory of 'the social and political history of mankind'.[15] I believe that Wagner structured *Götterdämmerung* as a 'replay' of *Das Rheingold* (working, of course, in reverse) to express his conviction that this history is cyclical, that because humanity never learns anything, it is doomed to repeat past errors until it finally destroys itself. Nothing (Wagner seems to say), not even love, can overcome man's insatiable lust for power, his overwhelming desire to enslave and dominate his fellow human being, and this aggressive instinct will eventually lead him to bring about his own annihilation.

The notion that because humanity is fatally afflicted with power-

---

[14] When Wagner showed Cosima the pencil sketch for this scene, he commented: 'When the ring was snatched from her [Brünnhilde] I thought of Alberich; the noblest character suffers the same as the ignoble, in every creature the will is identical.' *Diaries* i. 228 (entry for 4 June 1870).

[15] *I Saw the World End*, 246.

lust it is doomed endlessly to repeat its past errors is a pessimistic world view reminiscent of Schopenhauer. However, Wagner apparently formulated this *Weltanschauung* before he encountered Schopenhauer's writings.[16] Nevertheless, Schopenhauer gave Wagner the conceptual terms with which to articulate this world view: man's power-lust is really the universal Will manifesting itself as the Will to Power. More important, Schopenhauer offered a solution: the Will can be denied by one who recognizes the nullity of the phenomenal world.

Although a philosophical interpretation of the entire *Ring* obviously lies beyond the limits of this study, a recognition of the dramatic parallels between the first and fourth dramas, as well as an appreciation of their possible significance, will facilitate an understanding of the dramatic genesis of *Das Rheingold*.

IV. THE EVOLUTION OF THE TEXT

This section discusses chronologically each of the textual manuscripts which bear most directly upon the genesis of *Das Rheingold*, in order to trace how the events sketched in the 1848 scenario ultimately coalesced into the 'Preliminary Evening' of the *Ring*.

1. The 1848 Scenario

Die Nibelungensage (Mythus) opens with a striking birth-image: the earth's interior is a 'womb of night and death' which spawns the Nibelungs. They dwell in Nibelheim or Nebelheim (literally, the 'home of mist'), a place of 'gloomy subterranean clefts and caverns'. The Nibelungs 'burrow through the bowels of the earth (like worms in a dead body)'. Thus the earth is both a life-giving womb and a corpse whose intestines are consumed by scavengers. This rather revolting mixed image was perhaps inspired by the Eddaic passage in which the dwarfs first emerge and come to life as maggots in the body of the dead frost-giant Ymir, from whose corpse the world was formed. In this sense the Nibelungs (dwarfs) are truly born from 'the womb of death'. Their restless activity never ceases: 'they smelt, refine, and smith hard metals.'

---

[16] In an undated letter to August Röckel (obviously penned in Feb. 1855), Wagner writes: 'In accepting unreservedly the profound truths of his [Schopenhauer's] teaching I was able to follow my own inner bent, and although he has given my line of thought a direction somewhat different from its previous one, yet only this direction harmonized with the profoundly sorrowful conception I had already formed of the world.' *Richard Wagner's Letters to August Röckel*, trans. Eleanor C. Sellar (Bristol, n.d. [1897]), 124.

The second sentence immediately contrasts the foregoing with the 'pure, noble Rhinegold', which Alberich stole from the water's depths. However, mention is made neither of the Rhinedaughters nor of any necessity for renouncing love. Alberich used his cunning skill to forge the gold into a ring which gave him power over 'his entire race' (not, apparently, over the rest of the world). He became the lord of the Nibelungs and forced them to work for him alone, assembling the immeasurable Nibelung hoard. He forced 'his own brother, Reigin (Mime-Eugel)' to make the Tarnhelm, which enabled him to take on any shape at will. Thus equipped, Alberich set out to gain mastery over the entire world.

The fact that the above information is presented in three sentences will give the reader an idea of the density of this draft. All these details ultimately found their way into *Das Rheingold* Scene 3 except for Alberich's theft of the gold, which became the climactic event of Scene 1.

There follows a brief description of the race of giants—'defiant, powerful, primally begotten'. Again, this sounds more like the Eddaic frost giants than the two giant brothers of *Das Rheingold*. However, the mention of 'their monstrous strength, their simple mother-wit' suggests characteristics which obviously survived in Fasolt and Fafner. The giants feel themselves no match for the dwarfs, who are forging wondrous weapons—weapons which human heroes will one day wield to bring about their downfall. The concept of dwarfs forging weapons was of course taken over into *Siegfried* (where Mime makes a sword), as was the notion of a human hero (Siegfried) wielding one to kill a giant (Fafner). However, the concept of a wholesale war against the giants was dropped, and the notion of eternal enmity between the Nibelungs and giants was compressed into a few dark hints in *Das Rheingold* Scene 2.

Next the draft introduces the race of gods, 'already waxing to supremacy', which takes advantage of this strife. Playing upon the giants' fears, Wodan[17] bargains with them to build a fortress from which the gods may order and rule the world securely. After completing this work, the giants demand the Nibelung hoard as payment. The gods cleverly capture Alberich (how, the draft does not specify), and force him to ransom his life with the hoard. The dwarf wants to keep the ring, but the gods take that also, 'knowing full well that in it lies the secret of Alberich's power'. Alberich curses the ring, that 'it shall be the ruin of all who possess it'. Wishing to assure his absolute

[17] In this section, each character is referred to by the name he or she bears in the manuscript under consideration.

power, Wodan attempts to withhold the ring from the defiant giants, but finally 'Wodan yields on the advice of the three women of fate (Norns), who warn him of the downfall of the gods themselves.'

All this material relating to the giants, the gods, and Alberich eventually found its way into *Das Rheingold* Scenes 2 and 4, with obvious changes. At this point, only Wodan is distinguished from the rest of the gods; he deals with an entire race of giants, and is warned by 'drei Schicksalsfrauen' to relinquish the ring. There is no mention at all of Freia, Loge, Fricka, Erda, or any of the other gods. However, the resultant focus upon Alberich and Wotan was carried over into *Das Rheingold*, where the actions of these two protagonists trigger the dramatic development.

The giants now give the hoard and ring into the charge of a monstrous dragon (*Wurm*) on Gnitaheide (literally, the 'plain of envy'). The Nibelungs and Alberich remain in thrall to the ring, whose power the giants are too stupid to use. As the years pass, the race of giants withers and fades before the lustre of the gods; the Nibelungs toil miserably in fruitless labour; and Alberich broods incessantly over regaining the ring.

The foregoing lines more or less outline the events which occur between the end of *Das Rheingold* and the opening of *Die Walküre*; obviously a number of details were later to change. The giants leave the draft for good, and emphasis is placed upon the thraldom of the Nibelungs. We remember that the scenario ends with the liberation of Alberich and the Nibelungs through Brünnhilde's restoration of the ring to the Rhine.

The draft goes on to describe the beneficent aims of the gods, their guilt in the matter of the ring, and their need for a free hero who will take this guilt upon himself and atone for it through his own death. This plus the story of Siegfried has already been sketched, and because most of it does not directly concern the genesis of *Das Rheingold*, we will forgo a closer exegesis. However, several details *were* incorporated into the 'Preliminary Evening', and thus must be mentioned.

In the midst of a description of the Valkyries, the fallen heroes they bear home to Valhalla, and the Volsungs, mention is made of *Holda's apples* as a means of fructifying a barren Volsung marriage. Thus are born the twins Sigemund and Sigelind, whose incestuous coupling finally produces the hero Siegfried.[18] This is the first allusion

---

[18] In the original draft, this occurs 'after a long pregnancy', but in the fair copy it happens 'after a seven-year pregnancy in the wilderness'. Fortunately for Sieglinde, this afterthought was not carried over into any of the other *Ring* manuscripts, and does not appear in the *GS* version of the scenario.

in the *Ring* drafts to Holda's apples, which became a central dramatic symbol in *Das Rheingold*.

Towards the conclusion of the draft, Siegfried is warned of the curse by three mermaids with swans' wings ('drei Meerfrauen mit Schwanenflügeln'),[19] who implore him to cast away the ring. The mermaids foreshadow the Rhinedaughters, who, it will be recalled, were not mentioned at the beginning of the draft. They are here referred to as 'soothsaying daughters of the water's depths', from whom Alberich once stole the Rhinegold; however, they are not named, nor is any distinction made among them. The scene is reminiscent of that moment, early in the scenario, when Wodan yielded the ring to the giants on the advice of 'three women of fate (Norns)', who warned him of the downfall of the gods. Wagner thus establishes the aforementioned dramatic parallel between the three Norns ('drei Schicksalsfrauen') and the three Rhinedaughters ('drei Meerfrauen', 'weissagende Töchter'). Siegfried of course refuses, playing out his original role as the gods' redeemer; his necessary defiance of the immortals clinches the parallel between the Rhinedaughters and the Norns: 'I know three women wiser than you, they know [the place] where one day the gods will do battle in anxious fear: it is to the gods' advantage if they take care that I fight with them.' Clearly the Norns' mythological function of appearing to men and announcing the decrees of fate is here appropriated by the mermaids, who futilely warn Siegfried of his approaching doom. This parallel between the Norns and the Rhinedaughters (and by extension between Wotan and Siegfried) was built into the story from the beginning; it is one of the key factors which allowed Wagner to structure *Das Rheingold* as a dramatic analogue to *Siegfried's Tod*.

2. Siegfried's Tod

Just as *Lohengrin* had contrasted the historical world of tenth-century Antwerp with the mythical realm of the Grail, so *Siegfried's Tod* originally contrasted civilized society (Gibichung Hall) with the uncivilized wilderness (Brünnhilde's rock, the forest by the Rhine). This contrast was to be paralleled in *Das Rheingold* by the alternation of

---

[19] In the anonymous copy of the scenario which served as *Stichvorlage* for the *GS* printing, the phrase 'mit Schwanenflügeln' is crossed out; these words therefore do not appear in the printed version of the essay, nor were they carried over into the poem of *Siegfried's Tod*. This deletion obscures the meaning of Siegfried's remark to Hagen 'drei wilde Wasservögel | hätt' ich euch gefangen', which itself leads Hagen to ask Siegfried whether he understands the speech of the birds. This in turn motivates Siegfried's tale of the *Waldvogel*, culminating in Hagen's fatal question 'Verstehst du auch | dieser Raben Spruch?' Eliminating the mermaids' ornithological attributes weakened this logical progression.

scenes set in the environs of Valhalla (civilization) with episodes set in the Rhine and in Nibelheim (the wilderness).

The prose draft for *Siegfried's Tod* outlines the action of each scene in detail; some of this obviously changed as the poem underwent revision, but much of it is familiar to us from *Götterdämmerung*. The dialogues are sketched out in prose, and many of these serve the purpose of imparting to Wagner's intended audience information contained in the earlier portions of the 1848 scenario. The part which bears most directly upon *Das Rheingold* is Act II Scene 1, the confrontation between Alberich and Hagen. Not found in the 1848 scenario, this scene was apparently inserted to clarify Hagen's motivation.[20] Here Alberich recounts information originally presented in the first few paragraphs of the scenario (the Nibelungs, Alberich's theft of the gold, Mime and the Tarnhelm, the giants and the gods, the dragon), sometimes citing that draft word for word. The dwarf still inveighs against the gods as a group, not just Wodan. This scene contains the first physical description of Alberich, in that it mentions his 'long white hair and beard'.[21]

Wagner decided to preface his three-act drama with a Prologue in order to make clear the cosmic significance of Siegfried's mission. His sketch for the Norns scene describes these women as 'three tall female characters in dark, draped garments' who 'wind a golden rope'; this again suggests an affinity with the Rhinedaughters, 'three mermaids in swan garments' associated with the gold. The parallel eventually led Wagner to begin *Das Rheingold* with the three Rhinedaughters and, ultimately, to open both dramas with similar music.

The structure of *Siegfried's Tod* had now been finalized: a prologue plus three acts. This was also to become the structure of *Das Rheingold* (a preliminary scene plus three main scenes) and of the *Ring* as a whole (a prologue plus three dramas). Wagner's next step was to versify his drama, turning its prose dialogue into the alliterative *Stabreim*.[22] He laid out the text of *Siegfried's Tod* in

---

[20] The Hagen's Watch episode did not yet exist.

[21] In Act II Scene 2, Siegfried mentions 'Freija, die holde' (specifically associating her with Gudrun) as well as Frikka, 'Wodan's herrliche Gattin' (whom Brünhild in Act I Scene 3 had referred to as 'Frigga'). More importantly, Hagen in Scene 3 mentions four of the gods and the animals usually sacrificed to them: Wodan (steers), Fro (boars), Donnar (goats), and Frikka (sheep). In this way, Wagner gradually built up the cosmology of *Das Rheingold*, although at the time he certainly had no plans to set these gods upon the stage.

[22] Because *Stabreim* as an alliterative poetic technique has been treated so extensively in the Wagnerian literature (see, for example, Cooke, *I Saw the World End*, 74–8), we forgo a detailed explanation. Its consequences for Wagner's musical phraseology will be dealt with in Chapter 7.

three- and four-stress lines; later, he divided each four-stress line into a pair of two-stress lines. Again, the Alberich/Hagen scene is crucial to the evolution of *Das Rheingold*; Wagner in effect versified the opening paragraphs of the original scenario, as Alberich tells Hagen about the ring, the giants (who have now *created* the dragon which guards the treasure), and the gods. The mermaids are referred to as 'drei Wasserfrauen', but are still unnamed and have apparently lost their ornithological attributes.[23]

3. Der junge Siegfried

That the prose sketches for *Der junge Siegfried* have survived at all is a stroke of fate: Wagner used the large sheet of paper on which they were written as a wrapper for the verse draft! In the middle of this sheet[24] are three brief entries, one for each act, as well as a note pertaining to the entry for Act II. At the top of the sheet are two further expansions of the Act II events; these were made at the time of the initial entries. At the bottom of the sheet are three more entries, the first relating to the game of riddles between Wodan and Mime, the second and third to Wodan's confrontations with the Wala and Siegfried; these entries were made later than the others.

The entries for Act II show that Wagner originally planned to introduce the Nibelungs *en masse*, not just Alberich and Mime. Alberich calls them forth from the earth, whereupon they rail against him as the cause of their enslavement. Encouraging them to hinder Mime's plot, Alberich sets them upon his brother, who in turn promises to free them as soon he comes into possession of the ring. Upon seeing Siegfried, the Nibelungs recognize him as lord of the ring, but the hero orders them to retreat. Apparently Wagner intended to employ the Nibelungs as a sort of choral background to the dispute between Alberich and Mime. He quickly thought better of this, crossing out the reference to the Nibelungs in the main entry (but not the two supplementary notes). However, he later used the Nibelungs in *Das Rheingold* Scenes 3 and 4; in the latter, Alberich calls them forth from the earth, just as he was to have done in Act II of *Der junge Siegfried*.

The earlier entries refer to the dragon as 'Fafner'; however, there is as yet no suggestion that he is a transformed giant. The jottings for Act III show the gradual emergence of the notion of the gods' self-

[23] Certain changes in spelling occurred: 'Brünhilde' and 'Gudrun' became 'Brünnhilde' and 'Gudrune', 'Gnitaheide' was now 'Neidheide' (later still to become 'Neidhöhle'), while 'Fro' and 'Donnar' became 'Froh' and 'Donner'.

[24] WWV 86C Text I; transcribed in Strobel, *Skizzen und Entwürfe*, 66–8.

destruction: the earlier entry reads 'Wodan and the Wala: end of the gods', while a later one runs: 'Wodan and the Wala.—Guilt of the gods, and their necessary downfall: Siegfried's destiny.—Self-destruction of the gods.' Although not yet named, the goddess Erda has finally appeared in the *Ring* drafts.

This is not the place to offer a detailed exegesis of the prose draft and poem of *Der junge Siegfried*, nor to describe how the latter differs from the present *Siegfried*.[25] For our purposes, the most significant moment in the prose draft is the encounter between Wodan and the Wala, which contains many features subsequently incorporated into the Erda episode of *Das Rheingold*; these will be discussed in Chapter 10. We turn now to our most important documents: the sketches and drafts for *Das Rheingold*.

4. Das Rheingold *and* Die Walküre

As explained in Chapter 2, the remaining two dramas were conceived more or less simultaneously, the manuscripts suggesting that the prose sketch for *Das Rheingold* preceded that for *Die Walküre*. In addition, Wagner made supplementary prose sketches for both dramas in a pocket notebook.

The brevity of the prose sketch and the supplementary notes for *Das Rheingold* permits them to be translated in full. The former[26] originally began as follows:

I. The three Rhinedaughters. Wodan (bathing)—(Fricka is the Rhine-daughters' aunt.) Alberich from the depths. He woos all three women, one after another, and is rejected.—The gold glows. 'How to win it?' 'He who renounces love.'—Alberich steals the gold.—Night.[27]

However, Wagner later inserted after 'Wodan (bathing)' the remark 'W. knows about the gold's properties.'

The second paragraph originally ran as follows:

II. Wodan. Fricka. Giants (Windfahrer and Reiffrost) have built the fortress. They demand Freia:—finally they content themselves with as much gold as will cover Freia. Theft of the Nibelung hoard resolved upon.

Wagner later inserted after 'will cover Freia' the explanatory parenthesis '(whom they keep as a hostage)'.

---

[25] For a penetrating account of the differences between the two versions of the poem, see Daniel Coren, 'The Texts of Wagner's *Der junge Siegfried* and *Siegfried*', *19th Century Music*, 6 (1982), 17–30.

[26] Transcribed in Strobel, *Skizzen und Entwürfe*, 203.

[27] All translations from Wagner's textual manuscripts are my own.

No substantial alterations were made to the third paragraph, which reads:

III. Alberich as lord of the Nibelungs. Mime has just been forced to forge the tarncap [*tarnkappe*] for him. He puts it on and immediately disappears: from afar he is heard scolding and driving: from all sides the Nibelungs bring out the hoard.—Wodan and Loke(?) call upon Alberich. The latter boasts about the hoard and about his power: L. persuades him to demonstrate the power of the Tarnhelm also: A. transforms himself into a toad; L. captures him in this state, and tears the Tarnhelm off him. Alberich in his natural form is dragged as a prisoner through the ravines to the rocky heights. He pays as ransom the hoard and finally also the ring—which he curses.—The giants obtain the hoard, and also the ring—which Wod. first wanted to keep, but which, after being warned, he also gives up, whereupon Freia is handed over. A dispute immediately breaks out over the ring: one of the giant brothers slays the other. Wodan: 'Remember Alberich's curse.'

Among other things, this sketch shows that Wagner originally planned to introduce Wodan into the very first scene, presumably in order to witness the theft of the gold. The mermaids are now referred to as 'die drei Rheintöchter', but are still unnamed; their relationship to the gods was of course dropped as the drama evolved, but suggests yet another parallel to the three Norns. The name of Wodan's spouse is now spelled 'Fricka', and two new gods have entered the lists: Freia, whose relationship to the others is as yet unspecified; and Loke, who, true to his Eddaic namesake, assists Wodan in his deceitful plans. The giants are given names which once again suggest the Eddaic frost giants, and the murder of one by the other (not mentioned in any of the earlier manuscripts) is obviously intended to demonstrate the power of the curse. The manner in which the gods trick Alberich is now specified, but the latter's transformation into a serpent is missing; clearly Wagner had not yet planned for the surviving giant to change himself into a dragon, so he had no need to demonstrate how this might take place. Wodan is now 'warned' by an unnamed person or persons to relinquish the ring.

Most significantly, the motif of the renunciation of love has appeared. Wagner emphasized the importance of this concept in a letter to Liszt, which will be discussed in Chapter 7. Deryck Cooke has pointed out that Wotan too threatens to renounce love by bartering Freia away to the giants; thus it is perhaps no accident that Alberich's renunciation of love and Freia as the giants' hostage enter the *Ring* manuscripts at the same moment.

The prose sketch for Acts I and II of *Die Walküre*[28] contains little

---

[28] WWV 86B Text Ia; Strobel, *Skizzen und Entwürfe*, 204–5.

that directly affected the evolution of *Das Rheingold*. However, the outline of the argument between Wodan and Fricka (including the latter's charges of marital infidelity) shows Wagner developing the essential adversary relationship between these two characters.

Let us now consider the supplementary notes for *Das Rheingold* which Wagner entered in a pocket notebook.[29] Entitled *Der Raub* (*The Theft*), these run as follows:

Wodan as yet knows nothing about the power of the gold. Fasolt and Fafner demand the Rhinegold as ransom for Freia (the Rhinedaughters have already mentioned that the giants too had coveted it); they as yet know nothing about Alberich's theft. Wodan and Loke go first to the Rhinedaughters; here they learn what has happened, and are solicited for help and restitution. Only now do they go to the Nibelungs.—Alberich receives the Tarnhelm from Mime, and then goes into the depths, swinging the whip.— They learn about the power of the ring; Wodan desires to win it for himself.—When Alberich demands it back and the giants insist upon it, Wodan is momentarily willing to give up Freia for the sake of the ring: the Wala appears and advises against it—the gods beseech him: he gives up the ring, Freia returns. (He reflects upon the benefit which, as ruler, he has gained through the fortress.)—Lament of the Rhinedaughters.

:after the first transformation:

Daybreak: the rising sun strikes Valhalla. Wodan is awakened from sleep by Fricka. Fear: the fortress is completed:—Freia is forfeit. Where tarries Loke, who recommended the treaty with the giants? The gods assemble in apprehension and anxiety: Freia seeks protection from Wodan.—The giants enter, etc.—The giants fix the Rhinegold as ransom*; as they depart with Freia,** loud wailing breaks out among the gods: mists envelop them, Valhalla darkens. Wodan and Loke disappear into the twilight to go to the Rhine.

(*Loke has proposed this ransom)

**they intend to enquire again before sundown.

In conclusion: Wodan—'we gave away the gold—now we need iron.'

During the dispute over Freia, Loke finally arrives: in answer to Wodan's reproaches over his absence (since he promised to get rid of the Giants) he informs them about the lament of the Rhinedaughters, who have complained to him about Alberich's theft. The giants stop short when they hear about the gold; Loke finally offers them the gold in exchange for Freia (more argument—finally resolution).

These jottings tell us much about the further evolution of the drama. For one thing, it becomes apparent that Wagner had already decided to postpone Wodan's intial appearance until the opening of Scene 2, mercifully eliminating the 'bathing' episode. However, this

---

[29] Strobel, *Skizzen und Entwürfe*, 209–10.

necessitated some other mechanism by which Wodan could learn about Alberich and the ring. Wagner first considered making Wodan hear about the events of Scene I from the Rhinedaughters instead of directly witnessing them himself. Ultimately he made Loke the agent who informs Wodan about Alberich and the gold. This eventually blossomed into Loge's magnificent narration, the musical highlight of Scene 2.

Loke, meanwhile, has begun to control and direct events. At first, the giants themselves were to fix the Rhinegold as ransom, but Wagner later added a note to the effect that it was Loke who proposed it. Loke also recommended the treaty and promised Wodan that he would get rid of the giants; however, there is still no suggestion that he is a god of fire. The giants are named Fasolt and Fafner, suggesting that Wagner had by now decided upon the Fafner/dragon transformation (perhaps when writing out a non-extant prose sketch for *Die Walküre* Act III). Donner and Froh have not yet appeared, and it is now the *Wala* (not the Norns, as in the 1848 scenario) who warns Wodan to surrender the ring. One of the supplementary prose sketches for *Die Walküre*[30] gives the Wala's name as 'Erda', a rubric postulated by Jacob Grimm as the name of the ancient German earth goddess. The cosmology of *Das Rheingold* was by now almost complete.

The long prose draft for *Das Rheingold*[31] elaborates the story down to its smallest detail, including much dialogue (still cast in prose); this document will be referred to frequently in Chapters 7 to 10. Although a few important changes did occur during versification, the prose draft essentially presents the story in its final form. Freia's brothers now appear, and her relationship to Fricka is specified. The Nibelungs make two appearances; Wagner had by now solved the vexing problem of how to transfer the hoard from Nibelheim to the mountaintop. The transitions between scenes are outlined, dividing the action into four parts rather than the original three. Alberich transforms himself into a 'Riesenschlange', in order to prepare (dramatically as well as musically) for Fafner's transformation into a dragon.

Nevertheless, the prose draft does differ in some respects from the poem. The Rhinedaughters are still nameless, differentiated only as 'the first', 'the second', and 'the third'. However, the left margin of p. 1 contains two groups of names: first Bronnlinde, Flosshilde, and Wellgunde, then Woghilde, Wellgunde, and Flosslinde. The second

---

[30] WWV 86B Text Ib; Strobel, *Skizzen und Entwürfe*, 211.
[31] Strobel, *Skizzen und Entwürfe*, 213–29.

group of names was carried over into the verse draft, but altered in that manuscript to the familiar Woglinde, Wellgunde, and Flosshilde.

According to Fafner, the gods will grow old and die if Freia is taken away from them, but he makes no mention of Freia's golden apples; apparently Wagner had not yet hit upon the idea of using these as a symbol of eternal youth. In addition, although Loke's role is now fully fleshed out, he still has no connection with fire. This strongly suggests that when Wagner wrote out the prose draft of *Das Rheingold*, he had not yet decided to end the tetralogy by destroying the gods and the world by fire.

In addition, there is, amazingly, no mention of Wodan's spear! In the completed opera, Wotan uses this weapon to prevent Donner from braining the giants with his hammer, thus interposing the force of law. However, when Donner first threatens the giants (Scene 2), the prose draft reads simply 'Wodan steps between them: nothing through force: he must protect the treaty.' Considering the symbolic and musical ramifications of the spear, its complete absence in the prose draft is truly astonishing.

The prose draft of *Die Walküre*[32] did not appreciably affect the genesis of *Das Rheingold*. However, we may note that although Wodan now has his spear firmly in hand (as he did in the prose sketch for this opera), and although he waves it to make fire spring up from the rocks, he does not call upon Loke, nor does he give his final speech about 'he who fears the point of my spear' being unable to cross the fire. Neither fire nor spear had yet acquired their final dramatic significance.

The last document for consideration is the verse draft of *Das Rheingold*. Here all the elements are in place, including Freia's apples and Wodan's spear (the latter in its dual role as a symbol of law and a weapon of force). Yet apart from a rather cryptic remark to Alberich in Scene 3, there was at first still nothing in the verse draft to connect Loke with fire. However, after completing the versification, Wagner entered as a marginal addition to the manuscript Loke's last speech, in which the trickster contemplates turning back into flame and consuming the gods. The passage towards the close of *Die Walküre* wherein Wotan commands Loge to blaze up around Brünnhilde's rock was also an afterthought, as the final page of the verse draft[33] reveals, and was perhaps added at the same time as the *Rheingold* insert. We can thus pinpoint fairly precisely the moment when Wagner decided to destroy the gods by fire—after he had completed

---

[32] WWV 86B Text II; Strobel, *Skizzen und Entwürfe*, 231–51.
[33] WWV 86B Text III.

the verse draft of *Die Walküre* (1 July 1852) but before he revised the Norns scene of *Siegfried's Tod* (November or December 1852). In order to prepare for this conflagration, he expanded Loke's attributes by making him a god of fire; he changed 'Loke' to 'Loge' while writing the verse draft of the revised Norns scene.[34]

---

[34] WWV 86D Text VIb.

4 Analytical Positions

> The person who, in judging my music, divorces the harmony
> from the instrumentation does me as great an injustice as the one
> who divorces my music from my poem, my vocal line from the
> words!
>
> (Wagner to Theodor Uhlig, 31 May 1852)

This chapter summarizes some of the more important trends in
Wagner analysis, as a context for the ensuing discussion. It lays no
claim to being a comprehensive survey of Wagner criticism; rather, it
outlines the analytical methods with which, implicitly or explicitly,
this book is in dialogue.

I. THEMATIC ANALYSIS

Thematic analysis in Wagner is inevitably bound up with the concept
of the leitmotif. 'Leitmotif' may be defined as a recurrent musical
idea which has been invested by its composer with semantic content.
The concept, although not the name, goes back to Wagner himself.

In Part III of *Oper und Drama*, Wagner set forth his suggestions
on how poetry and music might be combined to produce drama. The
primary vehicle for dramatic expression is the singer's *verse-melody*
(*Versmelodie*). A particular thought is announced by a particular
verse of the poem. However, every thought is necessarily associated
with some feeling or emotion; this emotion is expressed by the vocal
melody to which the verse in question is set. Thus, in a verse-
melody, the words express the conceptual idea or thought, while
the melody expresses the emotion necessarily associated with that
thought. The orchestra, however, is an independent element, which
according to Wagner avoids the verse-melody itself but realizes its
harmonic implications.

As a pure organ of the feeling, the orchestra possesses the ability
to utter that which words alone cannot express. In this way, it is
closely allied with the dramatic element of *gesture* (*Gebärde*). A
gesture may accompany a verbal expression or be resorted to when
words fail; in either case it expresses what words cannot. But to be
effective, this gesture (whether or not associated with words) must

be accompanied by the orchestra, which says to the ear what the physical motion says to the eye, and thereby expresses the feeling behind the gesture.

The orchestra also possesses the power of *reminiscence* (*Erinnerung*). As mentioned above, a verse-melody expresses the emotion associated with the thought announced by a particular verse. By recalling this melody, the orchestra recalls that emotion, thereby also recalling the thought associated with it. In this way, orchestral melody can function as 'a messenger of the very thought itself', transmitting that thought wordlessly to the feeling. But this is possible only if the emotion conveyed by the melody has been 'conditioned' (*bedingt*) by a definite object, either a verbal or a visible one (that is, associated with either words or gesture).

Finally, the orchestra can present a *foreshadowing* (*Ahnung*) of something as yet unspoken. This musical presentiment will then be defined (after the fact, as it were) by association with an appropriate gesture or object.

The true drama, then, consists of a chain of organically developing dramatic/musical 'moments' (*Momente*), in which the most important dramatic motifs generate the most important melodic moments of reminiscence and foreshadowing. The composer then distributes these musical root-motifs throughout the drama so that 'their necessary play of repetition will furnish him quite of itself with the highest unity of musical form'.[1]

Although Wagner did not refer to these melodic moments of reminiscence and foreshadowing as 'leitmotifs' (*Leitmotive*), he did call them 'musical motifs' (*musikalische Motive*);[2] the term 'motif' must here be understood, not in its narrow sense as a short pitch and rhythmic cell, but as a melodic/harmonic idea of variable length. It should be noted that Wagner stresses the emotional association of the motif rather than its semantic content; the latter (the original 'thought' behind a particular line of verse) is transmitted only secondarily, through its original association with the emotion expressed by the verse-melody. In the case of an orchestral motif which originally

---

[1] *Richard Wagner's Prose Works*, trans. William Ashton Ellis (London, 1892–9), ii (*Opera and Drama*), 347; *Gesammelte Schriften und Dichtungen von Richard Wagner* (Leipzig, 1887–8; repr. Hildesheim, 1976), iv. 201. For the reader's convenience, references to *Oper und Drama* cite both the Ellis translation (*RWPW*) and the second (1887–8) edition of Wagner's *Gesammelte Schriften* (*GS*); most subsequent *GS* printings follow the pagination of the second edition, which differs from that of the first (1871–83).
For a fuller summary of Wagner's argument, see Frank W. Glass, *The Fertilizing Seed: Wagner's Concept of the Poetic Intent* (Ann Arbor, Mich., 1983), 47–52.
[2] *GS* iv. 185; *RWPW* ii. 329.

accompanied a wordless physical gesture, the emotional association would be visible rather than verbal in origin.

Hans von Wolzogen, in his 1876 analysis of the *Ring*, laid almost exclusive stress upon the semantic content of these motifs. In other words, he interpreted them semiotically, as musical signs referring to objects, characters, concepts, and specific emotions (love, hatred, anger, etc.). Emotion was thus simply one type of signified among others, not an inevitable and specific concomitant of every motif. Having found and labelled the '*Leitmotive*',[3] Wolzogen used them to illustrate his exegesis of the text.

It is easy to criticize Wolzogen's enterprise by pointing out that he recklessly transformed Wagner's 'melodic moments of feeling' into musical signs, thereby ascribing to them a function never claimed by their composer. But we should be wary of using *Oper und Drama* as an authority for the analysis of *Das Rheingold*, let alone the later music dramas. Wagner wrote this treatise during the winter of 1850–1, and did not begin the musical composition of *Das Rheingold* until November 1853. The discursive style of the essay suggests that even as he wrote them down, Wagner's ideas were in a state of flux; any attempt to ground a discussion of his thematic, tonal, and formal procedures in an exegesis of this prose work would necessarily be highly problematic. In fact, a study of the music dramas suggests that Wagner *did* employ his musical motifs as signs, as much for their semantic content as for the emotions originally associated with them. This is particularly true of the motif of 'foreshadowing', which normally is invested with semantic content ('is conditioned', to use Wagner's expression) through its association with a scenic or visual phenomenon, and is subsequently employed to remind us of that phenomenon directly, not through the mediation of a concomitant emotion. Consider, for example, the Valhalla motif. Because this theme is heard in the orchestra before the rising sun illuminates the fortress, it functions initially as a motif of 'foreshadowing', arousing in the listener emotions which are satisfied when the theme is 'conditioned' by the visual image. However, the motif's subsequent appearances often signify the fortress itself, the power it represents, or Wotan as its lord, and do not necessarily evoke this original

---

[3] Wolzogen does not use this term in *Thematischer Leitfaden* (1876), as Dahlhaus and others imply; here he refers simply to '*Motive*'. He first speaks of '*Leitmotive*' in 'Die Motive in Wagner's *Götterdämmerung*', an article which appeared in three numbers of *Musikalisches Wochenblatt* during 1877–9. Wolzogen may have found this term in Otto Jähns's 1871 catalogue of Weber's works. See Dahlhaus's discussion of leitmotif in *The New Grove Wagner*, ed. John Deathridge and Carl Dahlhaus (New York and London, 1984), 111–14; see also the entry 'Leitmotif' (by John Warrack) in *Tne New Grove Dictionary of Music and Musicians*, ed. Stanley Sadie (London, 1980), x. 644–6.

emotion. The theme functions as a musical sign, addressed directly to the intellect rather than the feeling. The same is true of the Gold fanfare; originally a motif of foreshadowing given concrete meaning by the spectacle of the gold's awakening by the sun in *Das Rheingold* Scene I, it functions henceforth as a sign signifying the gold in its natural state.

However, some themes *do* function as 'reminiscence' motifs in the way Wagner described. For example, the reappearances of the Renunciation of Love theme seem intended to evoke the tragic emotion associated with the concept of renouncing love in favour of power; this emotion in turn recalls the concept. Hence, when Wagner in Act I of *Die Walküre* makes Siegmund sing the 'Renunciation' melody at the very moment when the hero is supposedly *affirming* his love for Sieglinde, he apparently wants the melody to evoke this tragic emotion, in order to suggest that Siegmund has been drawn unwittingly into the tragic complications originally set in motion by Alberich's *Liebesfluch*. A more complex example is the Sword theme, which first appears towards the close of *Das Rheingold* as a motif of 'foreshadowing': Wotan is suddenly inspired with a 'grand idea' of how to save Valhalla and the gods, but he keeps both Fricka and the audience in the dark as to the exact nature of this idea. In *Die Walküre*, the same arpeggio is associated with the sword Nothung as the agency of Wotan's plan, and is 'conditioned' by the appearance of the weapon itself. Henceforth the motif may function in one of two ways: as a sign referring directly to the sword as a physical object, or as a reminiscence motif evoking the emotion which originally accompanied Wotan's 'grand idea'. It is in the latter sense that the motif appears, with shattering effect, at the climax of Siegfried's Funeral Procession.[4]

Wolzogen was justly accused of omitting a number of important leitmotifs and mislabelling others. Nevertheless, his guides to the *Ring* and the other music dramas became models for a certain type of Wagner 'analysis', which contented itself with locating, describing, and naming recurrent thematic shapes, sometimes accepting Wolzogen's findings, more often expanding and/or correcting them. Scant attention was paid to the transformation or interrelationship of themes, other than to point out that some occurred in more than one form and that others displayed melodic similarities.

---

[4] Christopher Wintle posits a multiplicity of contexts evoked by the reappearance of the Sword motif in Siegfried's Funeral Procession; see 'The Numinous in *Götterdämmerung*', in *Reading Opera*, ed. Arthur Groos and Roger Parker (Princeton, NJ, 1988), 202–11. Cogently argued though it is, Wintle's interpretation seems to me to miss the main point: namely, that Wotan's 'great plan' for moral regeneration lies in ruins.

It soon became commonplace to complain about the narrowness of Wolzogen's labels while continuing to use them or replacing them with equally narrow labels. Ernest Newman, whose work best exemplifies the English language variety of thematic guide,[5] often gave the impression that Wagner sometimes used the wrong theme in the wrong place. Deryck Cooke attempted to rectify Newman's errors by pointing out that some of them were based upon Wolzogen's blatant mislabellings.[6] For his pains, Cooke was recently excoriated for having 'merely preached a rewriting of the dictionary, with truer identifications provided for every thematic scrap'.[7] In actuality, Cooke's investigations ran much deeper than this: they demonstrated that Wagner derived the hundreds of leitmotifs in the *Ring* from a small number of 'basic motifs' (an arpeggio, a scale, a distinctive chord progression, etc.), and that each 'basic motif' represents one of the central symbols of the drama (Nature, Power, Magic, etc.), generating other motifs to represent different aspects of the central symbol.[8] This may be what Wagner meant when he wrote that the melodic moments of reminiscence and foreboding 'will necessarily have blossomed only from *the weightiest motifs* of the drama'.[9]

However, not all analysts were satisfied with explicating the semantic content of the leitmotifs or demonstrating their interrelationships; some maintained that these ideas served a structural function as well, behaving analogously to the themes of a symphonic work. The *locus classicus* of this sort of thinking is, of course, Alfred Lorenz's monumental *Das Geheimnis der Form bei Richard Wagner* (1924–33), discussed at greater length in the third section of this chapter. Lorenz viewed each of Wagner's music dramas as a mighty edifice of formal architecture, a musical labyrinth of forms-within-forms. These formal patterns are articulated by the leitmotifs through the principles of thematic correspondence, variation, and contrast. Lorenz did not deny the semantic content of the motifs, and he often made illuminating remarks on this account; but he did feel that, in addition to its dramatic role, each motif plays a decisive part in the articulation of multi-level musical structures.

Other analysts took a middle-of-the-road position, arguing that,

---

[5] To be fair, his book *Wagner Nights* (London, 1949; repr. 1961, 1977), published in America as *The Wagner Operas* (New York, 1949; repr. 1963), is much more than a thematic catalogue. It offers much valuable background material on the operas.

[6] Cooke's chief target was the so-called 'Flight' motif, which he interpreted as a musical sign for the emotion of love (*I Saw the World End*, 48–64).

[7] Carolyn Abbate and Roger Parker, 'Introduction: On Analyzing Opera', in *Analyzing Opera: Verdi and Wagner* (Berkeley and Los Angeles, 1989), 8–9.

[8] *An Introduction to 'Der Ring des Nibelungen'* (Decca Records RDN, S-1, 1969), 7.

[9] *RWPW* ii. 347; *GS* iv. 201.

while some thematic ideas are used primarily to create formal shape (although on a much smaller scale than Lorenz assumed), others are employed referentially, as signs that appear at the prompting of the text, and possess no formal implications. There thus emerged the dialectic of 'form-defining themes and referential motifs', which, as Carolyn Abbate has pointed out, 'was already in the nineteenth century a commonplace of Wagnerian criticism'.[10] Abbate herself has made the extraordinary claim that 'Wagner's motifs have no referential meaning; they may, and of course do, absorb meaning at exceptional and solemn moments, by being used with elaborate calculation as signs, but unless purposely maintained in this artificial state, they shed their specific poetic meaning and revert to their natural state as musical thoughts.'[11] This deliberately provocative statement seems to me totally without foundation. Obviously the 'semiotic baggage' (to use Abbate's words) is not 'somehow immanent in the motif'; clearly the motifs possess no *intrinsic* referential meaning (there is nothing in a triadic fanfare that necessarily signifies 'gold'). Yet once Wagner has deliberately invested a musical idea with semantic meaning, there is simply no way he can withdraw this meaning, however he may subsequently employ the motif (the Gold fanfare will always denote the gold on some level, even if this signification is not its main task at a given moment). Clearly leitmotif exegesis has gone too far, but this sort of exaggerated overcorrection does not seem helpful.

Cooke accepted (and praised) Lorenz's work, but his own analysis of the *Ring*, had he completed it, would have taken a much different course. He proposed to follow Wagner's own suggestion in *Über die Anwendung der Musik auf das Drama* (1879) that the transformation of each motif should be pursued carefully 'through all the changing passions of the four-part drama'.[12] This task, said Cooke, 'would involve clarifying the psychological implications of all the motifs, and tracing their changing significance throughout the whole of their long and complex development'.[13] Unfortunately Cooke died before he could carry out this task, and no one else has attempted it.

As the reader will soon realize, the analytical portion of this book concentrates upon formal/tonal structure; thematic discussion is largely confined to an investigation of compositional genesis. Never-

---

[10] 'Wagner, "On Modulation", and *Tristan*', *Cambridge Opera Journal*, 1 (1989), 42. She is probably referring to the writings of Christian von Ehrenfels.

[11] ' "On Modulation" ', 45.

[12] '... durch alle Wechsel der Leidenshaften, in welchen sich das ganze viertheilige Drama bewegt' (*GS* x. 190). Quoted and trans. by Cooke in *I Saw the World End*, 45.

[13] *An Introduction*, 7; quoted by Colin Matthews in his preface to *I Saw the World End*.

theless, it is hoped that this approach, along with the foregoing remarks, will provide a foundation for those interested in undertaking a more exhaustive thematic analysis of the opera.

II. TONAL ANALYSIS

Wagner had definite thoughts about the role tonality should play in 'the drama of the future'. In Part III of *Oper und Drama* he related the role of harmonic modulation to that of *Stabreim*: just as the alliterative poetic technique can link together speech-roots of either like or unlike emotional content and present them as related words directly to the feeling, so modulation can render this kinship even more perceptible through the musical kinship of related keys. When dealing with a verse expressing a single emotion, such as 'Liebe gibt Lust zum Leben' ('Love gives joy to life), the composer would have no cause to modulate. But in setting a verse of mixed emotion, such as 'die Liebe bringt Lust und Leid' ('Love brings joy and sorrow'), the musician would feel obligated to relinquish the key expressing the first emotion for one expressing the second. If this verse were followed by 'Doch in ihr Weh auch webt sie Wonnen' ('But in her woe she also weaves raptures'), he would return to the first tonality at the point where the second emotion gives way to the first. This modulatory procedure is justified by the poetic intent, without which it would seem arbitrary and unintelligible.[14]

Throughout his career, Wagner emphasized the difference between absolute music (which could encompass both the operatic set piece and the Beethovenian symphonic movement) and his own textually driven dramatic music, which he felt was richer, more daring, and inexplicable in purely musical terms. In *Zukunftsmusik* (1860), he referred to his music as bizarrely constructed and even illogical if considered from a purely musical point of view. An undated fragment entered in the '*Tristan* sketchbook' reads: 'On modulation in pure instrumental music and in drama. Fundamental difference. Swift and free transitions are in the latter often just as necessary as they are unjustified in the former, owing to a lack of motif.'[15] In *Über die Anwendung der Musik auf das Drama* (1879) he reiterated his conviction that a rapid series of modulations must be grounded in the drama in order to be intelligible, and that his own modulatory techniques were unsuitable for symphonic composition. Apparently Bruckner and Mahler paid little heed.

[14] *GS* iv. 152–3; *RWPW* ii. 291–3. See Glass, *The Fertilizing Seed*, 44.

[15] Quoted in Abbate, ' "On Modulation" ', 37. The '*Tristan* Sketchbook' is presently in the Bayreuth Archives (B II a 5).

Lorenz was interested less in how Wagner handled tonality on the level of the phrase or verse-melody than in the composer's use of tonality to delineate large structural blocks. The latter is bound up (Lorenz thought) with Wagner's concept of the 'poetic–musical period', discussed in the next section. However, Lorenz did accept Wagner's 'poetic' use of modulation, and extended this concept in a somewhat different direction. He observed that D major, the key in which Siegfried reforges Nothung, is the parallel major of D minor, the key of his father's misery (and that in which the sword was shattered). Whereas Siegfried's love scene with Brünnhilde is in C major, that between his parents closes in G (as Lorenz puts it, 'The seed of C major lies in its dominant!'). Hagen's tonality of B minor appears in the same relationship to Siegfried's D major as Alberich's key (B♭ minor) to that of Wotan (D♭ major). In other words, Lorenz interpreted certain keys as tonal symbols.[16]

Both Wagner's 'poetic' use of modulation and Lorenz's rudimentary key symbolism find echoes in the tonal theories developed by Robert Bailey and his student Patrick McCreless. Following Bailey, McCreless posits four independent tonal principles at work in Wagner's music: 'classical tonality', 'associative tonality', 'expressive tonality', and 'directional tonality'. 'Classical tonality' is simply the traditional tonic–dominant tonality as defined by Heinrich Schenker. 'Associative tonality' involves the consistent association of specific keys with particular dramatic symbols or ideas; invested with semantic content, these keys, like Wolzogen's leitmotifs, function as musical signs. 'Expressive tonality' employs structural progression by ascending or descending whole tones or semitones in order to create an expressive intensification or relaxation, which in turn reflects some aspect of the dramatic situation. 'Directional tonality' features an interplay between two different tonal centres, both of which can function as tonic (the so-called 'double tonic complex'), and usually involves a gradual progression from the first key to the second. According to McCreless, the tonal structure of the *Ring* is marked by the interaction of these four tonal principles. For example, a structural progression based upon 'directional tonality' may be interrupted by keys which appear purely for 'expressive' or 'associative' reasons, at the prompting of the text. Thus tonality as well as leitmotifs may be either form-defining, referential, or both.[17]

---

[16] *Das Geheimnis der Form bei Richard Wagner*, i: *Der Musikalische Aufbau des Bühnenfestspieles 'Der Ring des Nibelungen'* (Berlin, 1924; repr. Tutzing, 1966), 49–50.

[17] *Wagner's 'Siegfried'*, 88–95. McCreless's discussion of 'associative' and 'expressive' tonality is based largely upon Bailey's 'The Structure of the *Ring*', 48–61. For the 'double tonic complex', see Bailey's 'An Analytical Study of the Sketches and Drafts', in Richard Wagner,

While Bailey's tonal theories have exercised considerable influence in America, German Wagner scholars have found difficulty extricating themselves from the tangles of Hugo Riemann's harmonic system, even though many—beginning perhaps with Ernst Kurth[18]— have long recognized harmony and tonality as a central formal category in Wagner's music. In this regard the work of Carl Dahlhaus must be mentioned, in particular his celebrated essay 'Issues in Composition'.

Appropriating concepts introduced by Arnold Schoenberg, Dahlhaus characterized Wagner's harmony as 'wandering' or 'centrifugal', in contrast to Brahms's harmony, which is 'expanded' or 'centripetal'. Dahlhaus felt that in Wagner's music 'the keys, or fragmentary allusions to keys, do not always relate to a constant center' but 'should rather be seen as joined together like the links in a chain, without there necessarily being any other connection between the first and third links than the second'. Thus 'the characteristic function of Wagner's use of harmony is to establish not hierarchies but an order of succession'. By contrast, Brahms's music displays 'tonal centrality created by the enrichment of the fundamental bass and regional connections'; although a piece may begin 'on the tonal periphery the music's sole ambition is to reach its center'. The 'centrifugal' effect of Wagner's music derives from his frequent use of real or modulating sequence as an expository rather than a developmental device, while the 'centripetal' nature of Brahms's tonality is closely linked with the composer's use of 'developing variation'.[19]

This sounds plausible until Dahlhaus offers a demonstration. He first cites Schoenberg's rather bizarre harmonic analysis of an eight-bar passage from Act I of *Tristan* (beginning with the words 'War Morold dir so wert'). Condemning as 'ingenious but not particularly illuminating' Schoenberg's interpretation of this segment as a tonally integrated period in B minor, Dahlhaus offers a truly idiosyncratic reading of the passage as a piece of 'wandering tonality', characterized by sequential repetition and symmetrical division of the octave, but lacking a unifying tonic. In actuality, the passage, although highly chromatic, is a composed-out I^6-ii^6-V-i progression in $G^\flat/F^\sharp$ major/minor, in which the bass unfolding of the lower third

Prelude and Transformation from 'Tristan und Isolde', ed. Robert Bailey (New York, 1985), 113–46.

[18] *Romantische Harmonik und ihre Krise in Wagner's 'Tristan und Isolde'* (Berne, 1920).

[19] 'Issues in Composition', in *Between Romanticism and Modernism: Four Studies in the Music of the Later Nineteenth Century*, trans. Mary Whittall (Berkeley and Los Angeles, 1980), 65–75. This essay was originally published in 1974.

Ex. 4.1

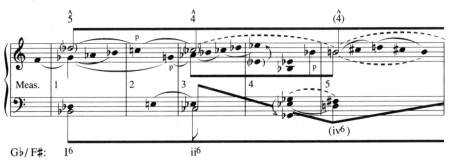

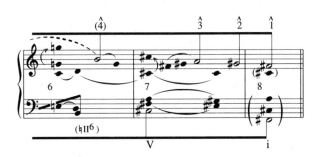

of ii⁶ (C♭–D–B) successively supports ii⁶, iv⁶, and ♮II⁶ (Ex. 4.1). In
his Riemannesque insistence upon vertical sonorities and functional
labels, Dahlhaus misses the way in which the well-defined contrapuntal motion of the outer voices clearly expresses a single tonality.[20]

If the Riemannians of Germany have had difficulty with Wagner's
tonal procedures, how have the Schenkerians of America and Great
Britain fared? Heinrich Schenker's own antipathy towards Wagner's
music is well known; he felt that Wagner was simply incapable of
composing-out a fundamental structure over a long period of time
by means of complex diminutions,[21] and he railed against the composer's 'overemphasis on the musical foreground due to theatrical
requirements'.[22] For the most part, his followers appear to have
tacitly agreed that the complete Schenkerian model is inapplicable

---

[20] 'Issues in Composition', 67–8.
[21] *Free Composition*, trans. Ernst Oster (New York, 1979), 106.
[22] 'Organic Structure in Sonata Form', trans. Orin Grossman, in *Readings in Schenkerian Analysis and Other Approaches*, ed. Maury Yeston (New Haven, Conn., 1977), 52.

to Wagnerian opera, and have generally confined their analyses to relatively brief instrumental passages, the *Tristan* Prelude being a perennial favourite.[23]

In my opinion, the Schenkerian model is more applicable to Wagner's texted dramatic music than has generally been recognized. At the very least, a judicious use of Schenkerian techniques might help prevent the Dahlhaus syndrome of drawing grand conclusions from bungled analyses. However, the Schenkerian model is by no means the only analytical weapon needed to stalk the structural complexities of Wagnerian opera. Wagner clearly used other methods of tonal organization when his dramatic purposes demanded them, and it is here that the concepts of expressive, associative, and directional tonality (including the double tonic complex) can be very helpful. Yet we must beware of applying these concepts mechanically or in a wholesale manner, a pitfall McCreless does not totally escape. In addition, although Dahlhaus's notion of 'centrifugal' tonality seems grounded in his own analytical ineptitude, his concept of 'centripetal' tonality (in which a passage begins 'off-tonic', as it were, and slowly gravitates towards this tonic) may paradoxically be more applicable to Wagner's music than to that of Brahms.

III. FORMAL ANALYSIS

In Part III of *Oper und Drama*, Wagner followed his explanation of the 'poetic' use of modulation with the description of a formal unit he called the 'poetic–musical period' (*die dichterische–musikalische Periode*). Such a unit comes into existence when the modulations, in order to realize the poetic intent, touch upon the most varied tonalities; however, all these keys appear in exact kindred relationships to the original tonality. Thus the principal key dominates all its related keys, just as the chief emotion dominates all its related emotions. If the resultant structure is termed the 'poetic–musical period', then the most completely expressive work of art is that which

---

[23] See, for example, William J. Mitchell, 'The *Tristan* Prelude: Techniques and Structure', in *The Music Forum*, i, ed. William J. Mitchell and Felix Salzer (New York, 1967), 163–203; and Allen Forte, 'New Approaches to the Linear Analysis of Music', *Journal of the American Musicological Society*, 41 (1988), 315–48. Recent attempts to apply Schenkerian analysis to texted passages include Matthew Brown, 'Isolde's Narrative: From *Hauptmotif* to Tonal Model', in *Analyzing Opera*, 180–201; Patrick McCreless, 'Schenker and the Norns', in *Analyzing Opera*, 276–97; and Warren Darcy, 'A Wagnerian *Ursatz*; or, Was Wagner a Background Composer After All?', *Intégral*, 4 (1990), 1–35. In an 'analytical postscript' to 'The Numinous', Wintle uses voice-leading graphs to demonstrate how two 'motivic' (or associative) tonalities are integrated into a governing key at the foreground level (231–4).

contains many such periods, each developing from and 'conditioning' the others.[24]

Alfred Lorenz based his entire enterprise upon this passage. Assuming that the length of the 'poetic–musical period' was flexible—that it could span anywhere from thirty measures to three hundred—he proceeded to carve up the four *Ring* dramas into an array of such periods, each displaying uniformity of tonal centre and dramatic content.[25] Each of Lorenz's periods is based upon one or more principal themes, and the majority are written throughout in the same metre and tempo. Furthermore, each exhibits an elaborate multi-level formal design, articulated primarily by thematic correspondence and contrast (the leitmotifs are thus 'form-defining' as well as 'referential'). Lorenz's elevation of *Bar* and *Bogen* to central formal categories is too familiar to require discussion.[26]

The impact of Lorenz's work can scarcely be measured; in fact, the history of subsequent Wagner scholarship could largely be written in terms of those who extended Lorenz's work and those who reacted against it. However, even analysts who begin by blasting Lorenz's project to smithereens generally continue by erecting something very similar in its place; this characterizes the work of Bailey and McCreless. Both appear to accept Lorenz's concept of the 'poetic–musical period', and feel it is valid for Wagner's works as far as Act I of *Tristan*. Beginning with Act II of that drama, however, the principle of the 'poetic–musical period' is replaced by a symphonic model: individual acts are composed as multi-movement 'symphonies' of four to six 'movements', each of which 'develops a particular dramatic issue and a particular aspect of the tonal plan of the act as a whole'.[27]

The concept of Wagner's music as 'symphonic' is not new, and in fact goes back to Wagner himself. However, as Abbate has pointed out, 'symphonic' procedure for Wagner meant motivic repetition and transformation, not the use of specific formal archetypes and large-scale tonal plans.[28] Wagner would have understood each of his music dramas, *Das Rheingold* included, as 'symphonic'.

[24] *GS* iv. 153–5; *RWPW* ii. 293–4. See Glass, *The Fertilizing Seed*, 44–5.

[25] Lorenz, *Der musikalische Aufbau*, 23–46.

[26] For a summary of Lorenz's method, together with critical commentary, see my unpublished doctoral dissertation 'Formal and Rhythmic Problems in Wagner's "Ring" Cycle' (University of Illinois, 1973), 13–51.

[27] McCreless, *Wagner's 'Siegfried'*, 187–90. The notion that the ideas of *Oper und Drama* apply to the operas from *Das Rheingold* to Act I of *Tristan*, after which they are overthrown, is derived from Bailey, 'The Genesis of *Tristan*', 6.

[28] 'Opera as Symphony, A Wagnerian Myth', in *Analyzing Opera*, 100–4.

The question, however, is not how many operas may be analysed in terms of the 'poetic–musical period', but whether Lorenz correctly interpreted Wagner's explanation of this concept. Dahlhaus felt that he had not. According to Dahlhaus, Wagner used the term 'period' in its generally accepted sense of a relatively short, tonally closed section;[29] in the vocabulary of *Oper und Drama*, a period would comprise several successive verse-melodies, and span no more than twenty to thirty-odd measures. In fact, Dahlhaus himself later applied the term in this sense to the operas of Richard Strauss.[30] Thus (according to Dahlhaus) Lorenz's huge tonal constructs can in no way be equated with Wagner's 'poetic–music periods', and Lorenz's labyrinthine formal edifices were figments of his own imagination.

If Wagner's music does not display the sort of 'architectural' form Lorenz posited, then what *is* its underlying formal principle? Dahlhaus found this in Wagner's concept of the 'symphonic web', a thematic network of related leitmotifs which stretches across the entire drama. 'Wagner renounced an architectonic foundation for musical forms . . . He was therefore forced to constitute his forms exclusively according to "logic", that is to emphasize the principle of thematic–motivic connection and development . . . Form as "architecture" was replaced by form as "web".'[31] This is closely allied with Wagner's rejection of symmetrically balanced phrases and cadential formulae (resulting in 'musical prose'), his notion that music must be thematically meaning-ful at every moment ('endless melody'), and his replacement of the antecedent–consequent principle by modulating sequence (creating the afore-mentioned 'centrifugal' tonality).

Dahlhaus's idea that Wagner renounced the 'architectural' basis of musical form is not borne out by an analysis of the music, as I hope to demonstrate in the following chapters. In fact, a central concern of this book is to debunk what might be termed 'the Dahlhaus myth' about Wagner, and to establish on a somewhat different basis from Lorenz the architectural nature of Wagner's dramatic/musical forms. Nevertheless, Dahlhaus was probably correct in his assertion that it is wrong to equate Wagner's 'poetic–musical periods' with Lorenz's large formal–tonal units; as suggested earlier, the attempt to ground an analysis of the music dramas in *Oper und Drama* is a highly

---

[29] 'Wagners Begriff der "dichterisch–musikalische Periode" ', in *Beiträge zur Geschichte der Musikanschauung im neunzehnten Jahrhundert*, ed. Walter Salmen (Regensburg, 1965), 179–94.
[30] *Nineteenth Century Music*, trans. J. Bradford Robinson (Berkeley and Los Angeles, 1989), 349.
[31] *The New Grove Wagner*, 126.

questionable one. However, this does not necessarily invalidate Lorenz's entire enterprise; it simply means that he had misinterpreted a small segment of *Oper und Drama*.[32] The implications of this for formal analysis will be discussed in Chapter 5.[33]

---

[32] As Thomas Grey puts it, '[Lorenz] cannot be primarily criticized for having misconstrued the "true" nature of the poetic–musical period, since Wagner's formulation of the concept resists any concrete definition. In any case, Lorenz's appropriation of the term would seem to be more a matter of convenience . . .' ('Richard Wagner and the Aesthetics of Musical Form in the Mid-19th Century (1840–1860)', Ph.D. diss. (University of California, Berkeley, 1988), 314).

[33] The American scholar Anthony Newcomb feels that the essence of Wagner's music lies in its formal fluidity: a given unit is not in any single form, but refers to, plays with, and intermixes various formal conventions. See 'The Birth of Music out of the Spirit of Drama: An Essay in Wagnerian Formal Analysis', *19th Century Music*, 5 (1981–2), 38–66.

5 *The Opera as a Whole*

> [*Das Rheingold*] has become a close-knit unity: there is scarcely a
> bar in the orchestra which does not develop out of preceding
> motifs.
>
> (Wagner to August Röckel, 25/26 January 1854)

Within the context of the *Ring* as a whole, *Das Rheingold* serves an
expository function; consequently, its poem is laid out as a quickly
moving series of external dramatic events, and contains few of the
reflective moments which characterize the next two dramas. This
feature of the poem greatly influenced its musical realization: the
opera is organized as a series of dramatic/musical 'episodes', each
built around one important dramatic event and governed (in most
cases) by a single tonality. The Structural Outline at the beginning
of this book displays the division of *Das Rheingold* into twenty
episodes, plus various transitions, interludes, etc.[1]

It should be emphasized that these 'episodes' are *not* the 'poetic–
musical periods' of *Oper und Drama*. As Dahlhaus and Abbate
have correctly pointed out, Wagner describes the latter as a longer
series of single, internally modulating lines, which would make each
'period' twenty to forty measures long at most. In any case, Wagner
wrote *Oper und Drama* almost two years before he began setting the
Rheingold poem to music, so that efforts by analysts to employ
the 'poetic–musical period' as a primary formal category are highly
questionable. It was mentioned in Chapter 4 that Lorenz misidentified
as Wagner's 'periods' the large formal/tonal units he himself had
observed. This does not, however, invalidate Lorenz's structures; it

---

[1] This Structural Outline is intended for initial orientation only, as a context for the detailed
discussion in Chapters 6 to 10. Readers may wish to copy this outline into their vocal scores
before proceeding further. Because sections are often elided or connected by transitions,
sharply defined structural breaks are not always present. Very brief transitions are not shown.
Only the controlling tonality of each episode is listed (not necessarily that in which it begins);
however, if an episode is controlled by two keys, moving from one to the other, both are listed.
The beginning of each section is given two ways in the 'Location' column: by reference to the
widely available Schirmer vocal score (page/system/measure number) and by measure number
from the beginning of the opera. References in successive diagrams and musical examples are
by measure number alone, but it is hoped that this initial double reference will enable readers
to orient themselves more quickly.

merely means that he was mistaken in believing that he could ground his own analyses in Wagner's prose writings.

If the episodes of the Structural Outline are not *Wagner's* 'periods', to what extent do they resemble *Lorenz's* 'periods'? In a general sense, they resemble them rather strongly, inasmuch as the episodes are for the most part quite long, often comprising hundreds of measures. In a specific sense, 'periods' and 'episodes' are not always congruent: Lorenz divides Episodes 2 and 13 into two periods apiece, combines Episodes 14 and 15 into one period, does the same with Episodes 16, 17, and 18, and places the division between Episodes 6 and 7 in a different place. Otherwise, Lorenz's formal articulations match those of the Structural Outline quite closely.

What justifies the analytical division into twenty episodes? First, the principle of structural tonality: with three exceptions, each episode is controlled by a single key, although this is not necessarily that in which it begins (the three exceptions, Episodes 6, 14, and 16, exemplify directional tonality). Also, in practically every case, each episode is set off from the previous one by a change of controlling tonality (Episode 7 constituting the sole exception). Although within an episode the principles of associative, expressive, directional, and classical tonality may interact, the controlling key always exerts a strong governing effect.

Secondly, each episode is unified dramatically, in that it works out a specific portion of the dramatic action; this often culminates in an important event, such as Alberich's theft of the gold (Episode 2), Wotan's use of his spear to impose the force of law (Episode 7), Alberich's capture by Wotan and Loge (Episode 13), or the dwarf's curse on the ring (Episode 14). The Structural Outline briefly indicates the dramatic content of each episode.

Thirdly, each episode displays thematic consistency. Frequently an episode begins by introducing a new theme or thematic complex which is then developed across the length of the episode. Although the thematic discussion usually involves previously heard material, there is normally little doubt as to what constitutes the principal musical idea of a given episode. This procedure correlates with the essentially expository nature of *Das Rheingold*, in that it sets forth the basic thematic material which the later dramas develop and transform. However, once a theme has been presented, it is henceforth available for future citation and development, so that the thematic structure of the opera is essentially cumulative. This ensures that the integrity of the separate episodes does not result in an overly segmented macrostructure, a 'number opera' masquerading as 'music drama'.

In addition to dramatic, tonal, and thematic consistency, each episode displays a clear internal formal design. However, these interior forms are generally *not* the bars and *Bogen* so beloved of Lorenz. Wagner has recourse to a wide variety of formal procedures, drawn from both opera and instrumental music. In every case, however, the formal design grows naturally out of the structure and content of the text, and was usually latent in the text from the beginning; some designs have no recognizable counterparts in either operatic or instrumental music, and can be explicated *only* in terms of the text. Thus, Dahlhaus is incorrect when he states that 'Wagner renounced an architectonic foundation for musical forms', that 'form as "architecture" was replaced by form as "web"'. It is one thing to make such a claim, quite another adequately to demonstrate it, and this, in my opinion, Dahlhaus has not done. Wagner's forms are certainly 'logical' in the Dahlhausian sense (that is, they 'emphasize the principle of thematic–motivic connection and development')—few scholars would dispute this. Yet they are also highly 'architectural', and it is to the demonstration of this thesis that Chapters 6 to 10 are primarily devoted.[2]

It may be asked whether the opera as a whole is 'architectural'; that is, whether it displays an overall formal/tonal plan or whether the twenty episodes are merely strung together like beads on a string. This question will be addressed in Chapter 11, after an examination of the individual episodes.

Now, however, it is time to plunge into the depths of the Rhine and investigate the genesis and structure of one of the most remarkable passages of music ever written: the *Rheingold* Prelude.

---

[2] I realize that this claim leaves me open to the charge of attempting to resuscitate Lorenz's 'discredited' analytical techniques, or of employing them under a different name. Although I am not particularly concerned about 'distancing' myself from Lorenz, I can only hope that a careful perusal of Chapters 6 to 10 will reveal the difference between his approach and my own. Of course, there will always be those who immediately label as 'neo-Lorenzian' *any* attempt to discern architectural structures in Wagnerian opera; in the face of such critical myopia, one can do little but cheerfully accept the label, realizing that it is by no means the worst epithet with which one could be pelted.

6 Creatio ex Nihilo: *The Prelude*

> Just imagine—the *entire* instrumental introduction to *Das Rhein-*
> *gold* is built upon the single triad of E♭!
>
> (Wagner to Franz Liszt, 4 March 1854)

I. THE CONTROVERSY

Wagner's own account of the genesis of the *Rheingold* Prelude is well
known. The impetus to begin the music allegedly occurred on 5
September 1853 in the Italian town of La Spezia, according to a
section of *Mein Leben* dictated in 1869:

Returning home in the afternoon, I stretched out dead tired on a hard sofa,
to await the long-desired hour of sleep. It did not come; instead I sank into
a sort of somnolent state, in which I suddenly felt as if I were sinking in
rapidly flowing water. Its rushing soon represented itself to me as the
musical sound of the E♭ major chord, which continually surged forward in a
figured arpeggiation; these arpeggios appeared as melodic figurations of
increasing motion, yet the pure E♭ major triad never changed, and seemed
through its persistence to impart infinite significance to the element in which
I was sinking. Feeling as though the waves were now roaring high above me,
I awoke in sudden terror from my half-sleep. I recognized instantly that the
orchestral prelude to *Das Rheingold*, as I had carried it about within me
without ever having been able to pin it down, had risen up out of me; and I
also quickly grasped how things were with me: the vital stream would not
flow from without, but only from within.

I immediately decided to return to Zurich and begin the composition of
my great poem.[1]

This chapter is a revised, somewhat expanded version of my article '*Creatio ex nihilo*: The
Genesis, Structure, and Meaning of the *Rheingold* Prelude', *19th Century Music*, 13 (1989),
79–100.

[1] Richard Wagner, *Mein Leben: Erste authentische Veröffentlichung*, ed. Martin Gregor-
Dellin (Munich, 1963), 580. All translations in this chapter are my own, although in this case I
have freely consulted *My Life*, 499 and Deathridge, 'Cataloguing Wagner', 193–5.
  Wagner also mentions this incident in the 'Annalen' for 1853; see Richard Wagner, *Das
braune Buch: Tagebuchaufzeichnungen 1865 bis 1882*, ed. Joachim Bergfeld (Zurich, 1975),
122. Beginning 17 July 1865, Wagner dictated *Mein Leben* to Cosima, using as a basis notes
written in the so-called 'Red Pocket-Book' (*Rote Brieftasche*), only the first four pages of which
have survived. After dictating from these notes up to Easter 1846, he wrote fresh notes in

Wagner also mentioned this experience to Emilie Ritter in a letter of 29 December 1854:

Already in Spezia I had a complete vision: . . . when I had sunk for a moment into a sort of half-sleep, the instrumental introduction to *Das Rheingold*—about which I could never before quite make up my mind—suddenly stood before me with such clarity and exactness that I realized all at once what was wrong with me. At that moment, I decided to return home and renounce everything connected with the external world.[2]

For years, this story was accepted at face value by scholars like Otto Strobel, Ernest Newman, and Curt von Westernhagen. Recently, however, John Deathridge has questioned Wagner's account on the grounds that it does not square with either his correspondence or his musical sketches. First, since the 1854 letter to Emilie Ritter contains the earliest surviving reference to the La Spezia 'vision', Wagner most untypically let more than a year elapse before communicating this earthshaking event to anyone. Second, in the autumn of 1854 (a few months before the letter to Ritter), the poet Georg Herwegh introduced Wagner to two works of Arthur Schopenhauer, *Die Welt als Wille und Vorstellung* and *Parerga und Paralipomena*; a section in the latter entitled 'Versuch über das Geistersehen und was damit zusammenhängt' discusses the allegorical significance of dreams and may well have influenced Wagner's account of his La Spezia 'vision'.

However, Deathridge feels that the most damning evidence is offered by the complete draft of the opera (begun 1 November 1853); here Wagner sketched the Prelude in a version which only roughly approximates its final form and lacks (according to Deathridge) the 'clarity and exactness' described to Emilie Ritter. In addition, some time after drafting the Prelude, Wagner inserted a remark at the top of the page suggesting that he had second thoughts about the musical content and length of the opening. The Prelude did not assume its final form until the *Partiturerstschrift* (begun 1 February 1854), and even in this document passages are crossed out and altered. Finally, not until 4 March 1854 did Wagner enthusiastically write to Liszt: 'Just imagine—the *entire* instrumental introduction to *Das Rheingold* is built upon the single triad of E♭'[3] (the letter contains nothing

---

February 1868, presumably basing them upon the 'Red Pocket-Book', which he then apparently destroyed. These new notes are the so-called 'Annals', which span the period 1846–68, and are contained in the 'Brown Book' (*Braunes Buch*), first published in 1975 (Eng. trans. 1980). In view of this, we cannot be absolutely certain that the note describing the La Spezia 'vision' was entered in the Red Pocket-Book at the time it occurred; it could have been entered for the first time in the Brown Book in 1868, as a piece of 'creative autobiography'.

[2] *SB* vi. 308. The date of this letter is often given incorrectly as 25 Dec.

[3] *Liszt–Wagner Briefwechsel*, 365.

about a 'vision'). Taken as a whole, Deathridge concludes, the evidence strongly suggests that Wagner

did not conceive [the Prelude] in its final form until well after the rest of *Das Rheingold* had been composed—rather in the traditional way of completing an opera by composing the overture last. . . .

Whether he really felt 'flowing water' and heard the 'pure' triad of E-flat major in his 'somnolent' state cannot be said for certain. It seems more likely, as his sketches and correspondence tend to suggest, that he was back-dating at least one crucial musical idea (the low E flat at the beginning of the Prelude) and combining it with an experience of some other kind in order to heighten the aura of the work—once again—with a powerful autobiographical image.[4]

A close examination of Wagner's musical sketches and drafts for *Das Rheingold* does indeed reveal that the genesis of its Prelude is nowhere near as simple and straightforward as Wagner claimed. Furthermore, it appears as if Strobel and Westernhagen, in their published studies, were less than honest about the content of these documents.[5] Nevertheless, although the manuscripts do not confirm Wagner's account of a precompositional 'vision', they do not contradict it, either.

Although the *Ring* has called forth books without number, no author to date has offered a convincing interpretation of the compositional genesis, musical structure, and metaphorical meaning of the *Rheingold* Prelude, an account that takes into consideration all relevant documentary sources. This chapter attempts to provide such an interpretation.

---

[4] 'Cataloguing Wagner', 195–7.

[5] Strobel strongly implied that the complete draft lacks any sort of instrumental introduction, and that Wagner did not notate the Prelude at all until, after finishing the complete draft, he immediately wrote it out in full score. This deliberate deception was facilitated by the lack of published facsimiles. In an early article on the *Ring* manuscripts, Strobel actually wrote: 'the draft, which for the reasons given above, begins immediately with the first scene . . .' ('Die Kompositionsskizzen zum *Ring des Nibelungen*: Ein Blick in die Musikwerkstatt Richard Wagners', *Bayreuther Festspielführer* (1930), 117). To have revealed that Wagner did draft the Prelude on 1 Nov. 1853, and that three months later he wrote out a substantially different version, eventually altering and correcting even this one, would have compromised the image of the composer which Strobel wished to present: the heaven-inspired genius who effortlessly translated his creative visions directly into full score.

Westernhagen was not above concealing evidence, either. In *The Forging of the 'Ring'*, he transcribed two items from an undated sketch sheet (WWV 86A Musik Ib) but omitted a third, perhaps because it could have undermined his theory about the genesis of the Prelude. This omission was revealed by Deathridge in 'Wagner's Sketches for the "Ring"', *Musical Times*, 118 (1977), 387.

Ex. 6.1

II. THE COMPLETE DRAFT VERSION OF THE PRELUDE

In late July or early August 1850, Wagner made some musical sketches for *Siegfried's Tod* (WWV 86D Musik Ib–d); these comprise the entire Norns scene and the first portion of the following duet, as well as thematic material associated with the Valkyries. On 12 August, he began an ink draft of the Prologue (WWV 86D Musik Ie), breaking off a bit earlier than in the preceding sketch.

The *Siegfried's Tod* sketch begins as shown in Ex. 6.1.[6] The Eb minor tonality, compound metre, and figuration of the underlying harmony also characterize the very different Norns scene which opens *Götterdämmerung*, composed nineteen years later.[7] Equally important, however, is the relationship between the opening of this sketch and the beginning of the *Rheingold* complete draft (see transcription[8] in Appendix). Although this similarity has been pointed out, its significance has not been sufficiently appreciated. In transferring to the Rhinedaughters certain musical gestures conceived in connection with the Norns, Wagner underscored musically the dramatic parallelism between these two sets of sisters.[9] When during the composition of the Erda episode of Scene 4 he associated *different* material with the Norns and their mother, he felt compelled to go back and incorporate this new material into the Rhinedaughters

---

[6] This transcription is taken from Bailey, 'Wagner's Musical Sketches', 472.

[7] In the later ink draft, Wagner changed the 12/8 metre to 6/4 and the semiquavers to quavers, creating an even stronger resemblance to the opening of *Götterdämmerung*; see Bailey, 'Wagner's Musical Sketches', 485.

[8] All transcriptions in the Appendix were made from WWV 86A Musik II. A reasonably clear facsimile of fo. 1r (containing the Prelude) appears in Westernhagen, *The Forging of the 'Ring'*, 18–19. My transcription agrees with Bailey's in all essentials ('Wagner's Musical Sketches', 473–4).

[9] See Ch. 3.

scene and its preparatory prelude. The final version of the *Rheingold* Prelude thus owes much to the composition of the Erda episode, just as its original version is indebted to the *Siegfried's Tod* sketches.

An examination of this original version may aid our attempt to reconstruct Wagner's creative process and facilitate an analysis of the Prelude's musical structure. The draft begins with a two-bar animation of the E♭ major triad, marked 'Bl[äser]' ('winds'). The range suggests that Wagner was thinking of bass clarinet and bassoons, with possibly a contrabass tuba on the low $E♭_1$. Although the passage is notated in 6/8 metre, the articulations initially imply 3/4. The indication 'Steigend' ('rising') implies that this oscillation is to expand through the upper wind instruments, forming a pulsating harmonic background to the string figurations which follow.

These wavelike semiquaver patterns (similar, as mentioned, to the figurations depicting the Norns' weaving in the *Siegfried's Tod* sketch) are marked 'Str[eicher]' ('strings'), but their range precludes any instrument other than the cellos; it is unlikely that Wagner expected the basses to double such a rapid passage. After the initial two-bar pattern and its repetition, the figurations rise and fall through the E♭ triad in a symmetrical arch shape (see Ex. 6.2). This sixteen-bar unit is then marked for repetition an octave higher, doubled by the violas; it is to be repeated again by second violins and violas, and finally taken up a fourth time, forte, by strings in triple octaves.[10] The final measure is altered to lead, diminuendo, into Woglinde's vocal entry.

The opening sixty-six bars of the *Rheingold* complete draft thus display a strophic design (Table 6.1). This suggests a set of variations in timbre on a sixteen-bar theme, coupled with an expansion in range, texture, and instrumentation. As we shall see, this structure is remarkably similar to that of the final version; apparently Wagner had already settled upon the form and shape of his instrumental opening.

It is illuminating to re-examine Wagner's account of the genesis of this passage in the light of the complete draft version. In the first documented reference to the La Spezia 'vision', the letter to Emilie Ritter of December 1854, Wagner speaks of the 'clarity and exactness' of his conception. Could not this 'clarity and exactness' have embraced the notion of an extended E♭ major triad, swirling string figurations, and a fourfold statement of a sixteen-bar 'theme', without necessarily implying that the thematic material was fixed in every detail? Similarly,

---

[10] Westernhagen speculates that Wagner was reserving the double basses for the low $E♭_1$, a pitch that, apart from the opening measure, is not notated (*The Forging of the 'Ring'*, 20).

Ex. 6.2

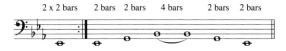

TABLE 6.1 Strophic design of complete draft version of Prelude

2 bars	16 bars	16 bars	16 bars	16 bars
Intro.	A^1	A^2	A^3	A^4
				Vn. 1
			Vn. 2	Vn. 2
		Va.	Va.	Va.
	Vc.	Vc.		Vc.
Winds ———————————————————————————————————————→				

the *Mein Leben* account refers to 'arpeggios' which appeared as 'melodic figurations of increasing motion'. The terms 'arpeggios' (*Brechungen*) and 'increasing motion' (*zunehmender Bewegung*) might seem to refer to the final form of the Prelude, whose arpeggiated theme is subjected to rhythmic diminution. Yet even in the draft, the semiquaver figures sometimes arpeggiate the triad, and the gradual addition of instruments, expansion of range, and 'rising' wind oscillations do indeed suggest 'increasing motion', even if the actual note values remain unaltered.

In fact, the complete draft form of the Prelude represents an *initial musical prototype* that, *pace* Deathridge, does not at all contradict Wagner's story of a precompositional 'vision' (it does not, of course, confirm it either). Although Wagner was later to expand this structure, change its thematic content, elaborate its instrumentation, and deepen its metaphorical significance, the basic shape was there from the beginning.

Sometime after completing this draft of the instrumental opening, Wagner added the note at the top of the page 'Voraus, langsam Vorbereitungen auf das Rheingoldmotiv' ('before this, slow preparations for the Rhinegold motif'). Westernhagen's contention that 'das Rheingoldmotiv' refers to the opening horn theme of the revised Prelude (an idea which, in all likelihood, had not yet been sketched) is, in my opinion, highly improbable.[11] It is far more likely that

---

[11] *The Forging of the 'Ring'*, 17.

Wagner was here referring to the horn fanfare which, in the second half of Scene 1, announces the appearance of the gold, and that he added this remark while working on the latter passage.[12] In other words, Wagner decided to expand the two-bar introduction (animation of the Eb triad by low winds) and give it a definite thematic content; because the 'Gold fanfare' is a simple major arpeggio, it could easily be worked into the opening triadic oscillation. Although Wagner later abandoned the notion of beginning *Das Rheingold* with the gold fanfare, he stuck with his decision to expand the chordal introduction and invest it with thematic significance.

III. THE COMPOSITION OF THE ERDA EPISODE

Early in 1854 Wagner began setting the Erda episode of Scene 4 to music. No separate sketches for this passage survive; Wagner's personal copy of the 1853 printing, containing musical jottings and text changes made during composition, has been preserved, but the pages containing Erda's appearance are unfortunately lost. It is therefore impossible to ascertain exactly when or under what circumstances the Erda/Norn theme first occurred to Wagner. Yet one may reasonably assume that this simple arpeggiation of the minor triad was conceived from the very beginning in relation to Erda herself. It first appears on fo. 34^r of the complete draft: as Erda rises from the depths of the earth, the motif itself rises from the depths of the orchestra—a simple yet effective bit of tone-painting.

The complete Erda episode is transcribed in the Appendix, and its genesis is more completely described in Chapter 10.[13] Erda's appearance is preceded by a stormy passage in F minor (mm. 3452–5), during which the gods implore Wotan to relinquish the ring. At the change to 'Langsam', the bass of the complete draft arpeggiates a descending F♯ minor triad, out of which Erda's theme slowly emerges; this harmony then resolves as subdominant to the new tonic C♯ minor. C♯ is enharmonically the parallel minor of Db major, a key associated with Wotan's fortress Valhalla, and the draft reveals that Wagner originally intended to notate this episode in Db minor: the new signature of four sharps is written over the old one of five flats.[14] While working out the instrumentation, Wagner changed his mind

---

[12] The Gold fanfare begins with the upbeat to m. 516 (31/2/1, one bar before Woglinde's 'Lugt, Schwestern!') and is played initially by horn 2. In the complete draft, it first appears on fo. 4^r, system 4, which Wagner probably reached around the second week of November 1853.

[13] The transcription of the Erda episode was made from fos. 34–5 of the complete draft; it first appeared in my article '"Alles was ist, endet!" Erda's Prophecy of World Destruction', *Programmheft II ('Das Rheingold') der Bayreuther Festspiele 1988*, 87–91.

[14] Presumably Wagner would have inserted Fbs and Bbbs as necessary.

and decided to begin the episode with a second inversion *tonic* triad; he also deleted the second, plagally inflected statement of the motif, lightly crossing out these passages in the complete draft.

Beginning one bar before 'Drei der Töchter' (m. 3482), Erda's motif reappears, transposed to E major (an expanded mediant) and animated with a quaver figuration suggestive of the Norns' weaving. In the *Siegfried's Tod* sketches, Wagner had used a somewhat shapeless semiquaver figure (later changed to quavers) to depict the same thing; his derivation of the new figuration from the Erda theme enabled him to give it a more sharply defined profile. Both figures arpeggiate the underlying harmony, but whereas the earlier one rose and fell rather aimlessly, the new one rises inexorably. This section concludes ('sagen dir nächtlich die Nornen') with a transposition of motif and figuration to A major (an expanded submediant).

Erda's *Weltuntergang* prophecy 'Alles was ist, endet!' ('Everything that is, ends!') is ushered in by a restatement of her motif over a weakened C♯ minor tonic chord (m. 3498). A second restatement over submediant harmony leads directly into the musical climax of the episode: a melodic inversion of the Erda theme over a Neapolitan sixth chord (m. 3502). This inverted theme is usually known as the *Götterdämmerungmotiv* because it accompanies the words 'Ein düst'rer Tag | dämmert den Göttern'. It might, however, equally well be called the *Weltuntergangmotiv*: Wagner introduced it immediately after 'Alles was ist, endet!' as a musical reverberation of those words.

Despite Wotan's attempt to restrain the goddess, Erda gradually disappears; as she does, her tonality dissolves, eventually stabilizing on an E♭ half cadence (enharmonically V/v of the previous C♯ minor). Two reappearances of Erda's motif in E♭ minor[15] (mm. 3527 and 3543) accompany Wotan's futile attempt to reach within himself and grasp the full significance of this unexpected revelation. The moment is crucial because it marks the first time in the complete draft that the motif is notated in E♭; the final change from this E♭ minor to the E♭ major of the Prelude reminds one of the intended tonal link between the opening of *Siegfried's Tod* and that of *Das Rheingold*.

IV. THE UNDATED SKETCH SHEET

As mentioned, Wagner had already decided to expand the Prelude's two-bar chordal introduction and give it thematic significance. Before

---

[15] The melodic augmented second G♭–A recalls the linear progression A–B♯ in the F♯ minor statement which begins the episode. Wagner's subsequent alteration of the earlier statement destroyed this 'framing' effect.

Ex. 6.3

a.

Wei - a Wa- ga! Wal- le du　　Wo - ge, wo - ge zur Wiege

b.

[sic]

c.

Hörner in Es

[sic]

beginning a full ink score of the opera, he made two further decisions: to replace the string figurations of the *Vorspiel* with the Erda/Norn theme, and to transform the entire Prelude from a simple depiction of the depths of the Rhine into an orchestral metaphor for the creation of the world. These two decisions went hand in hand and originated in the composition of the Erda scene: if the inverted, descending form of Erda's motif symbolized the end of the world (*Weltuntergang*), then the original, ascending form could logically be associated with its beginning. Furthermore, the fundamental nature of Erda's theme—an ascending triad—could easily suggest a primordial beginning, while its 'Norns' figurations could represent flowing water in general and the aquatic activities of the Rhine-daughters in particular.

At this point, the third set of preliminary musical sketches enters the picture. These sketches are notated in brown ink on an oblong piece of staff paper, which has been cut (probably by Wagner's heirs) from the top of a larger sheet; they are transcribed in Ex. 6.3.[16]

Example 6.3a couples the 'Weia! Waga!' melody (Woglinde's initial vocal statement in Scene 1) with a text that differs from its final version; because this text assumed definitive form in the verse draft (begun 15 September 1852), one might logically assign this sketch an earlier date. The first page of the prose draft (begun 23 March 1852), contains several attempts at these lines in the left-hand margin, and Wagner may have conceived this melody at the same time. Such reasoning would suggest that this sketch of the 'Weia! Waga!' melody predates the La Spezia 'vision' (5 September 1853) by a year to a year and a half and the beginning of the complete draft (1 November 1853) by fourteen to twenty months.

The remaining two sketches are more difficult to date. The editors of *WWV* claim that Ex. 6.3b is an early version of the Nature motif (the horn theme which begins in m. 17 of the Prelude).[17] To be sure, this sketch consists of various triadic arpeggiations in 6/8 metre, and we might well assume a treble clef and a key signature of three flats. Because the penultimate pitch overlaps with the 'g' of the word 'Waga' immediately above, the *WWV* editors speculate that this sketch predates the first one. Magnification does suggest that the pen stroke of 'Waga' crosses over the last g^2 of Ex. 6.3b, and it is conceivable that Wagner indented the vocal melody as far as he did in order to avoid a collision with the preexisting arpeggio sketch. The matter, however, is not absolutely clear, and the 'Weia! Waga!' melody could have been notated first.

Example 6.3c contains a threefold statement of the complete Nature motif, marked 'Hörner in Es' and notated in C. The theme differs slightly from its final form: the initial interval is a major third rather than a perfect fifth, and the motif rises only to the root, rather than the third, of the triad. Deathridge cites this as evidence that Wagner 'miscalculated the overtone series'.[18] Westernhagen claims that 'the further development, with the transition to a higher octave, is an attempt to prefigure the rise in the dynamic tension'.[19] Westernhagen, however, fails to take account of the fact that the horn in E♭ trans-

---

[16] This transcription was made from WWV 86A Musik Ib; cf. Deathridge, 'Wagner's Sketches', 387 (complete) and Westernhagen, *The Forging of the 'Ring'*, 16 (Exx. 6.3a and c only); both normalize stem direction in Ex. 6.3a, m. 3, and both omit the crossed-out c^1 in Ex. 6.3c, m. 7. The autograph contains two questionable markings (possibly ink blotches or pen practice) in the first measure of Ex. 6.3a. Between staves 2 and 3, in the middle of the sheet, is written 'weia Waga!'; in addition, the sheet contains two notations which suggest that Wagner was practicing his signature.

[17] *WWV* 408.   [18] 'Wagner's Sketches', 387.

[19] *The Forging of the 'Ring'*, 17.

TABLE 6.2 Compositional genesis of Prelude: a suggested chronology

1853	5 Sept.	Wagner allegedly experiences a precompositional 'vision' at La Spezia.
	1 Nov.	Begins the *Rheingold* complete draft. The first version of the Prelude lacks the Nature motif and uses the Norns figurations from the *Siegfried's Tod* sketches.
	(2nd week of Nov.?)	Decides to expand the opening of the Prelude and give it thematic significance.
1854	1–14 Jan.	Invents the Erda/Norn theme and incorporates it into the Erda episode in Scene 4.
	1 Feb.	Begins the *Partiturerstschrift*. Sketches the new Nature horn theme, then incorporates it into the expanded opening of the Prelude. Also incorporates a major mode variant of the Erda/Norn theme into the body of the Prelude.
	Feb.	Revises the Prelude, changing the horn theme to its definitive form.
	15 Feb.	Begins the *Reinschrift der Partitur*, entering into it the final version of the Prelude.
	28 May	Finishes the *Partiturerstschrift*.
	Summer	Hires a copyist, but dismisses him after completion of the Prelude.
	26 Sept.	Finishes the *Reinschrift*.
Late 1854–	11 Nov. 1855	Friedrich Wölfel makes a copy of Wagner's *Reinschrift*.

poses up a minor third in the bass clef but down a major sixth in the treble; all three versions therefore sound exactly the same! Wagner was simply experimenting with different placements of the change from bass to treble clef, a purely notational feature which suggests that he notated this third sketch while working upon the *Partiturerstschrift*.

Although the matter is not totally clear, I suggest the chronology shown in Table 6.2. This chronology does not take the problematical Ex. 6.3*b* into account; however, an alternative explanation for this sketch (as well as for Ex. 6.3*a*) will be offered later.

V. THE *PARTITURERSTSCHRIFT* VERSION OF THE PRELUDE

Before discussing the *Partiturerstschrift*, certain discrepancies among Wölfel's copy of Wagner's *Reinschrift*, the anonymous copy of

TABLE 6.3 Transpositions of low brass

Instrument	Wölfel's Copy of Wagner's Reinschrift	Printed Score
Tenor Tubas	in E♭ (𝄞 M6 ↓)	in B♭ (𝄞 M2 ↓)
Bass Tubas	in B♭ (𝄞 M9 ↓ or 𝄢 M2 ↓)	in F (𝄞 P5 ↓ or 𝄢 P5 ↓)
Contrabass Trombone	Prelude: in C (𝄢 as written)	in C (𝄢 as written)
	Scenes 1–4: in B♭ (𝄢 M2 ↓)	in C (𝄢 as written)
Contrabass Tuba	in E♭ (𝄢 M6 ↓)	in C (𝄢 as written)

the Prelude, and the printed score should be noted. First, the transpositions of the low brass in Wölfel's copy differ from those in the printed score; the revisions (summarized in Table 6.3) were later entered into Wölfels' copy when it was used as *Stichvorlage* for the first printing.[20] In Wölfel's copy, the transposition of the contrabass trombone changes: in the Prelude it is pitched in C, but in the rest of the opera it is in B♭. However, the anonymous copy of the Prelude puts this instrument in B♭, except for a momentary lapse (mm. 81–7) into C. Perhaps, then, Wagner's *Reinschrift* (from which the anonymous copy was made) pitched this instrument in B♭ from the very beginning, and Wölfel, at the composer's request, changed the Prelude part to C when he prepared his own copy.[21]

A further discrepancy among the *Partiturerstschrift*, Wölfel's copy, and the published score concerns the instrumentation of the low E♭ and B♭ octaves in the Prelude. These differences are summarized in Table 6.4, from which we can see that the contrabass saxhorn in E♭ quickly became (within the *Partiturerstschrift*) a contrabass tuba in E♭, later pitched in C; the tuba or bass tuba (Wagner used both names) became a contrabass trombone in C; and the various trombone parts were freely exchanged.

Although several more features of the *Partiturerstschrift* differ from their counterparts in the printed score (notably the dynamics of the semiquaver cello figurations and the pitches of the flute parts), the following discussion focuses upon only the most important of these: the opening horn canon.

---

[20] Wölfel's transpositions of the Wagner tubas (in E♭ and B♭) do not square with a remark attributed to Robert Bailey by J. Merrill Knapp: 'The Wagner tuba parts are notated in B flat and F consistently in the final autograph scores and also in the printed parts' ('The Instrumentation Draft', 283 n. 32). Either Bailey was mistaken or Knapp incorrectly transmitted his remark.

[21] The horn, trumpet, and bass trumpet parts in Wölfel's copy correspond to those in the printed score.

TABLE 6.4 Instrumentation of pedal tones in Prelude

Measure	Pitch	Wagner's Partiturerstschrift	Wölfel's Copy	Printed Score
45 ff.	$E\flat$	Bass Clarinet	Bass Clarinet	Bass Clarinet
	$E\flat_1$	Contrabass Saxhorn in $E\flat$	Contrabass Tuba in $E\flat$	Contrabass Tuba in C
81 ff.	$E\flat$	Tuba or Bass Tuba	Contrabass Trombone in C	Contrabass Trombone in C
	$E\flat_1$	Contrabass Tuba in $E\flat$	Contrabass Tuba in $E\flat$	Contrabass Tuba in C
113 ff.	$E\flat$	Bass Tuba and Trombone 2	Contrabass Trombone in C and Trombone 2	Contrabass Trombone in C and Trombone 2
	$E\flat_1$	Contrabass Tuba in $E\flat$	Contrabass Tuba in $E\flat$	Contrabass Tuba in C
47 ff.	$B\flat$	Trombone 3	Trombone 1	Trombone 1
	$B\flat_1$	Tuba or Contrabass Trombone in $B\flat$	Contrabass Trombone in C*	Trombone 3
79 ff.	$B\flat$	Trombone 2	Trombone 1	Trombone 1
	$B\flat_1$	Trombone 3	Trombone 2**	Trombone 3
111 ff.	$B\flat$	Trombone 1	Trombone 1	Trombone 1
	$B\flat_1$	Trombone 3	Trombone 3	Trombone 3

* Later in the score (p. 4) this instrument is designated as Trombone 4.
** Later in the score (p. 5) this instrument is designated as Trombone 3.

Ex. 6.4

a. Partiturerstschrift, mm. 17 – 20: horn 8.

b. Partiturerstschrift, mm. 37 – 44: horn 8.

c. Partiturerstschrift, mm. 45 – 52: horn 8.

d. Partiturerstschrift, mm. 17 – 20: horn 8 (pencil revision).

e. Printed score, mm. 41–4: horn 8.

Wagner initially had horn 8 sequence the Nature theme through the ascending major triad, starting it successively on Eb, G, and Bb; the other horns followed in canonic imitation. Examples 6.4*a*–*c* transcribe the sequential statements of this motif as they appear in the *Partiturerstschrift*;[22] note that Ex. 6.4*a* follows the pattern of the undated sketch. The entire passage up to the entrance of the violoncellos was originally four bars longer than the final version due to the double statement in mm. 37–44 (Ex. 6.4*b*).

Pages 1 and 2 of the *Partiturerstschrift* contain pencil revisions, which bring the horn canon closer to its final form. At some point after completing the Prelude, Wagner altered the initial motif (Ex. 6.4*a*) to the version shown in Ex. 6.4*d*; this corrects his 'miscalculation of the overtone series', and ends the motif upon the third of the triad rather than the root. He also changed all the subsequent canonic entries. At m. 37, Wagner altered his first sequence of the motif (Ex. 6.4*b*, first 4 measures) so that it also conformed with Ex. 6.4*d*; obviously he needed to change only the first note this time. Wagner then crossed out mm. 41–4 (Ex. 6.4*b*, last 4 measures) so that his original m. 45 became the present m. 41.[23] In order to change his second sequence of the Nature motif (Ex. 6.4*c*) into the version we know (Ex. 6.4*e*), only the first two notes needed to be altered; however, Wagner left this passage unchanged in the *Partiturerstschrift*, probably altering it when he made his fair copy.

The end result of all these revisions was to eliminate the rising sequences and ground the entire horn canon on low Eb.[24] The fact that the canonic horn entries were originally structured as rising sequences has important consequences for our reconstruction of the Prelude's compositional genesis.

VI. STRUCTURE AND MEANING

Lorenz's analysis of the *Rheingold* Prelude as a set of strophic variations is difficult to criticize, even though it addresses only one aspect of the piece.[25] Lorenz divided the Prelude into seven sections, as shown in the right-hand column of Table 6.5; the following

---

[22] Examples 6.4*a*–*d* were transcribed from the first eight pages of WWV 86A Musik III.

[23] Knapp claims that 'between measures 40 and 41, there are four measures (an earlier version of mm. 41–4), which have been crossed out. Some of the notes in the following measures are a different arrangement of the triad' ('The Instrumentation Draft', 282). The crossed-out measures, however, are not an earlier version of mm. 41–4 at all, but an extension of mm. 37–40, which Wagner later chose to delete.

[24] The *Partiturerstschrift* lacks the 'immer *p*' that appears in the printed score at the point where each horn first plays its high *bb*[1].

[25] Lorenz, *Der musikalische Aufbau*, 108.

TABLE 6.5 Relationship between complete draft version and final version of Prelude

Complete Draft Version (1853)	Final Version (1854)
Introduction (2 bars) ⟶	Introduction (16 bars) Theme (32 bars)
Strophe 1: A¹ (16 bars) ⟶	Variation I (32 bars)
Strophe 2: A² (16 bars) ⟶	Variation II (16 bars)
Strophe 3: A³ (16 bars) ⟶	Variation III (16 bars)
Strophe 4: A⁴ (16 bars) ⟶	Variation IV (16 bars) Coda (8 bars)

discussion assumes the accuracy of this division. The strophic design of the complete draft version forms the core of the final version.

Having decided to write an orchestral metaphor for the creation of the world, Wagner produced the effect of moving gradually from timelessness into measured time, from amorphous sounds toward distinct musical shapes.[26] The sixteen-bar introduction and the thirty-two-bar horn canon are temporally indeterminate. Only with the regular pulse and sweeping arpeggiations of Variation I does experiential time begin; yet the absence of any higher-level design precludes a sense of formal arrival. This higher-level design materializes in Variation II, coupled with a reduction of note values; however, the instrumentation is purposely 'muddy' and indistinct, blurring the melodic shape. Clarification begins in Variation III and is completed in the clear orchestral colours of Variation IV. The thematic fragmentation, increased rhythmic activity, and crescendos of the coda are abruptly cut short by a sudden drop in dynamics, texture, and instrumentation, as well as a change of harmony, at Woglinde's vocal entrance.

It is as if the enormous musical build-up of the Prelude has suddenly compressed inself into this single human figure. First singing nonsense syllables, the Rhinedaughter smoothly modulates into intelligible verbal phrases. Wagner has given us the ultimate demonstration of musical organicism: from a single musical pitch (the initial low E♭) he has gradually created life itself. In so doing, he has also demonstrated an essential part of his world-view: that the ultimate goal of nature is to evolve into human consciousness. The tragic events of the *Ring* ensue exactly because humanity loses touch with its natural origins.

[26] It goes without saying that all nineteenth-century 'creatio ex nihilo' openings—of which the *Rheingold* Prelude is but one example—share a common ancestor: Beethoven's Ninth Symphony.

The variation structure of the Prelude helps shape this evolutionary process, as follows:

1. Introduction (mm. 1–16; 1/1/1–1/2/4)[27]

In an ideal performance, the audience is unable to discern exactly when the initial contrabass tones begin; the listener only gradually becomes aware of a sound that, in effect, has *always* been there. Because the four second bassists are playing Eb_1 on an open string (tuned down a chromatic semitone), the third harmonic is audibly present during the first four measures; when the bassoons enter with *Bb*, they merely reinforce a pitch that was already sounding. At the same time, the ear clearly perceives *g*, the fifth harmonic, soon to be played by the French horn. This technique of anticipating a pitch through a prominent overtone lends a certain inevitability to the process and suggests that all life—the entire musical universe of the *Ring*—is latently present in the initial sound.

Wagner had long associated the interval of the perfect fifth with the spirit world, using it as a harmonic symbol for the Dutchman in *Der fliegende Holländer*, and later for the Tarnhelm in the *Ring* operas. Here, however, it functions less as an invocation of the supernatural than as an evocation of the endless void out of which a mythic world will soon be created.

Lorenz noted the gradual rhythmic animation of the Eb/Bb fifth through bow changes and tonguing:

Measure 1 2 3 4 5 6 7 8 / 9 10 11 12 13 14 15 16
     Eb   Bb   Eb Bb Eb Bb

The overlapping pulsations in mm. 9–16 persist for the remainder of the Prelude.

2. Theme (mm. 17–48; 1/2/5–2/3/3)

Wagner's alterations of the horn canon have already been described. His initial idea had been to sequence the arpeggiated Nature theme upward through the Eb triad, beginning it successively on Eb, G, and Bb. What suggested this procedure to him?

Certainly the process of sequencing an arpeggiated motif through an ascending triad is common enough in *Das Rheingold*. One example of this procedure, however, is so striking and occurs at such a crucial point, that it may well have provided the immediate model for the

---

[27] Again, the second entry in these double references cites the Schirmer vocal score (page/system/measure number).

Ex. 6.5

Complete Draft

[m. 3713]

horn canon. This is the so-called 'Rainbow' theme, which first appears on Gb toward the end of Scene 4 as Froh points the way to Valhalla (m. 3713; 208/3/1). As Ex. 6.5 shows,[28] the Rainbow theme rises triadically from Gb to db[1], then descends gradually toward its initial pitch; it is then sequenced thrice, beginning on the third, fifth, and root of the triad. At the opera's conclusion, this theme reappears on Db to accompany the gods as they cross over the rainbow bridge (m. 3883; 221/2/3); again it is sequenced on both the third and fifth of the triad.[29] The melodic ascent of this motif and its sequential treatment are so similar to those of the Nature motif in the *Partiturerstschrift* version of the Prelude that it is tempting to identify the first as the direct source of the second. In fact, Wagner may well have combined the *pitches* of the Rainbow theme with the *rhythm* of the Erda motif to produce the original form of the Nature theme, as Ex. 6.6 suggests. If this interpretation is correct, the Nature theme was sketched between 14 January and 1 February 1854.

Although Wagner's subsequent pencil alterations to the Prelude somewhat obscure this possible derivation, the 'framing' effect of the Nature/Rainbow complex has been felt by many musicians. Carl Dahlhaus correctly points out that by the time the Rainbow theme appears, the listener can no longer trust the 'reduction and simplification' of the major triad.[30] Nature has been ravished for the sake of

[28] Example 6.5 transcribes only the lower staff of a two-stave system of the complete draft (fo. 37r); the upper staff contains a suggestion of the accompaniment figure. On both staves, the key signature of 3/4 is written over one of 6/8. The rhythm of the third measure was originally ♩ ♩ ♫ and, as is often the case, the beginnings and endings of Wagner's slur marks are ambiguous.

[29] The final sequence was inserted later.

[30] *Richard Wagner's Music Dramas*, trans. Mary Whittall (Cambridge, 1979), 111.

Ex. 6.6

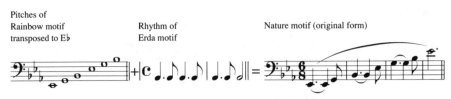

Pitches of
Rainbow motif   Rhythm of   Nature motif (original form)
transposed to E♭   Erda motif

power and wealth; civilization's achievement is hollow and morally bankrupt, making the rainbow's promise of hope a cruel illusion. This retrospectively adds one more layer of meaning to the *Rheingold* Prelude. In addition, such a musical frame satisfies the listener's desire for large-scale formal coherence.

The musical form of the Prelude's theme (mm. 17–48) is processive rather than architectural: canonic entries of the Nature motif occur at ever-decreasing temporal intervals, finally coalescing into a richly pulsating horn chord (major triad with emphasized third). This chord (which presumably could go on forever) suggests the perfect harmony that preceded mythic creation. By allowing linear strands to coalesce into a vertical sonority, Wagner suggests the identity of time and space and implies that organic life has not yet begun. Yet the eventual movement of the top 'voice' from g^1 to bb^1 (m. 44; 2/2/6) hints that change is imminent.[31]

3. *Variation I (mm. 49–80; 2/3/4–3/1/7)*

The complete draft version of the Prelude suggests that its introductory two-bar triadic oscillation was to expand through the upper wind instruments, forming a pulsating harmonic background to the string figurations. We have seen how Wagner enlarged this brief chordal opening to forty-eight bars (the sixteen-bar introduction followed by the thirty-two-bar theme), investing it with thematic significance and deepening its metaphorical meaning. He also preserved his original concept of allowing this harmonic background to persist as the figurations begin: both the low E♭/B♭ pulsations and

---

[31] The horn pitches in the Prelude are confined to partials 2, 3, 4, 5, 6, 8, 10, and 12 of the overtone series based upon Eb_1 as fundamental. Wagner, however, did not expect these parts to be played on natural horns in E♭; rather, they were to be executed on F horns using the second valve to lower the fundamental a whole step. For a detailed discussion of the matter, see Peter Nitsche, 'Transponierte Notation bei Wagner', in *Richard Wagner: Werk und Wirkung*, ed. Carl Dahlhaus (Regensburg, 1971), 231, 233–5.

Ex. 6.7

Climactic
pitches:

No. of bars: 4   4   4   4   4   4   2   2   1   1   1   1

the horn canon continue, while bassoons and flutes add yet another
layer to this background chordal structure.

Bassoons and cellos begin Variation I with a statement of the four-
bar Erda/Norn variant. Because the bassoon motif fills in triadic gaps
with passing tones (*eb–f–g* and *g–ab–bb*), it sounds like a figuration
of notes 3–7 of the Nature horn theme; we have already noted
the rhythmic identity of these two ideas. The quaver cello pattern
(suggestive of swirling water currents) adds yet another element
of figuration to the texture, making this section truly sound as a
variation of the preceding one. The regular pulses and clear motivic
profile suggest that experiential time has begun: the creation process
is under way.

The semiquaver cello figures in the corresponding portion of the
complete draft ascend and descend through the Eb triad (see transcription). In the *Partiturerstschrift* version, Wagner sequences the
four-bar quaver figure through the ascending triad (6 × 4 bars); he
then alters and shortens it, sequencing it downward (2 × 2 bars);
then shortens it again and continues the sequential descent (4 × 1
bar). The temporal contraction of this sequential unit and the rise
and fall of its climactic pitches correlate as shown in Ex. 6.7. The
overall shape is that of an asymmetrical arch, whose ascent occupies
three-fourths of the total length (24 + 8 bars). The rhythmic contraction of the descent produces a 'psychological accelerando' that
propels the music into Variation II.

The quaver figurations are, of course, passed through the entire
string family as the arch ascends and descends. Similarly, the slower-
moving Erda variant is gradually passed from bassoons to flutes; for
the first twenty-four bars (6 × 4 bars) the motif is sequenced upward
along with the string figurations, but during the eight-bar string
descent the winds repeat the last half of the motif in the manner of an
ostinato. Meanwhile bassoon 3, which for the first twenty-four bars
has reiterated a four-bar, three-note pattern, now compresses it into
two bars. This results in a flute/bassoon figure which repeats almost
mechanistically, further animating the Eb triad (Ex. 6.8). The winds'

Ex. 6.8

reiteration of eb^3 retains the climactic pitch of the string arch as the strings themselves descend.

If we now compare the reduction in Ex. 6.8 to the problematic sketch in Ex. 6.3*b*, we at once notice a striking similarity: the 'resultant melody' of Ex. 6.8 is identical to the upper line of Ex. 6.3*b*, mm. 1–2 (Wagner apparently began but discontinued a repetition in m. 3), while the bassoon parts of Ex. 6.8 suggest the lower line of Ex. 6.3*b*, mm. 1–2. Clearly Wagner could have sketched Ex. 6.3*b* while working out the wind parts of the *Partiturerstschrift*, a possibility which casts doubt upon it being an early version of the Nature motif. The fact that Ex. 6.3*b* appears on the same sheet as the horn theme (Ex. 6.3*c*), which clearly *was* jotted down during the making of the *Partiturerstschrift*, adds weight to this hypothesis. In fact, it is not beyond the realm of possibility that Ex. 6.3*a* was written at the same time also, as pen practice; Wagner could simply have made an error in the textual underlay. In this case, the writing sequence might have been: (1) Nature horn theme, (2) arpeggio sketch, (3) 'Weia! Waga!' melody. This chronology corresponds to the order in which these elements appear in the score.

4. Variation II (mm. 81–96; 3/2/1–3/5/4)

Through rhythmic diminution the Erda/Norn motif is compressed from four bars into two. The quavers become semiquavers, and the entire variation is only sixteen bars long, bringing it closer to its prototype in the complete draft. The figurations are given to cellos (reminiscent of mm. 3–18 of the complete draft), while the slower-moving Erda theme is played by clarinets. As mentioned, this results in a dark, somewhat 'murky' orchestral texture which obscures the melodic outline; it is as if the watery depths are struggling to give birth to their musical child.

Ex. 6.9

Rhine Theme (Clarinets)

The two-bar motif is spun out into a sixteen-bar theme (henceforth referred to as the 'Rhine theme') as follows (see Ex. 6.9):

1. The motif is stated twice, rising each time to g^1 (2 × 2 bars).
2. The motif is rhythmically varied; the syncopation across the bar-line reduces it from seven notes to five, so that it rises only as far as $b\flat$. This variant is also stated twice (2 × 2 bars).
3. The variant is spun out into six measures, during which the melodic line ascends only as far as $b\flat$, and continually doubles back on itself to g. The original arpeggiation has become cramped and crabbed (6 bars).
4. The motif 'straightens out' and reappears in its original form, ascending to g^1 (2 bars).

Lorenz analysed this theme as a *Reprisenbar*: two two-bar *Stollen* are followed by a ten-bar *Durchführung* and a two-bar *Reprise*.[32] A case for the *Reprisenbar* can be made, but it seems more logical to construe its proportions as:

Stollen 1   = 4 bars (2 × 2 bars): original form of motif.
Stollen 2   = 4 bars (2 × 2 bars): varied form of motif.
Abgesang = 8 bars $\begin{bmatrix} Durchführung = 6 \text{ bars: spinning-out of variant.} \\ Reprise \qquad = 2 \text{ bars: original form of motif.} \end{bmatrix}$

This structure, however, is perhaps best regarded as processive rather than architectural: after the original motif has been steadily contorted and bent back upon itself, it suddenly springs back into its original shape.

While clarinets and cellos unfold this sixteen-bar theme, the background harmony is animated through the superimposition of various overlapping ostinatos: the low $E\flat/B\flat$ pulsations, the descending horn canon, and the flute/bassoon figure.

---

[32] Lorenz, *Der musikalische Aufbau*, 108.

5. *Variation III (mm. 97–112; 3/6/1–4/3/4)*

This variation structurally parallels the preceding one; 'elements of figuration' involve changes in orchestration and density. The Rhine theme is played by oboes and cor anglais an octave higher than its previous statement. The double reeds cut through the background harmony much better than the low-register clarinets, sharpening the melodic profile of the theme; a gradual 'clarification' is under way. Clarinets continue to play the theme an octave lower, interlocking the original form with its inversion (Ex. 6.10). Wagner imaginatively exchanges melodic lines among the three clarinets so that each player takes a different linear strand whenever the pattern repeats.

Ex. 6.10

The semiquaver figurations are now divided into two parts, thus figuring both voices of the theme: second violins and violas play the upper part, while cellos play the lower in contrary motion. This recalls the third section of the complete draft version, in which second violins and violas were to take up the semiquaver scale patterns. The Eb/Bb pulsations, the horn canon, and the flute/bassoon figures continue from the previous variation.

6. *Variation IV (mm. 113–28; 4/4/1–5/1/4)*

This variation, structurally identical to the preceding pair, completes the clarification process. The sixteen-bar Rhine theme, now played by winds in three octaves, finally breaks through to the surface; its musical birth is complete. The two-part figurations involve the entire string family (as in the fourth section of the complete draft): first violins and violas double the previous second violin and cello parts an octave higher, so that the swirling arpeggiations begin to pass through each other. Upon this collage of background ostinatos, Wagner superimposes yet another: a trumpet pattern based upon the Nature rhythm (Ex. 6.11).

Ex. 6.11

7. *Coda (mm. 129–36; 5/2/1–5/3/4)*

In a sense the appellation 'coda' is a misnomer, inasmuch as these eight bars totally lack the sense of repose and closure traditionally associated with the term; on the contrary, they greatly intensify the rhythmic momentum.[33] Wagner here superimposes four different wind and string ostinatos (Ex. 6.12) over the horn canon and the

Ex. 6.12

[m. 129]

Fls.
Obs.
Cls.

Trpts.

Strs.

Strs.,
Winds

---

[33] The term 'transition' would be equally unsatisfactory, as it would imply a unit that stands outside the structural framework of the *Vorspiel*.

low pulsations. This collage of six different ostinatos, the majority repeating every two bars, creates an amazingly realistic suggestion of swirling water currents.

VII. CONCLUSION

The *Rheingold* Prelude simultaneously fulfils several dramatic/musical functions. Obviously it conjures up a picture of the depths of the Rhine, preparing the audience for the visual illusion of Scene 1, and it presents material which is developed during that scene. In conjunction with the Erda episode of Scene 4, it musically reinforces a dramatic parallelism between the Rhinedaughters and the Norns. Together with the concluding Rainbow theme, it provides a musical 'frame' for the entire opera, creating the impression of large-scale formal coherence. By unfolding the overtone series, it also suggests total organic unity, making it possible for all subsequent motifs (whatever their actual compositional origins) to be traced back to the opening bars. Finally, and most important, it serves as a musical metaphor for the creation of the world and depicts the gradual evolution of impersonal natural forces into human consciousness. Only the first of these functions was fulfilled by the complete draft version; the others resulted, directly or indirectly, from Wagner's composition of the Erda episode.

7 Scene One

My friend! I am in a state of wonderment! A new world stands revealed before me. The great scene in *Das Rheingold* is finished: I see before me riches such as I had never dared suspect. I now consider my powers to be immeasurable: everything seethes within me and makes music.

(Wagner to Franz Liszt, 14 November 1853)

I. SCENE I AS A WHOLE

Scene I stands outside the time-frame of the rest of the drama, and functions as a prologue to the story of the gods (Scenes 2–4). As such, it constitutes a relatively self-contained unit, a complete tragedy in miniature. Here, as elsewhere in the *Ring*, Wagner employs lighting effects to articulate large-scale structure.[1] The curtain opens upon greenish 'twilight' in the depths of the Rhine; eventually the gold begins to glow with a gradually brightening magical light; but Alberich's theft of the gold extinguishes this light and plunges the scene into impenetrable darkness. This progression (twilight–light–darkness) is expressed tonally by a background move from E♭ major through C major to C minor (Ex. 7.1). The crucial element in this key scheme is not the root movement by descending third (E♭–C), but the pitch-class fluctuation E♭–E♮–E♭. The 'brightening' effect created by chromatically raising scale degree $\hat{1}$ of E♭ and reinterpreting the result as $\hat{3}$ of C major is counteracted by depressing this $\hat{3}$ a chromatic semitone to ♭$\hat{3}$. As we shall see, the linear connection between $e♮^2$ and $e♭^2$ (and secondarily between $e♮^1$ and $e♭^1$) becomes an important structural and expressive element during the second half of the scene.

Scene I is organized symmetrically: two tonally closed dramatic units (Episodes 1 and 2) are flanked by an orchestral Prelude and Postlude[2] and separated by a modulatory transition (see the Structural

---

[1] On a much larger scale, the opera *Siegfried* may be understood as a long progression from the gloomy darkness of Mime's cave to the brilliant sunlight of Brünnhilde's mountaintop. This corresponds to Siegfried's extended tonal journey from B♭ minor (darkness) to C major (light).

[2] Wagner originally emphasized the parallelism between the Prelude and Postlude by basing both upon the same arpeggiated melodic figure; while scoring, however, he substituted different figurations. See Section V of this chapter.

Ex. 7.1

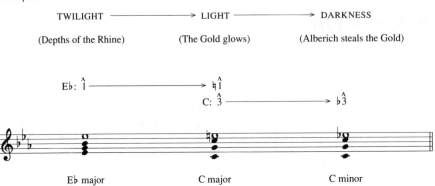

Outline). Scene I is thus tonally open, as it does not end in the key in which it began; it is also *harmonically* open, for while the Prelude's famous Eb major triad is ultimately understood as a tonic, the Postlude prolongs an unresolved dominant. By concluding Scene I on the dominant of the relative minor of its opening key, Wagner creates an effect of unresolved tragedy. As the tetralogy proceeds, these three keys acquire associative meanings: Eb becomes a tonal symbol for the natural world in general and the Rhine in particular; C major comes to represent light, truth, and ultimately love; while C minor signifies darkness, death, and the tragedy born of renouncing love.

II. EPISODE I (MM. 137–447; 5/4/1–27/2/4)

I. *The Episode as a Whole*

Episode I contains four distinct dramatic phases. As Wagner set this segment of his poem to music, he correlated these four phases with the musical processes of statement, contrast, interpolation, and return (Table 7.1). The whole suggests a ternary (ABA′) structure with a lengthy digression or interpolation (X) separating the contrasting section (B) from the recapitulation (A′).

A closed tonal unit in Eb major, this episode is governed at the background level by a I–iii–V–I tonic arpeggiation (Ex. 7.2).[3] However, a linear–harmonic interruption produces the specific middle-

---

[3] The analytical discussion in Chapters 7 to 11 assumes some familiarity with the work of Heinrich Schenker (1868–1935), especially *Free Composition*.

TABLE 7.1 Episode 1: Structural outline

Meas.	Dramatic Phase	Musical Process	Section
137	1. The Rhinedaughters appear and sport with one another.	Statement	A
182	2. Alberich appears and declares his amorous intentions.	Contrast	B
231	3. Alberich woos each of the sisters, and is thrice rejected.	Interpolation	X
421	4. The Rhinedaughters mock Alberich.	Return	A′

Ex. 7.2

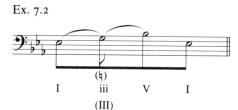

Ex. 7.3

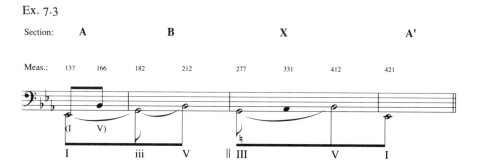

ground form I–iii–V ‖ III–V–I (Ex. 7.3). This correlates with the
formal structure as follows: Sections A and B move from I through iii
to V, the dividing dominant. The interpolation (X) backs up only as
far as III, substituting the major mediant for the minor; it leads a
second time to V, which finally resolves to I at the beginning of
Section A′. In addition, Section A moves from the initial tonic to an
applied divider, or backwards-relating dominant, creating a subor-

dinate I–V progression, and the interpolation (X) connects III and V
with a passing IV.

The length and complexity of this episode demand that each section
be discussed separately.

2. Section A (mm. 137–65; 5/4/1–7/3/1) and Transition

Section A is a marvel of dramatic economy. In only nineteen short
lines of verse, Wagner introduces and names the three Rhinedaughters,
contrasts Flosshilde's rather serious demeanour with her sisters' fri-
volity, mentions the mysterious gold whose sleep the nixies guard,
and intimates that these playful creatures may come to rue their
carefree behaviour. The nineteen lines group into four stanzas, each
with its own dramatic content:

Stanza 1:	Woglinde's song to the waves	5 lines
Stanza 2:	Wellgunde's appearance	4 lines
Stanza 3:	Flosshilde's appearance	5 lines
Stanza 4:	Flosshilde's warning	5 lines

The precise wording of stanza 1 gave Wagner some difficulty. The
prose draft reveals that he originally intended to open the drama with
a nameless Rhinedaughter singing a wordless song to the waves.[4]
Changing his mind, he began to work out a text for this vocalise in
the left-hand margin:

Prose Draft (A)	*Prose Draft (B)*
Weia! Wala!	Weia! Waga!
Woge du Welle!	Woge du Welle!
Walle zur Woge,	Walle zur Woge,
Weia! la la Walla	Waga la Weia!
Walla la wei!	Wallala weia la wei!

Wagner's revision (B) leaves lines 2–3 of the original version (A)
intact, preserving a textual exchange between 'Woge' and 'Welle'/
'Walle'; it reduces the fourth line to the same syllabic pattern as the
previous two, and expands the fifth into the only three-stress line in
the stanza.[5] In addition, Version B creates a new textual exchange
between 'Weia' and 'Waga' in lines 1 and 4.

The stanza assumed definitive form in the verse draft, although

---

[4] The prose draft reads: 'sie singt (ohne Worte) eine wohlige wellenweise dazu.' See WWV
86A Text II, p. 1; cf. Strobel, *Skizzen und Entwürfe*, 213.

[5] This transcription was made from WWV 86A Text II, p. 1; a facsimile appears in Strobel, *Skizzen und Entwürfe*, facing p. 214. Throughout this book, my transcriptions of textual variants constitute *interpretations* of Wagner's crossings-out and overwrites, not literal
reproductions.

changes in punctuation and capitalization appear in the fair copy and 1853 printing:

Verse Draft	Fair Copy/1853 Printing
Weia waga!	Weia! Waga!
Woge du welle,	Woge, du Welle,
walle zur wiege!	walle zur Wiege!
Waga laweia!	Wagalaweia!
Wallala weiala weia!	Wallala weiala weia!

The undated musical sketch transcribed in Ex. 6.3*a* differs textually from all these versions; it could either pre-date the prose draft marginalia or form a link between them and the verse draft. However, as suggested in Chapter 6, Wagner could have jotted it down as pen practice while he drafted the ink score, making an error in the textual underlay. This last hypothesis is suggested by the capitalizations, the word 'Wiege', and the fact that the sketch appears on the same sheet as Ex. 6.3*c*, which clearly *was* made while scoring.

Stanzas 2–4 assumed definitive form in the verse draft, and were carried over without change into the fair copy and 1853 printing.[6] However, unlike its predecessors, stanza 4 is not based upon any statement in the prose draft; these dramatically crucial lines (Flosshilde's warning about the gold) apparently occurred to Wagner at the last minute, during the act of versification. The fact is all the more remarkable in that, as will be demonstrated, Wagner throws the musical weight of the entire section onto this fourth stanza.

The syllabic patterns of the first four stanzas are displayed in Table 7.2. The preponderance of two-stress over three-stress lines is typical, as is the use of a three-stress line to close a stanza. Flosshilde's entrance in line 10, coupled with the end-accented rhythms of lines 9 and 19, suggests a binary (2 + 2) partitioning of the four stanzas, a formal grouping partially supported by the music.

Wagner's initial musical setting of these lines is transcribed in the Appendix. His major concern here was setting the text; the lower staff contains only the bass line and a sketch of the harmony, but remarkably little in the way of texture or figuration. Even at this early stage, Wagner had decided to separate stanzas 2 and 3 by a two-bar orchestral link (articulating the binary grouping mentioned above), and to clinch the move to the dominant by a reprise of the sixteen-bar Prelude theme. While scoring, he of course substituted the new Rhine theme from the revised Prelude for the original semiquaver figure.

[6] Wagner did, of course, make changes in capitalization and punctuation.

TABLE 7.2 Episode 1: Syllabic scheme of Section A, stanzas 1–4

Line	Upbeat	Stress 1			Stress 2			Stress 3	
1		Wei-	a!		Wa-	ga!			
2		Wo-	ge,	du	Wel-	le,			
3		wal-	le	zur	Wie-	ge!			
4		Wa-	ga-	la	wei-	a!			
5		Wal-	la-	la	wei-	a-	la	wei-	a!
6		Wog-	lin-	de,	wach'st	du	al-	lein?	
7	Mit	Wel-	gun-	de	wär'	ich	zu	zwei.	
8	Lass'	seh'n	wie	du	wach'st.				
9		Sich-	er	vor	dir.				
10		Hei-	a-	ha	wei-	a!			
11		wil-	des	Ge-	schwi-	ster!			
12		Floss-	hil-	de,	schwimm'!				
13		Wog-	lin-	de	flieht:				
14		hilf	mir	die	Flies-	sen-	de	fan-	gen!
15	Des	Gol-	des		Schlaf				
16		hü-	tet	ihr	schlecht;				
17		Bes-	ser	be-	wacht				
18	des	schlum-	mern-	den	Bett,				
19	sonst	büsst	ihr		bei-	de	das	Spiel!	

This passage provides a good example of how Wagner's poetic rhythms determined his musical phraseology, and will thus be examined in some detail. Within duple metre, a syllabic setting of a two-stress line will normally produce a one-bar unit (two beats); a three-stress line will normally generate one and a half bars (three beats), but usually Wagner will extend it to two bars (four beats) by lengthening the final duration or following it with a rest. Thus, within 6/8 (compound duple) metre, stanza 1 naturally suggests the vocal rhythm shown in Ex. 7.4. This comes very close to what Wagner actually wrote (see transcription), although he rhythmicized the first beat of line 5 differently. However, he augmented the end of line 5 ('wei-a!') to twice its normal length, extending this final unit from two bars to three, and making the entire phrase seven bars long instead of six; this augmentation throws into relief the important appoggiatura figure $f^2-e\flat^2$ (heard locally as $\hat{6}-\hat{5}$ of A♭). Such deviations for expressive purposes are not uncommon in *Das Rheingold*, but they depend for their effect upon a pre-established rhythmic norm (just as, in music of the Classical era, the four- or eight-bar phrase serves not as a musical strait-jacket, but as a structural norm against which expan-

Ex. 7.4

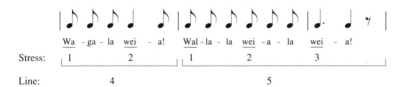

sions and extensions can make themselves felt). Thus Wagner's substitution of *Stabreim* for *Endreim* did not lead to the automatic
disintegration of symmetrical phrase structure; it simply transferred
the rhythmic norm to a lower structural level.[7]

After notating Woglinde's pentatonic melody, Wagner supported it
with a pianissimo Eb in the lower staff; he then sketched an Ab major
triad above this, as a realization of the tune's harmonic implications.
The overlapping violin arpeggiations (based upon the Norn figurations
of the revised Prelude) were of course added much later, while
working out the instrumentation.

Wagner's successive attempts to rhythmicize lines 6 and 7 (each
containing three stresses) are revealing. He began with a 'normative'
setting of line 6 (Ex. 7.5*a*). He then lengthened the first stress,
perhaps to emphasize the Rhinedaughter's name, and continued with
line 7, shaping it to match this second version (Ex. 7.5*b*). While
scoring, he shifted line 6 by one and a half measures, so that it fits
within the barlines and leaves an empty vocal measure between lines
5 and 6; he then compressed the beginning of line 7 (Ex. 7.5*c*).

Lines 8 and 9 are rhythmicized normally, each two-stress line
generating a two-beat unit; the final beat of line 9 ('dir!') elides with

---

[7] That is, the symmetrical four- and eight-bar phrases so characteristic of Wagner's earlier
operas (especially *Lohengrin*) are replaced in *Das Rheingold* by rhythmic regularity at the level
of the subphrase.

Ex. 7.5

a

b

c

the two-bar orchestral link. Thus, in the final version, the vocal units become successively shorter: in terms of measures, 2 + 1.5 + 1 + 1 (or 2 + 1.5 + 1 + 0.5 if one takes into account the effect of the elision). At some point, perhaps while scoring, Wagner sketched a few harmonies in the treble staff (see transcription, mm. 148–50); these make explicit the rising line $eb^2–f^2–g^2–ab^2–bb^2$, and help punctuate the cadence. Like its predecessor, this second phrase (which really begins with the empty vocal measure before 'Woglinde') is seven bars long, but its internal structure is obviously quite different.

Stanza 3 (Flosshilde's appearance) receives an entirely normative rhythmic setting; the vocal line arpeggiates the Eb^5_3 triad, although Wagner changed some pitches while drafting the score. Each two-stress line generates a one-bar unit, while the concluding three-stress line generates a two-bar unit through the customary procedure of

Ex. 7.6

a

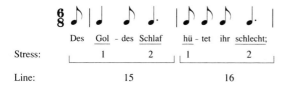

b

c

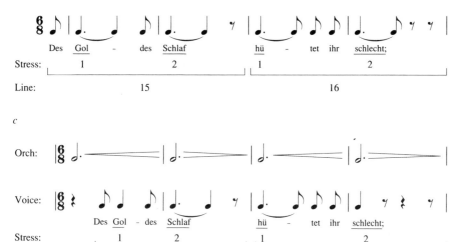

lengthening the final syllable. The resultant third phrase is thus six bars long.

Stanza 4 (Flosshilde's warning) forms the dramatic crux of the entire section, and Wagner clearly wished to highlight it musically. He accomplished this through a harmonic change to C minor (the first time since the beginning of the opera that the bass has left E♭) coupled with an augmentation of the vocal rhythms. Lines 15 and 16 would normally generate the pattern shown in Ex. 7.6*a*; however, Wagner expanded each stress so that it occupies two beats instead of one (Ex. 7.6*b*). While scoring, he condensed the rhythm of line 15, projecting the two-bar length in the orchestra (Ex. 7.6*c*). Lines 17–19 received a normative rhythmic setting (2 + 2 + 3 stresses → 1 + 1 + 2 bars), making the entire phrase eight bars in length. The lower staff of the complete draft (see transcription, mm. 158–65) contains more than usual in the way of harmonic elaboration: the first four bars

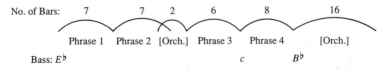

FIG. 7.1 Episode 1: Phrase structure of Section A' and Transition

Ex. 7.7

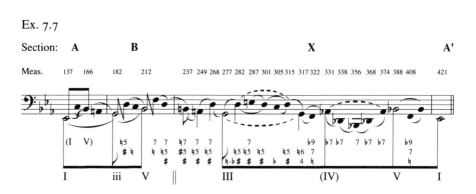

display a $\frac{5-6}{3-4}$ neighbouring motion within the C minor triad, while the last 4 contain the chromatic passing motion $g–gb–f$ as well as the addition of the tritone eb^1/a to the harmony. The resultant applied chord resolves to Bb, and Wagner indicates a reprise of the sixteen-bar Prelude theme at the level of the dominant.

Thus far, Wagner's phraseology has been determined primarily by the vocal rhythms, which in turn are generated from the stress patterns of his text. The only exceptions to this principle are the orchestral links: the two-bar elided unit which separates Phrases 2 and 3, and the sixteen-bar unit which follows Phrase 4 (Fig. 7.1).

Let us now consider the large-scale tonal motion of this section. It will be recalled from Ex. 7.3 that Section A moves from the initial tonic to an applied divider, and that this creates a subordinate I–V progression. Example 7.7, a more detailed middleground graph of the entire episode, shows that the root of the dominant (Bb) is preceded by its upper neighbour (c); this neighbour supports a C minor triad (Eb:vi) which functions as pre-dominant harmony between I and V.

The initial tonic is animated by $\frac{5-6}{3-4}$ neighbouring motion at Wog-linde's vocal entrance (m. 137; 5/4/1). Despite its striking effect, this $^6_4$ sonority functions less as a second inversion subdominant (IV$^6_4$) than as a linear expansion of the tonic.[8] However, it does cause the appoggiatura figure $f^2–eb^2$ ('wei-a!') to sound locally like $\hat{6}–\hat{5}$ (of Ab), a scale-step progression that reverberates throughout the *Ring*.

To underscore Flosshilde's warning about the gold, Wagner emphasizes the dark colour of the C minor chord—the first real harmonic change thus far—through scoring (double reeds) and range (melodic emphasis upon eb^1 in Oboe I). Although this chord functions locally as pre-dominant harmony between I and V, it also forecasts a large-scale tonal move to C minor, the key in which Alberich will renounce love and steal the gold. The decisive arrival at V is clinched by the following orchestral statement, a 'misplaced' fifth variation of the Prelude's sixteen-bar Rhine theme.

Obviously Wagner had to recompose this transitional passage (mm. 166–81; 7/3/2–8/3/1) when he drafted the score, incorporating the new Rhine theme and its arpeggiations. The low fifth, now Bb/F, is assigned to bassoons and clarinets, which ornament their pitches with increasingly frequent chromatic grace-notes. During the last four bars, contrabass octave pizzicati pull Bb down through A to G. The gradual accumulation of awkward grace-notes, coupled with the downward pull from Bb major to G minor, creates a gradual tonal darkening: Alberich negates the Rhinedaughters' joyful tonicization of the dominant by inflecting towards the darker waters of the mediant.

3. Section B (mm. 182–230; 8/3/2–12/1/5)

The poetic structure of Section B is somewhat more complex than that of A; it revolves around Alberich's three addresses to the Rhinedaughters, punctuated by the sisters' comments:

1. Alberich calls to the Rhinedaughters.	6 lines
The sisters investigate.	7 lines
2. Alberich wants to join them.	6 lines (+ 1)
The sisters are incredulous.	2 lines
3. Alberich expresses his growing desire.	5 lines
The sisters' fear vanishes.	4 lines

Although Alberich addresses the mermaids directly, they speak largely to each other (except for the single line 'Was willst du dort unten?' which they interject into Alberich's second address). Their comments may therefore be considered parenthetical inasmuch as the dramatic focus now shifts to the Nibelung.

---

[8] This interpretation is confirmed by the beginning of Section A' (mm. 421 ff.; 25/1/2 ff.), where the passage is recapitulated following an extensive dominant preparation; the 'Ab$^6_4$ chord' clearly stands for the Eb tonic.

TABLE 7.3 Episode 1: Syllabic scheme of Alberich's addresses in Section B

Line	Upbeat	Stress 1			Stress 2			Stress 3
1	He	he!	Ihr		Nic-	ker!		
2		Wie	seid	ihr	Nied-	lich,		
3		neid-	li-	ches	Volk!			
4	Aus	Ni-	bel-	heim's	Nacht			
5		naht'	ich	mich*	gern,			
6		neig-	tet		ihr	euch	zu	mir!
1		Ihr,	da		o-	ben!		
	[Was	willst	du	da	un-	ten?]		
2		Stör'	ich	eu'r	Spiel,			
3	Wenn	stau-	nend	ich	still	hier		steh?
4		Tauch-	tet	ihr	nie-	der,		
5	mit	euch			toll-	te		
6	und	neck-	te	der	Nib-	lung	sich	gern!
1	Wie	scheint	im		Schim-	mer		
2	ihr	hell	und		schön!			
3	Wie	gern	um-		schlän-	ge		
4	der	Schlan-	ken		ei-	ne	mein	Arm,
5		schlüpf-	te		hold	sie	her-	ab!

* The verse draft, fair copy, 1853 printing, and complete draft all have 'euch'; it was eventually changed to 'mich', probably to avoid redundancy with line 6. However, the *GS* version retains 'euch'.

Because Wagner had outlined this passage rather clearly in the prose draft, he had little trouble with its versification. The syllabic patterns of Alberich's three addresses are displayed in Table 7.3; the six lines of his first address group syntactically as 3 + 3, a grouping which has important musical consequences. Wagner began this portion of his complete draft by sketching two bars of instrumental preparation. He then gave Alberich's six lines an entirely normative rhythmic setting, generating a seven-bar phrase (mm. 185–91; 8/4/1–9/1/3) which moves harmonically from i to V of G minor. When he scored this phrase, Wagner of course added the semiquaver figurations of the revised Prelude. However, he later decided that the three-bar hypermetre of Alberich's first subphrase (itself generated from the three-line poetic grouping) required preparation; he therefore expanded the orchestral introduction from two bars to three, inking this revision over the original pencil version in the *Partiturerstschrift* and adding the indication '3 taktigen Rhythmus'. This provides a specific instance of a poetic grouping exerting an effect upon a purely instrumental passage.[9] That Wagner considered the sisters' next three lines parenthetical is suggested by the fact that he crammed them into the end of Alberich's phrase as part of a cadential extension, structuring the entire phrase (mm. 182–93; 8/3/2–9/2/1) as: three-bar orchestral preparation plus seven-bar vocal phrase plus two-bar cadential extension.

The Rhinedaughters dive deeper in order to investigate. Wagner originally intended to represent this dive (indicated in the complete draft by the words 'Sie tauchen hinab') by a *descent* of the bass from *d* to *d♭* coupled with a restatement of the two-bar semiquaver motif over a diminished seventh harmony. Flosshilde's retreat was, logically enough, suggested by a rising scale whose climax coincided with the arrival of the bass on *C*, with an apparent half-cadence (V^{6-5}_{4-3}) in F minor, and with a restatement of the two-bar motif at this new tonal level. While scoring, Wagner replaced the first semiquaver motif by a melodic *inversion* of the two-bar Rhine figuration (mm. 194–5; 9/2/2–3), the descending pattern better suggesting Flosshilde's dive; and the second by the original, ascending form of the figure (mm. 199–200; 9/3/3–4), representing her secure retreat to the upper waters. In this case, a scenic event called forth a specific musical procedure (melodic inversion). Interestingly, Wagner left the ascending scale at Flosshilde's 'Hütet das Gold!' intact (mm. 197–8; 9/3/1–2), a rare survival into the finished score of the original semiquaver figure of the complete draft.

Whereas Alberich's first address ended on V/G minor, the sisters' scouting expedition pulled the tonality down a tone, to V/F minor; Alberich accepts this new tonal level, and addresses the nixies a second time. If the Rhinedaughters' reply (bracketed in Table 7.3) is omitted, Alberich's six lines group as 3 + 3, paralleling the structure of his first speech. This again suggests a triple hypermetre, but one which materialized in a somewhat different manner from its predecessor. In the complete draft, Wagner introduced Alberich's first line with an angular one-bar melody eventually assigned to cellos; Alberich's call and the sisters' reply (each a two-stress line) completed a three-bar structural unit whose final measure was eventually filled out with the Rhine arpeggiation (clarinets). Alberich's next two lines generated a second three-bar unit which Wagner eventually underlaid with a varied restatement of the previous orchestral pass-

---

[9] Knapp clearly misunderstands the purpose of this inking-over, and attributes to it a rather lofty structural significance it never possessed: 'After the opening measures of the Rhinemaidens' music, Wagner emphasizes the change from their carefree play by copying in ink the turn to G minor and the dissonance that accompanies Alberich's first appearance . . . and labeling it below: "3 taktigen Rhythmus"' ('The Instrumentation Draft', 285).

age (cello melody and clarinet figuration). The final 3 + 3-bar grouping (mm. 202–7; 10/1/2–10/2/2) would have been difficult to predict
from the text alone, and appears to have resulted from Wagner's
desire to recreate the earlier triple hypermetre. Alberich's last three
lines generate a predictable four-bar unit, at the conclusion of which
the bass moves through B♮ to B♭ (mm. 211–12; 3/3/2–3); this lowers
the tonal level yet another whole tone and marks a return to the
dominant of E♭, an important structural event articulated by Wellgunde
and Woglinde's parenthetical one-bar questions. Alberich's second
address thus generates a formal unit of 3 + 3 + 6 measures; in its
final version (mm. 202–13; 10/1/2–10/3/4) the overall similarity of the
first two segments suggests a bar form (aa′b), although this structure
is neither implied by the text nor evident in the complete draft
version.

Alberich again accepts the sisters' new tonal offering, but darkens
the modality, and begins his third address over V/E♭ *minor*. Wagner
originally underpinned his vocal line with nothing but a B♭ in the bass
staff; while scoring, however, he added $^{♭9-8}_{♭6-5}$ neighbour motion above
this, then sketched in the Rhine figuration. We thus catch Wagner
elaborating his accompaniment in the complete draft before working
it out in full score.[10] The cb^1–bb motif ($\hat{♭6}$–$\hat{5}$ of E♭) sounds like a
dark perversion of Woglinde's original joyous f^2–eb^2 ($\hat{6}$–$\hat{5}$ of A♭).
Alberich's third address ends, like his second, on a diminished seventh
chord (m. 219; 11/2/2); Flosshilde resolves this as an applied dominant
back to V/E♭ *major* ('Nun lach' ich der Furcht'). Her next line ('der
Feind ist verliebt!') moves vocally $\hat{5}$–$\hat{1}$, implying resolution to the
tonic; however, the deceptive resolution at 'ver-*liebt*!' (m. 223; 11/3/2)
deflects the music away from this tonic. The sisters decide to postpone their resolution to E♭, in order to toy with Alberich.

How are we to understand the tonal structure of Section B?
Alberich's three addresses are oriented around G, F, and E♭ minor.
Is this an example of what Bailey would call an 'expressive' tonal
descent? Hardly, for there is no convincing dramatic reason why
the tonal levels should descend; indeed, Alberich's growing passion
might rather suggest an *ascent*. It seems more profitable to consider

---

[10] Westernhagen apparently did not realize that Wagner sketched in the Rhine figuration
while scoring; i.e., *after* finishing the complete draft and revising the Prelude. Failing to
distinguish among the various layers in the complete draft, he assumed that Wagner wrote them
all at the same time. Thus he states that the accompaniment figures in the complete draft
'occasionally suggest' the Rhine motif, and goes on to say: 'In the score a solo clarinet enters
here in place of the strings. Although that instrument is not specified in the sketch, the sound of
the clarinet will have suggested this particular figure to Wagner's imagination' (*The Forging of
the 'Ring'*, 22). Obviously nothing of the kind happened, but this false conclusion is unfortunately all too typical.

two facts: first, that these three tonal areas are represented primarily by their *dominants*, and second, that the roots of these dominants participate in a chromatic bass descent from D (V/G) to B♭ (V/E♭). The descending bass move $D-(D\flat)-C_1-(B\natural_1)-B\flat_1$ is clearly sketched out in the complete draft, demonstrating that this large-scale motion was part of Wagner's initial conception. In other words, Wagner is here working out a large-scale progression from a tonicized iii (G) to an active V within the key of E♭ (see again Ex. 7.7). The pedal B♭ underlying Alberich's third address (mm. 214 ff.; 11/1/1 ff.) sounds like a dominant preparation following a period of increased harmonic activity, and prepares the listener for some sort of tonal (and perhaps even thematic) recapitulation. But at this point the sisters elect specifically *not* to recapitulate; rather, they deflect the tonality away from E♭ through a series of descending thirds $(F-D-B_1$ in the bass) in order to sport with the Nibelung. The resolution to E♭ is indefinitely postponed; the long digression which follows will travel back through G (III) in order finally to regain V/E♭.

4. The Interpolation (mm. 321–420; 12/2/1–25/1/1)

The Interpolation (Section X) features one of Wagner's most important formal procedures: cyclical structure. The prose sketch states that 'He [Alberich] woos all three women, one after the other, and is rejected.'[11] In a letter to Liszt dated 20 November 1851, Wagner expanded upon this statement: '*Alberich* comes up out of the depths of the earth to the three daughters of the Rhine; he pursues them with his loathsome attentions; rejected by the first, he turns to the second: joking and teasing him, they all spurn the goblin.'[12] These early documents already suggest a tri-cyclic structure: Alberich woos each of the three Rhinedaughters in turn, and is thrice rejected.

Because the mermaids deliberately tempt Alberich in order to ridicule his amorous advances, their behaviour often strikes the audience as unnecessarily cruel. Cruel, perhaps, but not really unnecessary— Wagner clarified this point in another passage from the afore-cited letter: '. . . but so that none may steal the gold, they themselves are appointed its guardians: the man who approaches them has indeed no desire for the gold; Alberich, at least, does not seem to desire it, since he behaves like a man in love'.[13] Thus the Rhinedaughters' function is to distract men's attention from the gold by inflaming their

[11] 'Er wirbt nach einander um alle drei frauen und wird abgewiesen.' See WWV 86A Text Ia, a facsimile of which appears in Strobel, *Skizzen und Entwürfe*, facing p. 204.
[12] *Selected Letters*, 238 (*SB* iv. 188).
[13] *Selected Letters*, 238–9 (*SB* iv. 188).

passions. The nixies do their job so well that Alberich does not even notice the gold until after his threefold quest for love has been thoroughly frustrated.

In his prose draft, Wagner fleshed out this cyclic structure so that each of the three cycles contains the same dramatic progression: (1) One of the Rhinedaughters calls to Alberich and dives down to him; (2) Alberich clambers towards her, as she herself draws nearer; (3) Alberich woos her with terms of endearment, and concludes by attempting to embrace her; (4) she mocks him and quickly escapes; and (5) Alberich expresses his disappointment.

In order to demonstrate how clearly the prose draft projects this cyclical structure, a translation of the relevant passage is laid out below according to the fivefold dramatic movement of each cycle:[14]

Cycle 1: Alberich woos Woglinde. (1) One of [the Rhinedaughters] lets herself sink onto a rock closer to [Alberich]: (2) hurriedly and with imp-like agility he clambers towards her (He finds the increasing dampness loathsome). (3) He flatters her and attempts to catch her: (4) she teases and ridicules him; as he believes himself on the point of seizing and caressing her, she escapes towards another rock. (5) Hastily he tries to climb after her;
    Cycle 2: Alberich woos Wellgunde. (1) Then the second maiden calls to him from the opposite side: he should really turn to her. (2) Delighted, Alberich clambers towards her; she comes somewhat closer. (3) Already he hopes to be happy; (4) she examines him more closely, describes his ugly appearance, and marvels at his being in love. As he attempts to seize her by force, she quickly soars upwards. (5) He stands alone again, is annoyed, and angrily calls after the vanished one.
    Cycle 3: Alberich woos Flosshilde. (1) Then the third encourages him: why so downcast? isn't she still there? she would like to comfort him. (2) Alberich is delighted to hear that; she dives down to him: (3) he becomes more and more trusting; she praises his handsome figure, his grace and tenderness. He becomes quite ardent, and wants to embrace her. (4) With insolent laughter she quickly swims away; all three ridicule him. (5) Enraged, Alberich scolds her.

While versifying this passage, Wagner *expanded* the second and third cycles in order to intensify the dramatic progression; such expansion in the service of dramatic intensification is characteristic of his cyclic structures. For example, Alberich's simple 'Mein Friedel sei, | du fräuliches Kind!' (Cycle 1) grows into his impassioned declaration 'Die schlanken Arme | schlinge um mich . . .' (Cycle 2) and culminates in the parodistical 'love duet' with Flosshilde (Cycle 3). Similarly, his reaction at being rejected begins as mere annoyance

---

[14] See WWV 86A Text II, 1–2; cf. Strobel, *Skizzen und Entwürfe*, 214. My translation.

(Cycle 1: 'Wie fang' ich im Sprung | den spröden Fisch? . . .'), turns into anger (Cycle 2: 'Falsches Kind! | Kalter, grätiger Fisch!'), and finally erupts into an outburst of despair and anguish (Cycle 3: 'Wehe! ach wehe! | o Schmerz! o Schmerz! . . .'). In terms of physical action, Alberich futilely pursues Woglinde, but is allowed to approach Wellgunde, and actually embraces and caresses Flosshilde; the latter's abrupt rejection produces almost the effect of *coitus interruptus*, especially after the warmly lyrical, lushly orchestrated passage which precedes it.

Because the tonal structure of the interpolation cannot be understood out of context, the reader is referred again to Ex. 7.7. Whereas Sections A and B moved from I (E♭) through iii (G minor) to V (B♭), the interpolation backs up to III (G *major*) and passes through IV (A♭) to regain the active V on B♭. However, III is approached through a series of descending fifths (A–D–G), and its dominant is prolonged by upper and lower neighbour motion (D–E–D–C–D); the A♭ functions locally as V^7/D♭, and is prolonged by a symmetrical progression of major–minor seventh chords (A♭^{7}–D♭^{7}–B♭^{7}–D♭^{7}–A♭^{7}); and the regained dominant is intensified through an applied chord ($V^{♭9}_7$/V). Thus A♭ functions less as a true subdominant than as a composed-out passing tone between III and V whose transitional nature is underscored by the surface seventh chord it supports.

This tonal structure correlates with the cyclical design as follows: Cycle 1 (the wooing of Woglinde) passes from V^7/E minor to V^7/D minor; Cycle 2 (the wooing of Wellgunde) resolves V^7/G to the tonicized III before inflecting to minor and neighbouring its dominant. Thus the initial V^7/E is understood in retrospect as an upper neighbour to the first member of the descending fifth progression, which itself forms a tonal anacrusis to G. Cycle III (the wooing of Flosshilde) pulls G up to A♭ and, after prolonging it with the symmetrical progression of seventh chords, moves on to the B♭ dominant preparation.

In Sections A and B, Wagner's musical phraseology was determined strictly by the vocal rhythms, which in turn were generated by the accentual scheme of the text. At the beginning of the interpolation, however, an important change occurs: Wagner composes the orchestral part first, then writes the vocal line to fit against it. The complete draft shows us exactly how this occurred (see transcription):

At the point where Alberich begins his clumsy scramble up the rock towards Woglinde (m. 231 of the final version), Wagner drew a double bar, changed the key signature from three flats to one sharp, wrote in 'Meno mosso', and, *retaining the 6/8 metre*, wrote out six bars of an angular melody supported by parallel thirds. Dissatisfied, he crossed out these six bars and continued with a different version; he then added the vocal line, crowding in the text. This second version is much better formed than the first: the original two-bar unit is expanded to three, the second three bars are a literal sequence of the first a whole tone higher, and the final six measures clearly expand the harmonic goal V/E minor. The entire twelve bars (mm. 231–42; 12/2/1–13/1/2) thus constitute a bar form of 3 + 3 + 6 measures, whose Stollen feature the triple hypermetre now associated with Alberich. In addition, the change from 6/8 to 2/4 metre heightens the sense of disruption already created by the change of key, texture, harmony, and instrumentation. Alberich's poetic accents fall upon the half-beat (quaver) rather than the beat, creating an effect of clumsy impetuosity; Woglinde's 'Prüstend naht | meines Freiers Pracht!' (mm. 243–4; 13/1/3–4) restores the beat (crotchet) as the basic accentual unit, and modulates back to the rhythmic smoothness of the preceding sections. At the foreground level the first six bars are harmonically non-functional, consisting largely of chromatic parallel $\frac{6}{3}$ chords, but on a middleground level they prolong the functional V/E. This contrast between a non-functional foreground which contrapuntally prolongs a functional middleground or background harmony (or an entire harmonic progression) becomes a frequent feature of Wagner's mature musical style.

The complete draft signals the beginning of Cycle 2 (mm. 266–330; 15/1/3–19/2/1) by a change of harmony (from V^7/D to V^7/G, the latter unfolded in the bass by the falling fifth $A–D$) and an expansion of the vocal rhythm. Woglinde's opening two lines suggest the rhythm of Ex. 7.8a, but Wagner set them as shown in Ex. 7.8b. The remarkable expansion of line 2 allows its initial vowel sound, a seductive chordal ninth, to float almost endlessly above the new dominant harmony. While scoring, Wagner sketched in a flute part based upon Wellgunde's descending fifth motif (first $c^3–f\sharp^2$, then $e^3–a^2$; the bass move $A–D$ may be interpreted as an augmentation of this vocal motif); he then elaborated this line into caressing wind chords and slackened the tempo to 'Ruhig im Zeitmass'. Having caught Alberich's attention, Wellgunde cadences decisively in G (m. 277; 15/3/3: 'meide!'), the first authentic cadence (ii–V–I) since the wooing episode began; this articulation marks a return to the mediant (III) of E♭ at the middleground tonal level.

The foregoing (mm. 266–77; 15/1/3–15/3/3) constitutes the first event (Wellgunde's call to Alberich) of Cycle 2; during the second event (Alberich's clambering towards her), the dwarf again darkens the tonal atmosphere, inflecting towards minor and initiating a bass descent from i to V of G (mm. 278–82; 15/3/4–16/1/3). Woglinde

Ex. 7.8

a

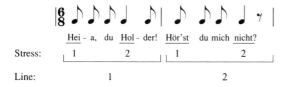

| Hei - a, | du | Hol - der! | Hör'st | du mich nicht? |

Stress: 1   2   1   2

Line: 1   2

b

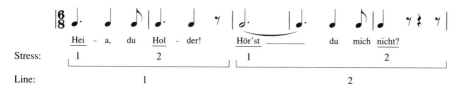

| Hei - a, | du | Hol - der! | Hör'st _____ | du | mich nicht? |

Stress: 1   2   1   2

Line: 1   2

inflects back to major (mm. 285–6; 16/2/2–3: 'Bin nun ich dir nah'?'), but Alberich abruptly wrenches the bass down to *E* (m. 287; 16/2/4: 'Noch nicht ge-*nug!*'). During the third event (Alberich's anticipation of amorous delights), the bass prolongs this *E* (mm. 287–94; 16/2/4–16/4/3), which functions as upper neighbour to V/G; its unstable character is created by chromatic lines which make it sound locally like V/A minor. In addition, the complete draft specifies that the initial portion of the semiquaver figuration from the original version of the Prelude is to run throughout this passage as an elaboration of the bass *E* (*E–D♯–E–F–E*, etc.); this figure actually survives in the final score, although the student unacquainted with the complete draft is apt to wonder where it came from.

Wellgunde initiates the fourth event of Cycle 2 (her closer examination and mockery of Alberich) by a remarkable rhythmic expansion of her two-stress lines (each ordinarily implying a two-beat unit):

Bist du ver-*liebt*	3 beats
und *lüs*-tern nach *Min*-ne,	4 beats
lass' *seh'n*, du *Schö*-ner,	5 beats

Her concluding line ('wie *bist* du zu *schau'n*?') suddenly snaps back to the normative length of two beats, followed by an expectant pause. While scoring, Wagner intensified the biting effect of this rhythmic contraction by inserting an extra bar and echoing Wellgunde's

last line in violas and stopped horn. The resultant musical mockery is
as devastating as the means by which it is created are simple.

Alberich expressed his romantic feelings on E, the upper neighbour of V/G; having resolved back to the dominant, Wellgunde now
moves to its lower neighbour (C) to deliver her stinging rejection. At
m. 314 (18/1/3: 'fest!') the resolution of the lower-neighbour c back to
V/G prepares a $\flat II^6$–V^7–I cadence; however, Wagner weakens the
effect by placing the crucial dominant in second inversion (mm.
315–16; 18/1/4–18/2/1). Wellgunde's vocal line cadences $\hat{5}$–$\hat{1}$ (mm.
316–17; 18/2/1–2: 'sonst fliess' ich dir fort!'), but in the complete
draft Wagner weakened the tonic resolution by embellishing it with a
$^{6-5}_{4-3}$ inflection. In the score, he weakened this resolution still further
by sustaining the $^6_4$ sonority for four bars (mm. 317–20; 18/2/2–18/3/1)
and eliminating the $^5_3$ resolution. His intent, obviously, was to depict
Wellgunde's unexpected escape by undermining the cadence: Alberich
thinks he has caught her (preparation for strong Neapolitan cadence)
but Wellgunde eludes his grasp (evasion of strong resolution). In
addition, the extended $^6_4$ chord recalls the referential sonority already
associated with the Rhinedaughters; while scoring, Wagner added the
new Rhine motif and the sisters' vocal laughter to the texture.

In the fifth event of Cycle 2, Alberich's rage at Wellgunde's escape
(mm. 321–30; 18/3/2–19/2/1) recalls and intensifies the declamatory
texture which concluded Cycle 1. His anger wrenches the bass chromatically downward from G to F; this F (m. 322; 18/3/3) supports a
minor ninth chord which locally implies B♭ minor. Alberich's vocal
line 'Schein' ich nicht schön dir, | niedlich und neckisch' (mm. 323–5;
18/3/4–19/1/1) is often interpreted as a rhythmic augmentation of the
cello figure which accompanied his scramble up the rocks in pursuit
of Woglinde (m. 233; 12/2/3).[15] Admittedly, the compositional origins
of these two ideas are quite different: the cello figure was conceived
as an instrumental accompaniment to a stage action, while the vocal
line was generated from the poetic rhythm. However, even if Wagner
did not consciously plan this musical affinity, he had certainly recognized it by the time he began Scene 3; there he clearly juxtaposes
the two motifs, whereby the implied B♭ minor orientation of the
vocal theme determines the tonality of the entire first half of the
scene. At the moment, however, there is no reason to suspect that
this melody will reappear, and the bass F soon rises chromatically
through passing ^{o7} and $^6_4$ chords to A♭ (m. 328; 19/1/4).

The arrival at A♭ initiates the third cycle (mm. 331–420; 19/2/2–
25/1/1), articulated in the complete draft by a change of key signature

---

[15] See, for example, Cooke, *I Saw the World End*, 41.

(from one sharp back to three flats), the direction 'achtel bewegung' ('quaver motion'), and an indication that the harp is to enter. As explained above, this cycle prolongs A♭, a large-scale passing tone (IV) between G (III) and B♭ (V), by means of the symmetrical progression $A♭^7-D♭^7-B♭^7-D♭^7-A♭^7$ (see again Ex. 7.7). The first event (Flosshilde's encouragement of Alberich) moves harmonically by fifth from $A♭^7$ to $D♭^7$ (heard locally as $V^7/G♭$), and features a significant expansion of the vocal rhythms:

Was *zank'st* du, *Alp*?	2 beats	$A♭^7$
Schon so ver-*zagt*?	3 beats	$A♭^7$
Du *frei*-test um *zwei*:	4 beats	$A♭^7$
früg'st du die *drit*-te,	6 beats	$A♭^7-D♭^7$
süs-sen *Trost*	4 beats	$D♭^7$
schü-fe die *Trau*-te *dir*!	6 beats	$D♭^7$

The langorous, seductive effect of this remarkable fourteen-bar phrase owes much to the insistent repetition of the appoggiatura eb^2 ('*drit*-te', '*süs*-sen', '*Trau*-te'); together with its resolution db^2, it suggests $\hat{6}-\hat{5}$ (over $V^7/G♭$), the scale-degree progression which began the entire scene. While drafting the instrumentation, Wagner sketched in a reiteration of this motif as a countermelody above the vocal line; this countermelody was ultimately assigned to solo violin, which begins by doubling Flosshilde's part, then continues independently with the carressing $\hat{6}-\hat{5}$ figure.[16] Reiterated wind chords (a realization of the 'achtel bewegung') complete the erotically charged texture.

The second event (Alberich's response and Flosshilde's dive) begins with yet another darkening of the tonal atmosphere: the violins' eb^2-db^2 becomes ebb^2-db^2, suggesting the minor mode ($♭\hat{6}-\hat{5}$). In the complete draft, Wagner originally notated this passage enharmonically in sharps, then wrote 'B tonarten' ('flat tonalities', here meaning really 'flat harmonies') to remind him to notate it correctly (i.e., in terms of the implied G♭ tonal centre). Alberich's two lines 'von vielen gefall' ich wohl einer, | bei einer kies'te mich Keine!'

---

[16] Again Westernhagen assumed that the countermelody was conceived simultaneously with Flosshilde's vocal line: 'Similarly, at Flosshilde's "süssen Trost schüfe die Traute dir", an upper part develops out of the vocal line in the sketch and continues above Alberich's gruff "Holder Sang singt zu mir her", and is assigned to a solo violin in the score.' After citing another example of this 'polyphonic flowering, quite spontaneous in effect', he concludes: 'The interesting thing is that these are not cases of ornamentation added to the score at a late stage, but instances of an innate tendency of Wagnerian melody to break out in polyphony from the moment of inception' (*The Forging of the 'Ring'*, 22–3). But the point is that they *were* 'added to the score at a late stage'! Westernhagen's theory of 'spontaneous polyphony' is, in fact, founded upon nothing more substantial than his own misreading of Wagner's drafts.

were originally set as parallel vocal units, the second a minor-mode variant of the first; Wagner later changed the second unit both melodically and harmonically. Alberich's invitation to Flosshilde to dive down to him ('Soll ich dir glauben, | so gleite herab!') wrenches the tonal level down a minor third, as the Db^7 chord (V^7/Gb) yields to Bb^7 (V^7/Eb) at m. 356 (20/2/5). In the complete draft, Wagner merely suggested Flosshilde's dive by the word 'hinab', followed by the first portion (the neighbour-note figure) of the original semiquaver figuration; in the score, he prefaced this figure with an inversion of the new Rhine arpeggiation.

Both the third and fourth events (during which Flosshilde first flatters Alberich, then cruelly taunts him) are structured as bar forms, whose AA′B organization is clearly articulated by the text. Lorenz's analytical extravagances have led to critical reaction against the notion of the bar form as a basic structural unit in Wagner's music. Certainly this form is not nearly as omnipresent as Lorenz claimed, yet it does appear often enough, on various structural levels, to warrant serious analytical attention. We have already noted the emergence of two *instrumental* bar forms, in the music accompanying Alberich's call to the Rhinedaughters (mm. 202 ff.; 10/1/2 ff.) and his clumsy scramble towards Woglinde (mm. 231 ff.; 12/2/1 ff.). In each case, an initial unit (A) was followed either by a varied repetition or a sequence (A′), then by a spinning-out of the material (B). This purely *musical* procedure of statement–repetition–development, which is obviously operative in the works of many composers (especially those of Beethoven) should be sharply distinguished from the *poetic* bar form, in which the AA′B structure is already implicit in the text. Events 3 and 4 are examples of the latter (the poetic version), as the outline in Table 7.4 suggests. By making Flosshilde reject Alberich in a compressed version of the same formal structure to which she originally flattered him, Wagner employs poetic/musical form to make a dramatic point.

Flosshilde's flattery of Alberich (Event 3) flowers into a miniature 'love duet' (mm. 360–87; 20/3/4–22/2/2) whose parodistic element (the sexual encouragement of an ugly dwarf by a beautiful mermaid) is seldom lost on its audience. Each Stollen comprises a lyrical major-mode phrase sung by Flosshilde, followed by a rather ugly minor-mode response from Alberich (three poetic lines apiece). Stollen 1 (mm. 360–7; 20/3/4–21/1/2: 'Wie thörig seid ihr . . .') prolongs the Bb^7 harmony (V^7 of Eb major/minor), while Stollen 2 (mm. 367–75; 21/1/2–21/3/2: 'O singe fort . . .') returns to Db^7 (V^7 of Gb major/minor); first violins heighten this tonal intensification by playing Flosshilde's Stollen 1 melody against her vocal variant. The Abgesang

TABLE 7.4 Episode 1: Interpolation, Cycle 3: Events 3 and 4
a. Event 3

Singer	No. of Lines	No. of Stresses	Formal Section and Harmony	
Flosshilde	3	2 + 2 + 3	} STOLLEN 1: V⁷/E♭	
Alberich	3	2 + 2 + 3		
Flosshilde	3	2 + 2 + 3	} STOLLEN 2: V⁷/G♭	
Alberich	3	2 + 2 + 3		
Flosshilde	2	2 + 2	St. 1	
↓	2	2 + 2	St. 2	
	1	2		} ABGESANG: V⁷/D♭
Alberich	1	2	} Abg.	
Flosshilde	1	2		
Alberich	1	2		

b. Event 4

Singer	No. of Lines	No. of Stresses	Formal Section and Harmony
Flosshilde	3	2 + 2 + 3	STOLLEN 1: V⁷/E♭ m
Flosshilde	3	2 + 2 + 3	STOLLEN 2: V⁷/E♭ m
Flosshilde	4	2 + 2 + 3 + 3	
Wog./Wellg.	Laughter		} ABGESANG: E♭: V⁷–[I]
Alberich	1	3	
Flosshilde	1	3	

(mm. 375–87; 21/3/2–22/2/2: 'Wie deine Anmuth...') is itself a miniature bar form, containing two similar vocal units sung by Flosshilde (two lines apiece) followed by a series of four short units (one line apiece) alternated between the singers. The reduction of poetic lines, with its concomitant shortening of vocal units, produces a rhythmic drive towards the more active harmonic motion of the Abgesang. The bass A♭ finally resolves to V⁷/E♭ minor (m. 388; 22/2/3), which marks the most crucial harmonic event of the interpolation—the regaining of the structural dominant.

Flosshilde's mockery (Event 4) is so clearly structured that little detailed discussion is necessary. As the dotted rhythms of her angular vocal phrases hammer home the relentless *Stabreim*, sharp staccato chords punctuate her merciless verbal assault. She pauses for a moment on $\hat{2} \atop V$ (m. 400; 23/2/3: 'seh'n!'), resuming the interrupted melodic/harmonic component from the end of Section B. The sisters' laughter and Alberich's retort energize this dominant harmonically and prepare to cadence on $\hat{1} \atop I$; however, a deceptive resolution to $_{♭}\hat{VI}$ 'at the end of the song' ('am Ende vom Lied!'—see m. 406; 24/1/1) post-

TABLE 7.5 Episode 1: Syllabic scheme of Section A′

Line	Upbeat		Stress 1			Stress 2			Stress 3
1	Wal-	la-	la!	La-	la-	lei-	a!	La-	lei!
2			Hei-	a!		hei-	a!	Ha-	ha!
3			Schä-	me	dich,	Al-	be!		
4			Schilt	nicht	dort	un-	ten!		
5			Hö-	re,		was	wir	dir	heis- sen!
6	Wa-		rum,	du		Ban-	ger,		
7			ban-	dest	du	nicht			
8	das		Mäd-	chen,		das	du		minnst?
9			Treu	sind		wir			
10	und		oh-	ne		Trug			
11	dem		Frei-	er,		der	uns		fängt.—
12			Grei-	fe	nur	zu			
13	und		grau-	se	dich	nicht!			
14	In	der	Fluth	ent-		flieh'n	wir	nicht	leicht.

pones this cadence once again and prepares for Alberich's tremendous outburst of despair (Event 5). The latter section, purely declamatory and almost recitative-like, functions much in the manner of a dominant preparation heralding a thematic/tonal reprise, while the emphasis upon V of the parallel minor (a classical retransitional procedure) heightens the effect of the eventual resolution to the tonic major.

5. Section A′ (mm. 421–47; 25/1/2–27/2/4)

Section A′, the first concerted passage in the opera, is a vocal trio during which the sisters mock Alberich's unsuccessful wooing. Although the prose sketch does not mention this trio, the prose draft contains a first attempt at its text: 'The maidens: "we came to you, you didn't hold us: now come to us, and choose [the one] who pleases you the best!"'[17] In other words, the sisters have not finished tormenting the poor dwarf; they goad him on to further pursuit. The verse draft of this passage is virtually identical with the 1853 printing, which is laid out schematically in Table 7.5; it comprises four three-line verses preceded by two introductory lines.

Wagner's setting of this passage follows the poetic structure to the

[17] 'Die Mädchen: "wir kamen zu Dir, Du hieltest uns nicht: nun komm zu uns, und wähle [die,] die dir am besten gefällt!"' WWV 86A Text II, p. 2; cf. Strobel, *Skizzen und Entwürfe*, 214.

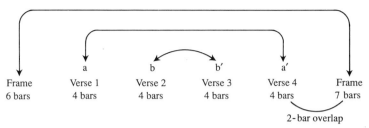

FIG. 7.2 Episode 1: Phrase structure of Section A'

extent of using each verse as the basis of a musical phrase, the 2 + 2 + 3-stress patterns yielding four-bar units (2 + 2 + 4 beats) through the by now familiar technique of lengthening the final stress. However, Wagner shaped these phrases so that the fourth resembles the first, and the third is almost identical to the second, thus superimposing a symmetrical abb'a' pattern upon the whole. He extended this symmetry by repeating the two introductory lines at the end, and accompanying both appearances of these lines by an orchestral statement of the 'Weia! Waga!' melody, creating a textual/musical 'frame'; the closing frame overlaps verse 4 by two bars. The entire section is therefore shaped as an arch (see Fig. 7.2).

Because a symmetrical structure is inherently non-dramatic (as opposed, for example, to the goal-oriented bar form), one might ask why Wagner felt justified in employing it here, especially since it is not implied by the text. First, the passage as a whole is internally static, allowing the composer to yield to a purely musical impulse—the desire for structural symmetry—without compromising the poetic intent. Second, the entire section functions at the background level as a thematic/tonal recapitulation, and such a function is perhaps best fulfilled by a unit which eschews complex internal development in favour of clear, easily perceived formal organization. In fact, it is this section's very formal integrity which allows it to function so convincingly as the 'structural downbeat' of the entire episode.

The complete draft of this section affords some fascinating insights into Wagner's compositional process (see transcription, beginning at m. 421). He set the text up to the word 'Fluth' (verse 4, line 3; m. 441) on two staves, then decided to overlap the 'Weia! Waga!' melody with the end of Phrase 4. He therefore crossed out the bass line for mm. 439–40, transferred it to an added third staff, and wrote out the 'Weia! Waga!' melody on the vacated second staff. His intention, obviously, was to frame the four vocal phrases with the orchestral melody, and this in turn probably suggested bringing back the introductory two lines of text.

The complete draft of Section A' contains another item which has hitherto gone unnoticed in published studies of this manuscript. It is often claimed that the pages of the *Partiturerstschrift* containing the scoring of Section A' (mm. 421–47) are missing. However, a glance at the complete draft reveals that Wagner sketched the instrumentation directly into this manuscript, bypassing the *Partiturerstschrift* altogether! The third staff of mm. 421 and 426 contains the violin arpeggiations (see transcription), while the lower staff of mm. 427 and 433–4 contains the viola figurations (the latter two bars must be read in the alto clef). In addition, the composition draft at this point contains markings (e.g., 32, 33, ⋈ , etc.) for page and system breaks in the *Reinschrift*. These markings appear regularly in the *Partiturerstschrift*, from which the *Reinschrift* was made, but appear in only this particular portion of the complete draft. Thus, in this one instance, Wagner worked directly from the complete draft to the *Reinschrift*. The fact that this passage is essentially a reprise of material already scored (mm. 137 ff.) allowed Wagner to forgo a more elaborate sketch of the instrumentation.

The entire reprise represents the resolution of the interrupted V (reached at the end of Section B and regained at the end of the interpolation) to I. However, Wagner prevents total closure; he weakens the E♭ tonic through the referential $^6_4$ sonorities, avoids a strong low bass, and uses relatively light scoring throughout. The final f^2 does not resolve to eb^2 (although the complete draft shows that Wagner originally intended this); rather, it is frozen in place until the abrupt disruption which signals the beginning of the following interlude.

III. TRANSITION (MM. 448–513; 28/1/1–31/1/2)

The Transition fulfils two functions: tonally, it modulates from the key of Episode 1 (E♭ major) to that of Episode 2 (C major), while dramatically it accompanies Alberich's desperate pursuit of the Rhinedaughters. Aside from the dwarf's initial 'Wie in den Gliedern . . .' and his final 'Fing' eine diese Faust!', this is a purely orchestral passage, whose musical gestures are closely synchronized with the pantomime it accompanies.

The brief prose sketch contains no mention of this chase, but the prose draft describes it in these words:

Now he [Alberich] begins to chase them with deperate exertion: with terrible agility he leaps and climbs from rock to rock; with laughter and

TABLE 7.6 Transition between Episodes 1 and 2: Verse-melodies

Cycle 1		Cycle 2	
Meas.	Music	Meas.	Music
448	'Wie in den Gliedern' (Alberich)	483	'Wie in den Gliedern' (orch.)
461	'Schein ich nicht schön dir'		
470	'Schäme dich, Albe!'		
473	'Weia! Waga!'	491	'Weia! Waga!'
476	Stumbling music	494	Stumbling music
479	'Heia, du Holder!'	502	Laughing music (dissipating)

derision they lure him here and there. Finally he loses patience: foaming with rage, he pauses and looks up at them with clenched fist.[18]

The verse draft expands this scenario somewhat; after Alberich's 'Wie in den Gliedern . . .' it reads:

He begins the chase with desperate exertion: with terrible agility he climbs from rock to rock, leaps from one to the other, tries to catch first one then another of the maidens, who always elude him with mocking laughter; he staggers, falls into the abyss, then clambers hastily aloft again, until finally he loses patience: foaming with rage, he pauses breathless and shakes his clenched fist at the maidens.[19]

The expansion in the verse draft already suggests the two clearly defined dramatic cycles of the final version. Each cycle contains four phases: Alberich chases the Rhinedaughters, they elude him, he stumbles and falls, and they mock him. The orchestra accompanies this dramatic progression with a succession of verse-melodies from Episode 1; it thus simultaneously fulfils two of the functions described by Wagner in *Oper und Drama*, that of allying itself with *gesture* (the chase) and bringing back the *reminiscence* of an emotion when the singer is not giving voice to it. Table 7.6 displays these verse-melodies to show the parallelisms between the two cycles; the words cited are those initially associated with each melody. Alberich's 'Wie in den Gliedern . . .', which he sings in mm. 448 ff. (28/1/1 ff.) for the first time, returns at the beginning of Cycle 2 (m. 483; 29/3/6) in bassoons and violas; both times it expresses Alberich's smouldering fury. In Cycle 1, the orchestra launches the chase with a sequential development of 'Schein ich nicht schön dir' (mm. 461 ff.; 28/3/4), but replaces

---

[18] WWV 86A Text II, p. 2; cf. Strobel, *Skizzen und Entwürfe*, 214–15.
[19] WWV 86A Text III, p. 6.

this in Cycle 2 by an extension of 'Wie in den Gliedern'. The Rhine-daughters' mockery in Cycle 1 is suggested by 'Schäme dich, Albe!' followed by 'Weia! Waga!', but in Cycle 2 this is curtailed to 'Weia! Waga!' alone. Alberich's stumbling is both times depicted by the chromatic fragments previously associated with his ungainly efforts; in Cycle 1, these scales merely descend for three bars, while in Cycle 2 they are sequenced upwards for eight bars. The sisters conclude Cycle 1 by musically thumbing their noses at the dwarf (mm. 479–82; 29/3/2–5: 'Heia, du Holder!'), Cycle 2 by laughing at him on the biting dotted rhythms associated with Flosshilde's mockery (mm. 502–3; 30/3/2–3). Alberich's final gesture of rage is punctuated by a fortissimo diminished seventh chord (m. 505; 30/4/2) which gradually dissipates, along with the dotted rhythms, and resolves to a G major triad (V/C).

These various themes are played at ascending tonal levels: the bass rises from the Eb which concluded Episode 1 through F (m. 461; 28/3/4), G (m. 466; 28/4/4), and A (m. 470; 29/1/2), finally arriving at Bb in m. 491 (29/5/4). While F, G, and A all support dominant ninth harmonies, Bb supports a $^6_4$ chord; the transition concludes on a G major $^5_3$ sonority.

The complete draft of this transition contains several points of interest. First, it shows Wagner working out a purely instrumental passage on two staves; for the most part he confined himself to sketching out the melody plus the bass line, sometimes filling in the harmonies. Second, he initially considered having the Rhinedaughters sing during the final appearance of the 'Weia! Waga!' melody (mm. 491 ff.; 29/5/4 ff.), but apparently thought better of it. Third, and most significant, are the abbreviated stage directions such as 'Alberich sturzt ab', 'lachen', 'zurückfallen', etc.; although not extensive, these jottings suggest that Wagner had mentally choreographed the entire pantomime, shaping the music to match envisaged stage actions. The resulting intimate connection between physical action and musical tone is one which no opera director can afford to ignore.

To understand the internal harmonic structure of the Transition, it is necessary to place it in the context of the entire scene. Scene 1 opens in Eb major and closes in its relative minor C; as Ex. 7.9a shows, this modulation is effected through a chromatic pivot (Eb:III = C:V). The G major pivot has been prepared, of course, through the prior emphasis upon III during Section X of Episode 1. At a slightly later level (Ex. 7.9b), the Eb:I is expanded by two unfoldings: Eb–Bb in the bass (changing the harmony from $^5_3$ position to a consonant $^6_4$) and g–eb^1 in an upper part. At a still later level (Ex. 7.9c), these unfoldings are expanded by parallel major tenths which

Ex. 7.9

allow the minor sixth $g-eb^1$ to be filled in by the same number of passing tones (three) as the perfect fifth $Eb-Bb$. At the foreground level, these passing tenths become dissonant dominant ninth chords, which momentarily suggest the keys of Bb minor (allowing 'Schein ich nicht schön dir' to appear at its original tonal level; cf. mm. 323 ff.), C minor, and D major; the final statement of 'Weia! Waga!' appears over the consonant Eb_4^6 chord. The resolution to C is complicated by a modal substitution which produces first C major, turning only much later (towards the end of Episode 2) to minor. This modal substitution results from the Eb–E♮ inflection (Eb:$\hat{1}$ → C:$\hat{3}$) mentioned at the beginning of this chapter, a crucial linear move first effected by Alberich's verbal outburst 'Fing' eine diese Faust!!' (mm. 504–5; 30/4/1–2: $eb^1-e\natural^1$). The subsequent decrease in harmonic tension and the dissipation of the dotted-rhythm 'laughing' motif perfectly reflect the gradual fading of the Nibelung's anger as his attention is drawn to the visual spectacle which now unfolds.

IV. EPISODE 2 (MM. 514–715; 31/1/3–52/1/1)

The prose sketch of Episode 2 reads simply: 'The gold gleams. "How to win it?" "He who renounces love."—Alberich steals the gold.—Night.'[20] In the afore-cited letter to Liszt of 20 November 1851, Wagner expanded this scenario as follows:

Then the Rhinegold begins to gleam; it attracts Alberich; he asks what use it serves? The girls declare that it serves for their enjoyment and sport; its gleam illumines the depths of the floodwaters with its rapturous shimmering; but many are the wonders that could be wrought by means of the gold, great are the power and might, the riches and dominion that could be won by the man who knew how to forge it into a ring: but only he *who renounces love* could understand that! but so that none may steal the gold, they themselves

[20] 'Das Gold erglänzt. "wie das zu gewinnen?" "Wer der liebe entsagt."—Alberich raubt das gold.—Nacht.' See WWV 86A Text Ia; cf. Strobel, *Skizzen und Entwürfe*, 215.

TABLE 7.7 Episode 2: Structural outline

Meas.	Section and Content	Refrain
514	*Introduction*: The gold awakens.	'Heiajaheia!'
540	*Trio 1*: The Rhinedaughters rejoice in the gold.	'Heiajaheia!'
569	*Dialogue Cycle 1*: The splendour of the gold.	'Wallala!'
593	*Dialogue Cycle 2*: The power of the gold (the ring) and the necessity of renouncing love.	'Wallala!'
645	*Trio 2*: The Rhinedaughters renew their mockery of Alberich.	'Heiajaheia!'
663	*Action Cycle 1*: Alberich approaches the gold.	'Heiajahei!' 'Ha ha ha!'
690	*Action Cycle 2*: Alberich steals the gold.	Alberich's laughter

are appointed its guardians: the man who approaches them has indeed no desire for the gold; Alberich, at least, does not seem to desire it, since he behaves like a man in love; they laugh at him anew. The Nibelung then grows angry: he forswears love, steals the gold and carries it off into the depths.[21]

Wagner's emphasis upon the notion of renouncing love suggests how central it had become to his entire dramatic conception.

The formal structure of Episode 2 marks an advance in complexity over that of Episode 1, and exhibits a synthesis of closed song, cyclical procedure, and refrain form. In its final version, the episode may be outlined as:

	A	B	A′	B′
Introduction	Trio 1	Two Dialogue Cycles	Trio 2	Two Action Cycles

On a more detailed level, it breaks down as shown in Table 7.7.

The introduction, an extended dominant preparation based upon canonic sequences of the Gold fanfare, presents the visual spectacle of the gold's awakening. The two trios are inset songs characterized by the dotted rhythms previously associated with the sisters' mockery; in fact, Trio 2 reprises the 'Schäme dich, Albe!' melody from the concluding section of Episode 1, transposed from E♭ to E major (a large-scale manifestation of the E♭–E♮ pitch-class inflection). Each dialogue cycle comprises a brief question by Alberich followed by a lengthy response from the mermaids; the information thus elicited enlightens the audience as well as the dwarf. Each action cycle comprises a threat and a violent gesture by Alberich, followed by a frightened reaction from the sisters; Alberich's theft of the gold

[21] *Selected Letters*, 238–9 (*SB* iv. 188).

(Cycle 2) constitutes the dramatic climax of the entire scene. Furthermore, each section terminates in one of two textual/musical refrains.
The 'Heiajaheia!' (Refrain 1) which concludes each trio is accompanied orchestrally by the Gold fanfare; the 'Wallala' (Refrain 2)
which punctuates each dialogue cycle is supported by the 'Weia!
Waga!' melody. Action Cycle 1 concludes by transforming Refrain 1
('Heiajahei!') into the 'Laughter' motif ('Ha ha ha!'), both characterized by dotted rhythms; Action Cycle 2 ends with Alberich's scornful
laughter, a final corruption of Refrain 1 which suggests the passing of
power from the Rhinedaughters (who sang all previous refrains) to
the Nibelung. The reiterated Gold fanfares of Action Cycle 2 (often
distorted by diminished seventh harmonies) hark back to the Introduction, whose V/C major is now replaced by V/C minor.

The reader will notice that the second dialogue cycle is fully twice
as long as the first and presents two items of information (the power
of the gold and the renunciation of love) to the former's one (the
splendour of the gold). This apparent imbalance is explained by the
fact that Wagner originally contemplated *three* dialogue cycles, each
presenting a single piece of information, but later merged the second
and third cycles into one. The tri-cyclical structure is found in the
prose draft; a translation of the relevant passage is laid out below:[22]

Dialogue Cycle 1: The splendour of the gold.
Alberich's eye is strongly attracted by the gleam. He asks what it is that
gladdens them with such radiant lustre.
The maidens: Where does he live, that he knows nothing of the Rhinegold?
In a gay exchange of song, they inform him of the power of the gold, the
radiant star of the watery depths, that alternately sleeps and wakes, but that
upon awakening greets them so gloriously that they like nothing better than
to play on the riverbed in the radiant gleam.

Dialogue Cycle 2: The power of the gold—the ring.
Alberich: Is the gold good only for their games, and otherwise of no use
to anyone?
The maidens: Their father told them to guard the gold well, for great
power lies within it. He who knew how to forge a ring out of the gold could
use its power to make the entire world his own.

*Dialogue Cycle 3 (merged with Cycle 2 in verse draft): The necessity for
renouncing love.*
Alberich: Why then has no one forged it into a ring?
The maidens: Only through magic can the ring be forged, and only he
who renounces love can gain that magic. But everything that lives wants to
love: certainly many covet the gold, but no one will give up love. We also

---

[22] See WWV 86A Text II, p. 2; cf. Strobel, *Skizzen und Entwürfe*, 215. My translation.

guard the gold well against you, Alberich: for love plagues you too, and it would indeed be very difficult for you to renounce it, lovesick as you are!

The verse draft compresses the second and third dialogue cycles into one by eliminating Alberich's third question ('Why then has no one forged it into a ring?') and allowing Woglinde to provide this information gratuitously. In the score, Woglinde's speech about the renunciation of love ('Nur wer der Minne . . .') occupies the central position of the lengthy second dialogue cycle, and is thrown into musical relief by a change of key, metre, tempo, and texture.

Not surprisingly, the versification of this 'renunciation' message gave Wagner some trouble. He first wrote:

> Nur, wem die Minne
> nie weidet den Muth,

He then changed the 'wem' to 'wer,' crossed out the second line, and continued as shown below on the left (Version A):

Verse Draft (A)	*Verse Draft (B)*
Nur, wer der minne	Nur, wer der minne
die macht entsagt,	macht versagt,
nur wer der liebe	nur wer der liebe
die lust verjagt,	lust verjagt,
nur dem erziehlt sich den Zauber	nur der erziehlt sich den Zauber
zu das gold zu zwingen zum reif.	zum reif zu zwingen das gold.

He revised Version A by twice crossing out the article 'die,' changing 'dem' to 'der,' and adding an alternative version of the last line in parentheses, thus creating the somewhat terser Version B.[23] This last version was carried over into the fair copy and the 1853 printing, as well as the complete musical draft. However, while working out the instrumentation Wagner inadvertently reverted to Version A and entered 'Nur, wer der minne | macht *entsagt*,' an error which found its way into all subsequent orchestral and piano/vocal scores. That Wagner still considered Version B as definitive is substantiated by a letter of 28 May 1854 to Marie Sayn-Wittgenstein, in which he quotes the word as 'versagt.'

Throughout Episode 2, the text receives a relatively normative rhythmic setting. The controlling metre is now compound triple (9/8), as opposed to the compound duple (6/8) which has dominated the opera thus far. The reader will recall that in duple metre, a two-stress line normally generates a two-beat unit (one bar), while a three-stress line often generates a four-beat unit (two bars) by lengthening the

---

[23] This transcription was made from WWV 86A Text III, p. 8.

Ex. 7.10

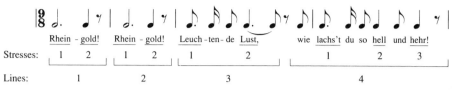

final stress or following it with a rest. In triple metre, however, a two-stress line often generates a three-beat unit (one bar) by lengthening either the first or second stress; a three-stress line may generate a three-beat unit also, but this is often expanded to six beats (two bars) by doubling the normal length of the first or second stress and tripling that of the third. Thus the Rhinedaughters begin their first trio on the rhythm of Ex. 7.10, while Alberich's first question is set as in Ex. 7.11; the latter continues the triple hypermetre associated with the dwarf.

The only relief from the prevailing compound metre occurs at Woglinde's 'renunciation' message (mm. 617 ff.; 43/1/1 ff.), where the change to 4/4 is emphasized by a slackening of tempo.[24] Wagner apparently felt that the essentially duple metre of this passage required preparation. Perhaps for this reason, the complete draft changes to 6/8 (compound duple) metre at Wellgunde's 'Weisst du denn nicht' (m. 614; 42/4/2; see transcription in Appendix); after the 'renunciation' speech, Wellgunde's 'Wohl sicher sind wir' (m. 625; 43/3/1) returns to 6/8, which yields to 9/8 only at the conclusion of the sisters' second trio (m. 653; 46/2/2: the refrain 'Heiajaheia!'). While scoring, Wagner decided to retain the triple metre throughout, so he rewrote the 6/8 passages in 9/8; this highlighted the 'renunciation' message still further

---

[24] The 4/4 metre is treated as a slow 2/2. Because the new crotchet is equivalent to the previous dotted crotchet, the beat has in effect doubled in length.

by surrounding its simple duple metre with compound triple.[25]

Although an exhaustive discussion of the complete draft version of Episode 2 lies beyond the scope of this study, the following variants are worth mentioning:

The Introduction (mm. 514–39; 31/1/3–33/1/4) originally lacked mm. 520 (31/3/1) and 524 (31/4/1), so that Woglinde's and Wellgunde's vocal lines overlapped the following horn fanfares; Wagner later (probably while scoring) made a note to insert these measures. In addition, m. 531 (32/2/2: 'Stern!') was immediately followed by the resolution to C major (m. 534; 32/3/3); however, Wagner jotted down 'länger dieser Takt' and expanded the single measure to three (mm. 531–3). As a result, the twenty-bar dominant preparation (V/C) is articulated by harp chords into five four-bar hypermeasures. At the tonic resolution, Wagner originally gave the Gold fanfare to three trumpets, played against a rapid semiquaver violin figure; while scoring, he assigned the fanfare to solo trumpet and deferred the violin figure until the beginning of Trio 1 (m. 540; 33/2/1). All these changes served to expand and intensify the introductory passage, during which the increasing momentum of the string oscillations suggests the ever brightening glow of the gold. The Gold fanfare is a 'motif of foreshadowing' given concrete meaning by a visual spectacle—the gold's awakening.

Trio 1 begins with the sisters' cry of 'Rheingold!'; this gesture expands the $\hat{6}$–$\hat{5}$ scale-degree progression introduced in Episode 1 by harmonizing it in C major with a vii°⁷–I progression over a tonic pedal. Wagner wrote out the vocal lines of Trio 1 (mm. 540–68; 33/2/1–37/3/2) in three parts on one staff; the lower of the two instrumental staves contains only the bass notes of the root position harmonies, while the upper staff is blank except for the violin figuration in m. 540. Although this new figuration (dubbed by Deryck Cooke 'Nature in Motion') continues almost unabated throughout Episode 2, it appears only four times in the complete draft: mm. 534 (eliminated in the final version), 540, 561, and 589. The handwriting suggests that these statements were added to the draft later, perhaps while scoring, and this hypothesis is strengthened by two facts: First, the Postlude to Scene 1 (mm. 716–43; 52/1/2–53/4/2) is based upon this new figure in the final score, but upon the original *Vorspiel* figurations in the draft. Second, Loge's narration in Scene 2 begins (in the score) with a slowed-down version of this new figure and concludes with its

---

[25] In addition, the complete draft contains certain motivic references which Wagner deleted from the final version. Measures 635–40 (44/2/2–44/4/1) originally contained Alberich's chromatic figure, while mm. 640–2 (44/4/1–3) featured his 'Schein ich nicht schön dir' melody.

Ex. 7.12

a. Complete Draft

Der Welt Er - be ge - wän - ne zu ei - gen, wer aus dem Rhein- gold schü - fe den Ring,

b. *Partiturerstschrift*

Der Welt Er - be ge - wän - ne zu ei - gen, wer aus dem Rhein - gold schü - fe den Ring,

c. *Partiturerstschrift*

Der Welt Er - be ge - wän - ne zu ei - gen, wer aus dem Rhein - gold schü - fe den Ring,

original fast form, but the figure is missing from both places in the draft. Thus two of the figurations which dominate Scene 1 and contribute to its distinctive colour or *tinta*—the Rhine figure and the Nature in Motion figure—were probably not conceived until well after the complete draft was finished.

Wagner sketched Dialogue Cycle 1 in a similar manner—vocal parts on one staff, bass notes plus an occasional harmony on another. At its conclusion, Wagner wrote in the 'Weia! Waga!' melody (mm. 587–8; 40/1/3–40/2/1) on the lower staff, followed by the gold fanfare in G on the lower and the violin figure on the upper (mm. 589–90). However, he then began Alberich's second question ('Eurem Taucherspiele . . .') immediately in the following bar. While scoring, he decided to extend the G major harmony for two more measures (mm. 591–2; 41/1/1–2), and to have the sisters sing 'Wallala . . .' as a refrain over this chord (mm. 589–92). This particular textual refrain thus does not appear in either the poem or the complete draft; it was added to the texture while scoring, perhaps to clarify the large-scale formal structure.

The complete draft of the second dialogue cycle begins, like that of the first, with vocal lines on the upper staff and bass notes plus a few indications of harmony on the lower. However, it suddenly becomes more complex at the point where the Ring motif first enters. This is one of the most frequently quoted themes in the tetralogy, and its initial shaping caused Wagner some trouble. In the complete draft, Woglinde's vocal line 'Der Welt Erbe . . . Ring' (mm. 600–3; 41/3/4–42/1/3; see Ex. 7.12a) differs somewhat from the final version, and is doubled at the lower tenth. While scoring, Wagner altered the vocal line rhythmically but kept the same pitch sequence (see Ex. 7.12b, transcribed from the *Partiturerstschrift*); he then restored the original rhythm but altered some of the pitches (Ex. 7.12c). Finally, he added the accompanying wind parts: the oboes double the voice at the unison and lower third, while English horn and bassoon double it at the lower octave and tenth. Wagner's aim in altering the vocal line was probably not, as Westernhagen suggests, to increase 'The effect of an incantation',[26] but to connect the three key words 'Welt', 'Rheingold', and 'Ring' by the same pitch (e^2), emphasizing the *Stabreim* of the second and third words.

Westernhagen has already pointed out some of the ways in which the complete draft version of Woglinde's 'renunciation' speech (see transcription) differs from the final score.[27] However, the most striking change made during scoring was the addition of the Wagner tubas, which here enter for the first time in the opera (mm. 618–21; 43/1/2–43/2/1). Because these instruments play such an important role in creating the distinctive sound universe of *Das Rheingold*, it is noteworthy that their first task is to harmonize the 'Renunciation of Love' theme. Despite the varied uses for which they are later employed, the sensitive listener will never quite forget this initial tragic association.

In the complete draft, Action Cycle 1 begins with Alberich's 'Der Welt Erbe . . .' (mm. 667 ff.; 47/4/3 ff.), sung to a variant of the Ring motif and doubled at the lower third; while scoring, Wagner revised this passage and prefaced it with two orchestral statements of the Ring motif. This is an excellent example of a 'reminiscence melody': the orchestra recalls the words originally attached to the theme before Alberich himself actually sings them. As Deathridge has pointed out, Westernhagen is wrong to conclude that Alberich's threat 'Erzwäng' ich nicht Liebe, | doch listig erzwäng' ich mir Lust?' is not addressed

[26] *The Forging of the 'Ring'*, 24–5. Knapp's contention that 'in the [*Partiturerstschrift*], however, Wellgunde's vocal line appears to have originally had C#'s in both measures 601 and 602' ('The Instrumentation Draft', 289) results from a misreading.

[27] *The Forging of the 'Ring'*, 25–6.

Ex. 7.13

Ex. 7.14

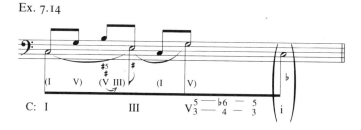

to the Rhinedaughters; the indication 'heimlich' (absent from the score) appears in the complete draft two measures earlier than Westernhagen places it, and clearly applies only to the lines 'Der Welt Erbe | gewänn' ich zu eigen durch dich?'[28]

The conclusion of Action Cycle 2 differs in the complete draft from the final version. Wagner originally accompanied the sisters' cries for help with tremolo violins cascading down various diminished seventh chords; he ultimately replaced this gesture with the new Nature in Motion figuration, sequencing it downwards over a dominant of C minor (mm. 708 ff.; 51/1/3 ff.).

The foreground tonal syntax of this episode is somewhat simpler than that of the first: long stretches of music are underpinned by tonic or dominant pedals. However, interpreting the background and middleground levels is a more complex matter. The following brief discussion may assist the reader in making a more detailed analysis.

The tonal background resembles that of Episode 1 (now transposed to C major): a I–III–V–I tonic arpeggiation (Ex. 7.13). Before V resolves, however, the mode changes to minor, and the final tonic is withheld (represented by the parentheses in Ex. 7.13). As a result, Episode 2 is *tonally closed* but *harmonically open*, a situation which becomes increasingly prevalent as *Das Rheingold* proceeds.

An early middleground level exhibits the complications shown in Ex. 7.14. The initial tonic is followed by an applied divider (V), while

---

[28] Deathridge, 'Wagner's Sketches', 389; cf. Westernhagen, *The Forging of the 'Ring'*, 27. However, Deathridge's transcription of mm. 667–71 (his Ex. 6) is itself flawed: he misreads rests as notes no fewer than three times, providing one with an editorial sharp!

Ex. 7.15

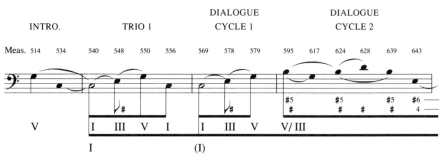

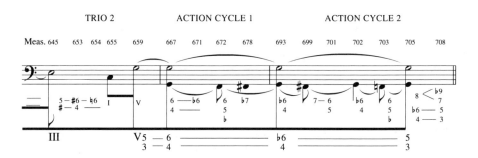

III is preceded by its own dominant (V/III), creating what Schenker calls an 'auxiliary cadence'.[29] The main V is preceded by a lower-level I, then expanded by $\frac{5-6-5}{3-4-3}$ neighbouring motion, during which the modal change occurs.

Example 7.15 displays the composing-out of this structure on a later middleground level, and relates it to the formal structure discussed above. The Introduction prolongs V in the manner of a traditional dominant preparation, then resolves it 'prematurely' (m. 534) to I; this 'premature tonic resolution' has almost the effect of a large-scale anticipation, and recurs later in the episode. Trio 1 contains a middleground replica of the background structure; that is, a lower-level I–III–V–I arpeggiation which composes out the initial I.[30]

---

[29] The applied divider and the auxiliary cadence are really mirror images of one another; both unfold the perfect fifth of the principal triad and use it to support a lower-level dominant, but an 'applied divider' *follows* the principal triad, while an 'auxiliary cadence' *precedes* the principal triad with its dominant.

[30] Schenker calls such a situation a *transference* of the fundamental structure (*Übertragung der Ursatz-Formen*) to a lower level; such transference need not always begin with the tonic, although here it obviously does.

Dialogue Cycle 1 reiterates this arpeggiation, but ends on V, the applied divider of Ex. 7.14. Dialogue Cycle 2 prolongs V/III by motion to its lower and upper thirds before resolving it—again, prematurely—to III^{6-5}_{4-3} (m. 643). Trio 2 expands III through $^{5-6}_{3-4}$ motion, then resolves to a weak I (m. 655); however, the structural motion is from III to V (m. 659). Action Cycle 1 begins the V^{5-6}_{3-4} neighbouring, changes the mode, and ornaments the $^{\flat6}_4$ with its own neighbour, $\text{ii}^{\varnothing6}_5$ (m. 672). Motion through $\text{vii}^{\circ7}$/V (expanded during mm. 678–92 by a rising chromatic progression) leads back to the $^{\flat6}_4$ (m. 693), which is subjected to further neighbour motion (at mm. 699 and 703). Finally, the $^{\flat6}_4$ resolves back to V, now intensified through the addition of $\flat9$ (m. 708), and the episode ends on an unresolved dissonance.

Before leaving this episode, we should consider the E♮–E♭ chromatic inflection which permeates the vocal lines and ultimately changes the mode to minor. As the sisters discuss the *possibility* of forging the gold into a ring, they continually stress the pitch e♮² (mm. 598 ff.; 41/3/2 ff.). However, as Woglinde explains the price of such power, she inflects to e♭² (mm. 618 ff.; 43/1/2 ff.), returning eventually to e♮² (m. 623; 43/2/3). During the ensuing discussion, the sisters alternate these two pitches (mm. 630 ff.; 43/4/3 ff.), ultimately reinterpreting e♭²–e♮² as d♯²–e♮² (mm. 642–3; 44/4/3–45/1/1). Trio 2 maintains e♮² throughout (mm. 645 ff.; 45/1/3 ff.); however, Alberich soon darkens the mood as he contemplates renouncing love, turning e♮¹ to e♭¹ (mm. 667 and 671; 47/4/3 and 48/1/3). He continually reiterates e♭¹ (mm. 690 ff.; 50/1/1 ff.), restating the e♮¹–e♭¹ move as he 'curses love' (mm. 699 and 702; 50/3/2 and 50/4/1). These two pitch classes function within three different foreground contexts: $\hat{3}$–♭$\hat{3}$ of C, $\hat{1}$–$\hat{7}$ of E (e♭² = d♯²), and $\hat{6}$–♭$\hat{6}$ of G; their reiteration helps subsume these contexts into the C major/minor tonal background. A recurrent pitch-class set of this sort, which maintains its identity during changing harmonic contexts, may be considered a sort of large-scale 'pitch motif', whose ability to unify and integrate long expanses of music is by no means negligible.

V. THE POSTLUDE (MM. 716–43; 52/1/2–53/4/2)

The Prose Sketch for Scene 1 ends with the single word 'Night' ('Nacht'). The Prose Draft expands this to 'The rocks disappear in the thickest darkness: the black water waves sink downwards, deeper and deeper.'[31] Wagner decided to represent this dark flood by an

---

[31] 'In der dichtesten finsterniss verschwinden die riffe: das schwarze wasserwoge senkt sich immer tiefer hinab.' See WWV 86A Text II, p. 2; cf. Strobel, *Skizzen und Entwürfe*, 216.

arpeggiated expansion of the dominant of C minor, but he altered the length and content of these figurations while scoring.

In both the complete draft and the final score, therefore, the orchestral Postlude prolongs V/C minor; however, the draft accomplishes this with twenty bars of the figuration from the original version of the Prelude (now written as quavers; see transcription in Appendix), while the score uses twenty-eight bars of the Nature in Motion figure. Both versions sequence their respective figurations upwards towards a climactic dominant ninth chord, then reverse the direction of the sequence, creating an arch shape. The melodic climax of the earlier version divides its twenty bars into 8 + 12 (a 2:3 ratio), while that of the later version divides its twenty-eight bars as 12 + 16 (a 3:4 ratio). As with the Prelude, Wagner hit upon his basic shape and musical process almost immediately, but enriched and expanded it while scoring. In the final version, the orchestral shriek on the V^9 chord (m. 728; 52/5/2) recalls in scoring and spacing the sisters' cry for their stolen gold (m. 712; 51/3/1: 'Weh!'), itself a debased form of their original joyous 'Rheingold!'. In fact, the entire Postlude can be understood as an expansion of mm. 705–13 (50/4/4–51/3/2, the culmination of the preceding Action Cycle); it thus functions as an 'aftermath' to Episode 2, just as the Prelude serves as preparation for Episode 1.

8 First Transformation and Scene Two

> Alberich and his ring could not have harmed the gods unless the latter had already been susceptible to evil. Where, then, is the germ of this evil to be found? Look at the first scene between Wodan and Fricka . . . The firm bond which binds them both . . . constrains them both to the mutual torment of a loveless union.
>
> (Wagner to August Röckel, 25–26 January 1854)

I. THE FIRST TRANSFORMATION

Although the prose sketch says nothing about this scenic transformation, the first major division of the prose draft concludes: 'Thus the scene changes imperceptibly into an open space on a mountain height.' The verse draft expands this into: 'Gradually the waves change into clouds, which little by little clear up, and as they finally disperse entirely, an open space on a mountain height becomes visible, at first still in twilight.' After 'disperse entirely', the fair copy of the poem adds 'as if into a fine mist', producing the version which appeared in the 1853 printing.

When Wagner reached this point in his complete draft, he drew a double bar and wrote in parentheses above the upper staff 'Walh[all]: Des-dur' ('Valhalla: D♭ major'), thus indicating the transition's thematic/tonal goal (see transcription in Appendix, beginning at m. 744). Between the staves he outlined the thematic progression in more detail: 'liebesfluch,—dann: welterbe—endlich Walhall' ('curse on love,—then: world inheritance—finally Valhalla'). By 'curse on love' Wagner meant the Renunciation theme; 'world inheritance' refers to the Ring motif, which first appeared as a verse-melody at Woglinde's words 'Der Welt Erbe | gewänne zu eigen.'

Wagner originally wrote out the Renunciation theme (mm. 744–8; 53/4/3–53/6/2) in doubled note-values under the influence of the previous Allegro tempo, so that it occupied ten bars instead of the present five; at the entrance of the Ring motif (m. 749; 53/6/3), he marked the tempo 'Lento' and specified that the present crotchet was to equal the previous minim. He sketched in the wind arpeggiations very roughly, and above the first set (mm. 751–2; 54/1/1–2) wrote 'Bl[äser]. (Nebel zertreuen)' ('Winds (mist dispersing)').

While scoring this passage, Wagner assigned the Renunciation theme (still in long note-values) to French horns and cor anglais; he replaced the original string figurations with the new Nature in Motion figure, but retained the quavers of the complete draft. Deciding to condense these ten bars into five, he scrawled a slur and the words '1 Takt' ('one bar') over each group of two bars. To accommodate this change, he indicated a broadening of the tempo at m. 744 (53/4/3): '(dasselbe viertel Zeitmass wie nachher) | (Langsam) | ♩ = langsamer wie zuvor ♩.' ('(the same quadruple tempo as later) | (slow) | ♩ = slower than the previous ♩.'). In the final score, m. 744 follows a ritardando and is marked simply 'Etwas langsamer', while m. 749 (marked 'Lento' in the complete draft and 'Langsam' in the *Partiturerstschrift*) bears no tempo indication.

The transformation of the swirling water currents into mist (as the string arpeggiations pass to flutes and harp) and the remoulding of the chromatic Ring motif into the diatonic Valhalla theme are justly famous and require little comment. The passage begins with the Renunciation–Ring combination, an orchestral 'reminiscence' of Woglinde's verse-melody from mm. 617–24 (43/1/1–43/2/4); as before, it leads from C minor to a first inversion half-diminished seventh chord on A. The latter previously resolved as $ii^{\emptyset6}_5$ to the dominant of E minor (Ex. 8.1*a*); it now leads as an applied chord to V/C major, thus retaining the tonal centre (Ex. 8.1*b*). A chromatic 5–6 shift transforms V/C into V/A♭ major (Ex. 8.1*b*), and the last eight bars (mm. 761–8; 54/5/1–8) prolong a dominant ninth over E♭. This low E♭ (cellos and basses) refers back unmistakably to the opening of Scene 1. However, the pedal tone is no longer harmonically static: Alberich's theft has set the tragedy in motion, and there can be no return to the original state of elemental nature.

II. SCENE TWO AS A WHOLE

As mentioned earlier, Scene 1 stands outside the temporal framework of the rest of the drama, and functions as a Prologue to the story of the gods. Scenes 2–4 are bound together dramatically by unity of time: the action takes place between dawn and dusk of a single day. Scenes 2 and 4 are set in the mountainous environs of Valhalla (suggesting the lofty aspirations of civilized society), while Scene 3 transpires in the gloomy subterranean vaults of Nibelheim (the 'womb of night and death', the self-regarding realm of evil). The D♭ major opening of Scene 2 (Episode 3) is mirrored thematically and tonally by the close of Scene 4 (Episode 20), while Scene 3 emphasizes B♭ minor (Episode 12). Thus, in a very general sense, Scenes 2–4

Ex. 8.1

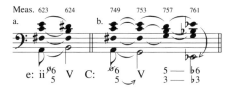

Ex. 8.2

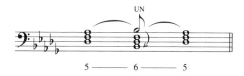

Ex. 8.3

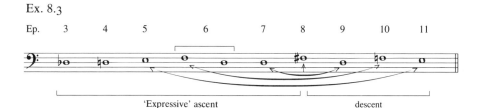

'Expressive' ascent   descent

constitute a large ABA′ ternary form supported by a move from D♭ major to its relative minor and back; this tonal progression may be viewed as a linear expansion of D♭ through 5–6–5 neighbour motion (Ex. 8.2). Further correspondences between Scenes 2 and 4 will be demonstrated in Chapter 11.

As shown in the Structural Outline, Scene 2 comprises nine dramatic/musical episodes (3–11); except for Episode 6, each is governed by a single tonality. The scene as a whole is not tonally closed, nor is it built around the tonic–dominant polarity of 'classical' tonality. Instead, the tonal background is controlled in three different ways (Ex. 8.3):

First, Episodes 5–11 form a symmetrical tonal pattern: E–F–D–F♯–D–F–E; as will become apparent, this symmetry is underscored dramatically and thematically. The return of the initial D♭ (Episode 3) is, of course, postponed until the end of Scene 4, where it articulates a larger tonal arch (see Chapter 11). D minor may be considered transitional, especially in view of the recitative-like texture of Episode 4; nevertheless, the D♭ major–D minor succession (Episodes

3–4) forms the model for the connection between the end of *Das Rheingold* and the opening of *Die Walküre*.

Second, the scene as a whole displays an 'expressive' chromatic rise from Db to F♯ (avoiding the Eb so prominent in Scene 1), followed by a descent to E; in both cases, D functions as a digression. The tonal intensification mirrors the rising dramatic tension as Wotan, attempting to cope with an ever-worsening situation, impatiently awaits the arrival of Loge. The F♯ climax (Episode 8) coincides with the fire god's belated entrance.

Third, each key possesses 'associative' or symbolic meaning. Db major is associated with Valhalla, the concrete symbol of Wotan's noble aspirations, while D minor refers somewhat negatively to the god's spear, the objectification of his egoistic will-to-power. F minor/major is the key of the giants (and later, in *Siegfried*, of Fafner-turned-dragon), while a highly chromaticized F♯ symbolizes Loge and his magic fire. Both E minor and D major are connected with Freia: the former symbolizes her distress, while the latter represents the goddess as the embodiment of love, youth, and beauty.[1] Thus the D minor/major relationship binds together the two central symbols of the drama: power (Wotan's spear) and love (Freia). In addition, F♯ lies a tritone away from the C major of Scene 1, thereby opposing falsity and deception (Loge) with purity and truth (the gold in its natural state).

III. THE NINE EPISODES

1. *Episode 3 (mm. 769–826; 55/1/1–58/1/4)*

The second paragraph of the prose sketch begins in the most cursory manner imaginable: 'Wodan. Fricka.' A supplementary note outlines the action of this episode: 'Daybreak: the rising sun strikes Valhalla. Wodan is awakened from sleep by Fricka.' The visual component was thus an integral part of Wagner's original conception: the rising sun's illumination of the fortress objectifies Wotan's dream of power. Possibly Wagner wished to demonstrate that an operatic sunrise could be dramatically vindicated, in contrast to the Meyerbeerian 'effect without cause' which he had criticized so scathingly in *Oper und Drama*.[2]

---

[1] Lacking a key of their own, Froh and Donner share their sister's D major.

[2] Wagner was referring to the sunrise in Act III of *Le Prophète*, which reveals the citadel of Münster to the troops of Jean de Leyde. According to Wagner, Meyerbeer's sunrise is a purely mechanical 'effect' which lacks any motivating poetic 'cause'. The supplementary prose sketch outlining the *Rheingold* sunrise postdates *Oper und Drama* by only a year, so that a 'cause and

TABLE 8.1 Episode 3: Structural outline

Meas.	Section and Content
769	*PRELUDE (Section A)* As Wotan and Fricka lie sleeping, the rising sun illuminates the fortress. The orchestra presents the Valhalla theme, modulating to the dominant (D♭: I–III–V$_t$).
789	*SCENE (Section B)* Fricka's attempts to awaken Wotan from his dream of power frame Wotan's musings, which prolong the tonicized dominant (A♭). The orchestra recalls the music from the end of the First Transformation (Ring/Valhalla motifs).
801	*Retransition*: Wotan awakens.
804	*ARIA (Section A')* Wotan apostrophizes his fortress over a varied reprise of the Valhalla theme, harmonically modified in order to cadence on the tonic (D♭: I–IV–V–I).

The prose draft expands upon the scenic description in a manner very close to the final text, then continues:

Fricka awakens: her gaze falls on the fortress; she is astonished and alarmed; 'Wodan, husband, awaken!'—Wodan speaks softly in a dream: the fortress hovers before him: joy, splendour, honour, and might!—Fricka shakes him; she scolds, there is no more time for dreaming, etc.—Wodan awakens. His gaze is powerfully fixed by the fortress; he revels in joy over the completed work.

Wagner experienced little difficulty turning this into verse; for instance, the line 'wonne, glanz, ehre und macht!' easily became: 'Der *Wonne* seligen Saal | bewachen mir Tür und Tor: | Mannes *Ehre*, | ewige *Macht* | ragen zu endlosem Ruhm!' The poetic content of the episode, then, is threefold: the rising sun's illumination of the fortress, Fricka's repeated attempt to awaken Wotan from his dream of power, and Wotan's apostrophe to the fortress.

When Wagner reached this point in his complete draft, he apparently decided to realize the threefold poetic content in a tripartite operatic form: a Prelude, Scene, and Aria structure, in which the Aria recapitulates the Prelude's thematic material following its development during the Scene (Table 8.1). This formula had already been employed to open Act II of *Tannhäuser*, and would resurface years later to begin Act III of *Die Meistersinger*. However, Wagner's adaptation of the form in *Das Rheingold* is more complex than might at first appear.

effect' relationship between these two sunrises cannot be ruled out. See *RWPW* ii. 96–9; *GS* iii. 302–5.

Wagner probably had his preliminary sketch (Ex. 2.2*a*) in front of him when he drafted the Valhalla theme (mm. 769–88; 55/1/1–55/5/4), writing it out on two staves free of corrections or alterations. The theme is marked 'Pos[aune]' ('trombones'), instruments already suggested by the tenor clef of the sketch, while the fanfares (now functioning as upbeats) are designated 'Tromp[eten]' ('trumpets'). In his *Partiturerstschrift* and ink score, Wagner assigned the theme to tenor and bass tubas in E♭ and B♭ respectively, supported by contrabass trombone in B♭ and contrabass tuba in E♭; for the printed score, he pitched the tubas in B♭ and F, and the contrabass instruments in C. The tubas are eventually joined by trombones and trumpets, while the trumpet fanfares are doubled by trombones. The whole suggests the 'herrlicher Bau' and 'blinkende Zinnen' of the fortress, yet the timbre of the 'Wagner tubas' inescapably recalls their original use—that of harmonic support for the Renunciation of Love theme.

The orchestral Prelude cadences in A♭, a tonicized dominant;[3] its recapitulation during Wotan's Aria 'Vollendet das ewige Werk' (mm. 804–26; 57/1/1–58/1/4) is extended and altered to close in the tonic. While drafting the Aria, Wagner wrote out the instrumental part first, then fitted the vocal line against it. While scoring, he notated the vocal line and the first harp chord but did not bother writing out the unchanged portion of the reprise. Only at the word 'wies' (m. 817; 57/4/1), where a new subdominant inflection begins, did he start to renotate the orchestral part.

As Westernhagen remarks, Wagner recomposed the cadence of the Aria (mm. 821–4; 57/4/5–58/1/2: 'hehrer, herrlicher Bau!'). Originally, a root position tonic entered at 'hehrer' after only one bar of IV–I oscillations, and persisted through the next two measures ('herrlicher Bau!'), followed by an orchestral V[7]–I cadence (Ex. 8.4*a*). Wagner scored this version in the *Partiturerstschrift*, but changed the bass of 'Bau' into a linear descent from D♭ (see Ex. 8.4*b*, a reduction of the *Partiturerstschrift*). Later he altered the cadence again, writing over the old version in ink: he changed m. 821 ('hehrer') from a tonic to a second bar of IV–I oscillations, moved the bass descent (D♭–C–B♭) forward into the 'herrlicher' measure, and crossed out the 'Bau' measure, simultaneously altering the vocal line (Ex. 8.4*c*). Some of these revisions were first entered into the complete draft (see again Ex. 8.4*a*). Their net effect was to expand the subdominant (mm. 818–21; 57/4/2–5) and link it more directly to the dominant (m. 823; 58/1/1); this suggests that Wagner heard the accented $\frac{5}{3}$

---

[3] This tonicized dominant is represented by the symbol 'V$_t$' in Table 8.1.

Ex. 8.4

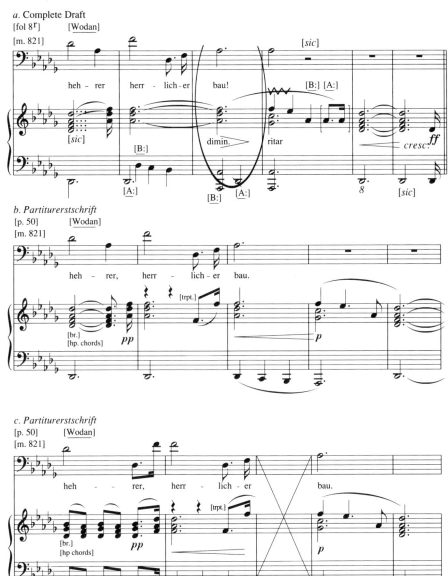

a. Complete Draft

[fol 8ʳ]   [Wodan]

[m. 821]

heh – rer   herr – lich – er   bau!   [B:] [A:]

b. Partiturerstschrift

[p. 50]   [Wodan]

[m. 821]

heh – rer,   herr – lich – er   bau.

c. Partiturerstschrift

[p. 50]   [Wodan]

[m. 821]

heh – – rer,   herr – lich – er   bau.

Ex. 8.5

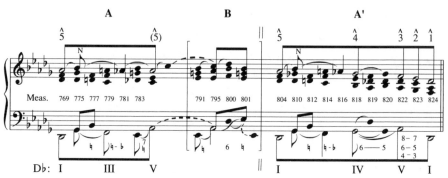

sonority of m. 822 (57/4/6) as an 'apparent tonic' representing a cadential $^6_4$.

Scene 2 begins with a tonal hiatus: the previous dominant on E♭ progresses directly to the new tonic D♭, omitting the connecting fifth A♭ (which is, however, represented by low string tremolos). The Prelude and Aria of Period 4 stand in an antecedent–consequent relationship, and represent a typical I–V ‖ I–V–I interruption scheme (Ex. 8.5). The Prelude itself suggests a miniature ternary form: the two-bar Valhalla motif is stated twice (mm. 769–72; 55/1/1–4), fragmented and sequenced (mm. 773–8; 55/2/1–55/3/2), and restated twice (mm. 779–82; 55/3/3–55/4/2), leading to a cadential coda (mm. 783–8; 55/4/3–55/5/4). The sequences expand IV, the reprise resolves this as upper neighbour to III, and the coda tonicizes V; the Prelude as a whole thus arpeggiates the tonic triad. The Aria adds a varied third restatement (mm. 818–19; 57/4/2–3) to the reprise, inflecting towards IV; this subdominant is expanded through m. 821 (57/4/5) and led directly to the V–I cadence (m. 822 representing the cadential $^6_4$).

The Scene (mm. 789–803; 56/1/1–56/4/4) functions as a sort of parenthetical interpolation between the Prelude and Aria, prolonging the A♭ dominant. Fricka violently disrupts the tonicized dominant with a diminished seventh chord—a typical recitative gesture—but her chord does not resolve. Instead, the music 'backs up' to the end of the Transformation (cf. mm. 791–4 (56/1/3–56/2/2) with mm. 761–4 (54/5/1–4): Wotan is still dreaming. This time, however, the E♭ dominant resolves to A♭ for a cadential reworking of the Valhalla motif, thus correcting the previous tonal hiatus (but retaining the E♭ pedal). Again Fricka disrupts the tonicized A♭, but this time her attempt to awaken Wotan is successful: her dissonant chord resolves into a ii⁶–V half-cadence (still in A♭). Low strings fill in a descending octave E♭ and move to D♭ for the Aria, recreating the episode's initial tonal hiatus.

Episode 3 thus reworks a standard operatic formula; it is controlled at the background level by a 'classical' I–V ‖ I–V–I interruption scheme, into which a dominant expansion is interpolated. The parenthetical nature of the Scene is corroborated by the fact that when, in 1862, Wagner incorporated this episode into a concert arrangement, he directed that mm. 789–803 (56/1/1–56/4/4) be omitted.[4]

2. Episode 4 (mm. 826–914; 58/1/4–63/3/1)

One of Wagner's supplementary prose notes reads: 'Fear: the fortress is completed:—Freia is forfeit.' The prose draft expands this line into the infamous dispute between Wotan and Fricka. The draft differs from the poem in two important ways. First, Wotan prematurely informs his wife that Loge had counselled him in his dealings with the giants; in the poem, he withholds this information until the last possible moment. Second, Wotan reminds Fricka that when he wooed her, he entered into a wager with her 'defiant kinsmen' whereby he risked losing his single remaining eye; the compression of this information in the poem has led to endless disputes over how Wotan lost his eye in the first place.[5] The verse draft, fair copy, and 1853 printing do not differ substantially from the final version.[6]

The complete draft differs from the score in several places. The timpani's adumbration of the Giants rhythm (m. 835; 58/4/1) was added while scoring, suggesting that the preliminary sketch of this motif (Ex. 2.2c) postdates the composition of Episode 4. Westernhagen has pointed out one reworking of Fricka's vocal line (mm. 852–3; 59/4/3–60/1/1);[7] another occurs in m. 873 (61/1/5), where her expressive falling seventh ('Wohnung') was originally a descending fifth.[8] The most interesting case occurs at mm. 901–2 (62/4/1–2), where Fricka's 'Liebe und Weibes Werth?' was originally supported merely by two sustained chords. While scoring, it occurred to Wagner to add the Renunciation theme; he sketched this into the complete draft, scored it for divided cellos, then decided to put all the cellos on the top line supported by violins and violas. Finally, the triplet violin figure in m. 911 (63/2/1) which anticipates Freia's motif is missing from the draft; perhaps Wagner had not yet sketched Ex. 2.2b.

---

[4] See the description of WWV 86A Musik VIIb in *WWV* 355–6.

[5] See, for example, Cooke, *I Saw the World End*, 151.

[6] The line 'so musst du mir Gotte schon gönnen' had to be altered to 'mir Gotte musst du schon gönnen' while setting it to music.

[7] *The Forging of the Ring*, 37.

[8] The same is true of Wotan's subsequent transposition of this melody; see m. 885 (61/4/3).

TABLE 8.2 Episode 4: Structural outline

Meas.	Section and Content
	PART 1 (First Dialogue Cycle): Fricka's Concern
826	1. Fricka worries about Freia; it is time to pay the giants.
835	2. Wotan tells her not to worry.
	PART 2 (Second Dialogue Cycle): Fricka's Anger
845	1. Fricka chides Wotan for secretly bartering away her sister.
859	2. Wotan reminds her that she too wanted the fortress.
	PART 3 (Third Dialogue Cycle): Fricka's Hope
865	1. Fricka admits she had hoped the fortress would keep her philandering husband at home (Arioso: F major→D minor).
884	2. Wotan replies that, if he is to be imprisoned in the fortress, he must be allowed to conquer the world (Arioso: E♭ major→C major).
	PART 4 (Fourth Dialogue Cycle): Fricka's Reproach
897	1. Fricka reproves Wotan for bartering away love in exchange for power.
903	2. Wotan reminds his wife that, in order to win her hand in marriage, he wagered his one remaining eye; thus, he can hardly be accused of not honouring women.

This episode utilizes yet another operatic convention, in that it is set as a through-composed recitative in four sections, the third of which blossoms into arioso (Table 8.2). In each section, a reproach by Fricka elicits a response from Wotan; this fourfold alternation is clearly outlined in the prose draft. The recitative style is evident not only from the character of the vocal writing and accompaniment, but also from the frequent use of that well-worn harmonic cliché, the $^6_3$ sonority.[9] The chordal accompaniment is occasionally enlivened by motivic references, notably the Spear motif (a 'foreshadowing') and the Renunciation melody (a 'reminiscence').

Not surprisingly, the tonal structure is very fluid, as befits a recitative. Although controlled by D minor, the episode really serves to connect the previous D♭ major with the upcoming E minor; D minor is literally a D-striving-towards-E. The tonal background is accordingly governed not by 'classical' tonic–dominant polarity, but by the linear 5–6 progression shown in Ex. 8.6a. Example 8.6b shows how this is worked out at a later (middleground) level.

---

[9] The very first verticality is a $^6_3$ chord on E (m. 827; 58/2/1); the complete draft reveals that this replaced a diminished $^4_3$ chord on E♭, which was to have followed a $^6_3$ chord on D♭ (later omitted).

Ex. 8.6

a

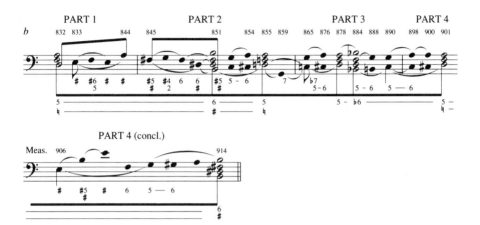

Fricka's initial statement moves directly from D♭ to V⁷/D minor (m. 829; 58/2/3: 'Freia!'), in which key low strings quietly announce the Spear motif (mm. 831–3; 58/3/2–4). The latter comprises a descending scale (beginning on ♭6̂–5̂, an echo of Alberich's 'Wehe!') checked by an E major triad; it thus encapsulates the fundamental D/E dialectic.[10] An interpretation of E major as V/A appears to be confirmed by the following augmented sixth chord on F (m. 834; 58/3/5); however, a reinterpretation of this as V⁷/B♭ (m. 835; 58/4/1) ushers in Wotan's reponse, itself underpinned by a B♭ major statement of the Spear motif. A repeat of the scale at original pitch leads again to the E major triad, which now resolves to A (a tonicized dominant).

Fricka's outburst 'O lachend frevelnder Leichtsinn!' (m. 845; 59/2/2) triggers an 'expressive' rise to V/B minor. Her ensuing tirade unfolds a B major triad, a large-scale expression of the chromatic 5–6 progression (see Ex. 8.6*b*). As she continues, however, she 'undoes' this progression, leading the music back to D minor (m. 854; 60/1/2: 'Freia') and beyond to G (m. 859; 60/2/4: 'Macht!'). This initiates yet

---

[10] This D minor/E major dichotomy becomes the controlling tonal force of *Die Walküre*, where it symbolizes the conflict between Wotan's will to power (objectified in Siegmund) and the compassionate love which Brünnhilde opposes to this will.

another recall of the 'dream music' from the end of the Transformation (cf. mm. 859–64 (60/2/4–60/4/1) with mm. 753–60 (54/2/1–54/4/2)) as Wotan reminds Fricka that she too asked for the fortress; this time the falling fifth motion D–G continues to C as V/F (m. 865; 60/4/2). As in Episode 3, the orchestra has indulged in a musical 'analepsis' or flashback, recalling and resolving a thwarted harmonic implication from the Transformation.

As Fricka waxes lyrical over the joys of hearth and home, the tonality momentarily stabilizes on V/F (mm. 865 ff.; 60/4/2 ff.); but at her memory of Wotan's power-lust, the music slides back into D minor and leads through a strong harmonic progression to an authentic cadence (mm. 876–83; 61/2/3–61/4/1). Wotan's response deftly deflates Fricka's argument by transposing her melody down a whole tone and leading from V/Eb to an authentic cadence in C, clinched by the Valhalla music. This is a good example of an 'expressive' tonal descent.

Fricka wrenches the tonality back to D minor, while the orchestra recalls both the Renunciation and Spear motifs (mm. 901 ff.; 62/4/1 ff.); the latter leads again to an E major triad, which this time is prolonged by its own dominant (mm. 906–8; 63/1/1–3). During Wotan's final refutation, the bass ascends linearly from E to B, and the episode concludes on a half-cadence in E minor (m. 914; 63/3/1).

Episode 4 thus works out a contrapuntal, 'progressive' background with middleground and foreground techniques which become more 'harmonic' at the very point where disputatious recitative shades into lyrical arioso. It offers an excellent example of Wagner's ability to breathe new life into an outworn operatic convention.

3. *Episode 5 (mm. 914–84; 63/3/1–68/1/1)*

After 'Freia is forfeit,' the supplementary prose sketch continues: 'Where tarries Loke, who recommended the treaty with the giants? The gods assemble in apprehension and anxiety: Freia seeks protection from Wodan.' As mentioned, Wagner originally incorporated the reference to Loge into the preceding argument between Wotan and Fricka, then decided to postpone it until after Freia's entrance. He also elected to defer the entrance of the other gods (Donner and Froh) until after the dispute with the giants. The prose draft outlines the action of Episode 5 in great detail, including a prose version of Freia's climactic plea for help.

The complete draft differs from the final version in several places. The initial ascent over the dominant pedal (V/E minor) originally occupied only one bar instead of three (mm. 914–16; 63/3/1–3);

TABLE 8.3 Episode 5: Structural outline

Meas.	Section and Content
914	*Introduction*: Fricka informs Wotan that Freia is coming.
922	*PART 1 (A)*: Freia runs in and pleads for help.
	PART 2 (B):
935	1. Fricka is dismayed that Wotan once again trusts Loge.
942	2. Wotan reveals that Loge promised to help him find a ransom for Freia.
960	*Retransition*: Fricka informs Wotan that the giants are coming.
967	*PART 3 (A')*: Freia renews her plea for help.
980	*Coda*: Fricka tells her sister that all the men have abandoned her.

Ex. 8.7

when he reached this point in the *Partiturerstschrift*, Wagner sketched out a rising line in thirds, then scored it for winds. He also altered the conclusion of the episode (mm. 980 ff.; 67/4/1 ff.) by giving this same rising line to Fricka (doubled by cellos), thus creating a musical frame. In addition, the complete draft lacks the 'flickering' Loge figurations in mm. 936–40 (64/4/3–65/2/1), suggesting that Wagner had not yet invented the fire god's music (the figurations are present in the *Partiturerstschrift*). Finally, the complete draft does contain a suggestion of the giants' dotted rhythm at 'Dort schreiten rasch | die Riesen heran' (mm. 962 ff.; 66/2/2 ff.); Wagner originally scored this for horns, then assigned it to timpani with horn afterbeats.

The formal/tonal plan resembles that of Episode 3: a tripartite ABA' structure (Table 8.3) is created by inserting a parenthetical interpolation into a 'classical' interruption scheme (Ex. 8.7). Here, however, the parenthesis comes *before* the end of the antecedent, and is not itself a dominant prolongation; this interpolation is therefore more disruptive than that of Episode 3. Freia sings during the A and A' sections, Fricka and Wotan squabble during Section B, while Fricka alone controls the introduction, retransition, and coda.

The episode is launched with a sudden change of tempo (marked 'All[egr]o non troppo' in the complete draft, 'Ziemlich lebhaft' in the score). After Fricka's introductory dominant preparation (mm. 914–21; 63/3/1–63/4/4), Freia runs in; the orchestra expresses her fear through an agitated rendition of the Freia motif (mm. 922–4; 64/1/1–3). This initiates the first phase of the interruption scheme; the E minor tonic is deliberately destabilized by a dominant pedal (producing a 'consonant' i_4^6). The bass ascent to V gets 'stuck' on a German augmented sixth chord[11] (m. 933; 64/3/5), which does not resolve until m. 960 (66/1/5); it is here (mm. 935 ff.; 64/4/2 ff.) that the interpolation occurs. As in Episode 3, this takes the form of an analepsis: Wotan and Fricka resume their argument from Episode 4, in its original key of D! D thus functions 'associatively' until it is absorbed into V/E minor at m. 960 (66/1/5), where the return of material from mm. 925–8 (64/1/4–64/2/3) wrenches the music (and Fricka's thoughts) back to the present. This retransition (mm. 960–6; 66/1/5–66/3/3) constitutes the interrupted dominant; the consequent (Section A′) begins with a root position statement of Freia's motif (m. 967; 66/4/1), which is now expanded to accompany her arioso-like plea for help. A restatement on G (III) leads to a final version of the motif over B (V); this time the $_4^6$ sonority embellishes the cadential dominant. Fricka's coda (mm. 980–4; 67/4/1–68/1/1) neighbours and resolves this dominant, closing out the interruption scheme.

4. Episode 6 (mm. 984–1127; 68/1/1–75/1/1)

Chapter 3 traced the textual metamorphosis of the giants, as they gradually shrank from an entire race into the brothers Fasolt and Fafner. The *Rheingold* prose sketch represents an intermediate stage in this process: 'Giants (Windfahrer and Reiffrost) have built the fortress. They demand Freia.' In the prose draft, however, most of the elements of Episode 6 are in place, with the notable exception of Freia's golden apples: according to Fafner, the mere act of removing Freia from the vicinity of the gods would cause them to wither and die. This portion of the prose draft is laid out as a series of exchanges between Wotan and the giants; the prose dialogue often approaches its versified form, which, of course, does incorporate Fafner's description of the apples.

Westernhagen has pointed out the difference between the final form of Fasolt's melody 'all' deinem Wissen fluch' ich . . .' (mm. 1057–60; 71/4/3–72/1/1) and that found in the complete draft.[12]

---

[11] The 'correct' spelling of this chord is C–E–G–A♯; Wagner respells the A♯ enharmonically as B♭ in order momentarily to suggest V⁷ of F major, the key of the giants. The preceding chord (m. 931; 64/3/3) is vii°⁷/V in E; the bass A♯ is also respelled as B♭.
[12] *The Forging of the 'Ring'*, 37.

TABLE 8.4 Episode 6: Structural outline

Meas.	Section and Content
	PART I: THE FORTRESS AND THE TREATY
984	*Solo No. 1*: Fasolt describes the building of Wotan's fortress (F major/minor).
1011	*Transition*: Wotan attempts to renege on the bargain.
1041	*Solo No. 2*: Fasolt warns Wotan that he must uphold the treaty (F minor).
1072	*Transition*: Wotan mocks Fasolt's desire to possess Freia.
	PART II: FREIA AS RANSOM
1081	*Solo No. 3*: Fasolt disdains Wotan's pursuit of power at the expense of love (D minor/major).
1106	*Transition*: Fafner mocks Fasolt's reason for wanting Freia.
1111	*Solo No. 4*: Fafner describes Freia's golden apples, without which the gods will wither and die (D major).

Otherwise, the latter does not diverge appreciably from the final version; nor did the composition of this episode cause Wagner much difficulty. It is likely that the preliminary sketch of the Giants motif (Ex. 2.2c) immediately preceded his drafting of this section.

Nevertheless, the *Partiturerstschrift* contains at least one point of interest. At Fasolt's 'Die dein Speer birgt', the Spear motif sounds fortissimo in the lower register of the orchestra (mm. 1034 ff.; 70/4/1 ff.). Wagner labelled this 'Tr[ompeten]' ('trumpets') in the complete draft, but he initially scored the scalar descent for three trombones doubled by cellos and basses, adding a triplet fanfare figure for trumpet and bass trumpet. He later subdued the effect by replacing the trombones with horns and bassoons, omitting the low string doubling, and assigning the fanfare to violins and violas. His apparent intent was to reserve the trombone/trumpet scoring for that moment in Episode 7 when Wotan first brandishes the weapon (one bar before 'Halt, du Wilder!': mm. 1163 ff.; 77/1/2 ff.). Thus the Spear theme, a motif of 'foreshadowing', gradually grows in volume until it is finally 'conditioned' by an imperious physical gesture.

Wagner conceivably could have set the repartee between Wotan and the giants in the same manner as the Fricka/Wotan altercation of Episode 4—as a dramatic dialogue carried out in through-composed recitative. Instead, he elected to 'heighten' several of the giants' statements into aria-like solos, connected by recitative (Table 8.4). Fasolt sings three tonally closed solos (in F major/minor, F minor, and D minor/major), while Fafner is allotted but one (in D major); Wotan's remarks are confined to the modulating recitatives. However, a 2 + 2 or binary grouping of the four solos is evident: the first two are in F and deal with the fortress and treaty, while the last two are in D and concern Freia. The period as a whole thus encapsulates the fundamental power/love dialectic, moving gradually from thesis to antithesis; this dramatic progression is paralleled by a corresponding tonal move from F to D.

Episode 6 is thus controlled by a double tonic complex (F/D); it may in fact constitute the first real example of this technique in the Wagnerian canon. One might, of course, object that the double tonic interpretation results from the way in which the boundaries of the episode were initially fixed: if we instead place the ending of Episode 6 at m. 1071 (72/2/6) and begin Episode 7 a few bars later (at the change to D), this interpretation evaporates. However, such a strategy wreaks violence upon the dramatic/musical continuity, and ignores the fact that implications of D are embedded within the very beginning of the episode. In fact, Episode 6 affords an excellent opportunity to study how the double tonic complex actually works.

Fasolt's first solo (mm. 984–1010; 68/1/1–69/2/2) is structured as an ABACA form, a sort of miniature rondo in which the Giants theme alternates with the Spear scale and the Valhalla motif. The Giants theme first suggests the Phrygian mode on C (a deliberate archaic touch), soon reinterpreted as $\hat{5}$ of F minor; it later appears on A (mm. 996 ff.; 68/3/3 ff.) and F (mm. 1009–10; 69/2/1–2). Thus this solo arpeggiates the descending F major triad. The Valhalla theme (mm. 1001 ff.; 68/4/3 ff.) expands B♭ as a neighbour of A; this neighbouring motion suggests a possible reading of A as V/D minor, especially since the parallelism with mm. 984 ff. implies that the repeated tone of m. 996 could function as both $\hat{1}$ of A Phrygian and $\hat{5}$ of D minor. The progression of mm. 1007–9 (69/1/4–69/2/1 ff.: 'zieh' nun ein . . .') encapsulates the tonal dichotony: I–V of D is followed

Ex. 8.8

directly by I–V–I of F. Thus, although the tonal background clearly articulates F, the foreground contains latent hints of D (Ex. 8.8).

After a typical recitative chord, Wotan's first question tonicizes V/F (mm. 1011–13; 69/2/3–69/3/1). Fasolt's indignant reply evokes the descending Spear scale, checked as usual by a chord on E; this resolves to A major for a lyrical excursus on Freia's motif (mm. 1017–22; 69/3/5–70/1/1). Previous associations with the Spear motif (cf. Episode 4) imply that A stands for a tonicized V/D; Freia is thus indirectly associated with the key of D major. Wotan's angry refusal wrenches the music back to F minor (m. 1025; 70/2/1); Fasolt's astonishment triggers some violent chromatic explosions, but Fafner's dark words (mm. 1038 ff.; 70/4/5 ff.) restore the tonal equilibrium and nudge Fasolt towards the dominant of F.

Fasolt's second solo (mm. 1041–71; 71/1/3–72/2/6) is tonally symmetrical, and moves from F through E♭ to D♭ and back; although this could be considered a linear expansion of F minor through 5–6–5 neighbour motion (Ex. 8.8), the F–E♭–D♭–E♭–F progression also represents an augmentation of the third bar of the Giants motif (cf. m. 986: C–B♭–A♭–B♭–C). From another perspective, E♭ sounds somewhat more secure than F minor: the pulsating root position horn chords in m. 1047 (71/2/5 ff.: 'Was du bist') create the impression that *this* is where the solo really beings, while the perfect authentic cadence at m. 1065 (72/1/6: 'Treu'!') sounds like its conclusion. The F minor passages (mm. 1041–6 and 1066–71; 71/1/3–71/2/4 and 72/2/1–6) frame this closed unit both textually and tonally, the closing frame 'correcting' the previous E♭ cadence. Nevertheless, F has been seriously weakened (E♭ threatens to 'burst' the F minor frame), and when the giants return in Scene 4 they re-enter in E♭ major.

F now simply collapses into D minor during the ensuing recitative (mm. 1072–80; 72/2/7–72/4/4); Fasolt's third solo (mm. 1081–1105; 72/4/5–73/4/4) articulates this key through a straightforward motion from i to V (mm. 1081–90; 72/4/5–73/2/2). This dominant is interrupted by a return to F ('Wir Plumpen'), which leads through G to A as V/D; in other words, F has now been absorbed into D minor as its mediant. The mode changes to major, the previous bass F is replaced by F♯ (thus marking the total obliteration of F), and this again moves through G (m. 1100; 73/3/7) to A (mm 1103; 73/4/2). The passage ends on an unresolved dominant as Fasolt is interrupted by his brother.

Fafner seizes the moment and repeats the preceding bass move (now F♯–G–G♯–A) to prepare for his solo (mm. 1111–27; 74/2/1–75/1/1). His description of Freia's apples is structured as a clear *Reprisenbar*: Stollen 1 = Apples motif twice (2 + 2 bars); Stollen 2 = variant of

Apples motif, again twice (2 + 2 bars); Durchführung = 'Twilight' variant of Apples motif (7 bars); Reprise = Apples motif once (2 bars). The tonal motion is from I (mm. 1111–18; 74/2/1–74/3/4) through bII^6 (expanded chromatically in mm. 1119–24; 74/4/1–74/5/2) to V–I (mm. 1125–6; 74/5/3–4). Fafner has 'clinched' D major (now unambiguously associated with Freia), even while incorporating the 'threatening' Eb as its Neapolitan. A brief transition built upon the Giants motif (mm. 1128–34; 75/1/2–75/3/1) passes from D through C and Bb to A for the dominant preparation that launches Episode 7.

5. Episode 7 (mm. 1134–83; 75/3/1–77/4/1)

As pointed out in Chapter 3, none of the *Ring* manuscripts prior to the *Rheingold* prose draft mention Donner and Froh as playing any part in the action of the 'Preliminary Evening'. The prose draft itself reads:

Donner and Fro come quickly: Freia beseeches them for help. Fro protects Freia in his arms. Donner threatens with his hammer. Wodan steps between them: nothing through force: he must preserve the treaty. Fricka reproaches him with his cruelty.

It should again be noted that the passage makes no mention of Wodan's spear. The verse draft prefaces Wotan's 'Halt, du Wilder!' with the direction 'Wodan | (stepping between them.)', thus paralleling the prose draft. However, the conclusion of Wotan's speech, which actually mentions the spear, is followed by 'he has stretched out his spear between the combatants'; the fair copy moves a variant of this direction—'Wodan | (stretching out his spear between the combatants)'—to the head of the speech.

The version of Donner's challenge which appears in the verse draft, fair copy, and 1853 printing is somewhat longer than the one in the printed score:

Original Version	*Printed Score*
Schon oft zahlt' ich	Schon oft zahlt' ich
Riesen den Zoll;	Riesen den Zoll.
schuldig blieb ich	
Schächern nie:	
kommt her! des Lohnes Last	Kommt her, des Lohnes Last
geb' ich in gutem Gewicht!	wäg' ich mit gutem Gewicht!

As outlined below, lines 3 and 4 of the original version were actually set in the complete draft, but later deleted.

Perhaps surprisingly, the composition of Episode 7 caused Wagner

Ex. 8.9

considerable difficulty. The reader is referred to the Appendix, which contains a full transcription of the complete draft version of this episode (beginning at m. 1133).

Wagner first drafted five bars of dominant preparation based upon the Freia motif, beginning at Fasolt's 'folg' uns *fort!*' He then tried to compress every pair of measures into one bar by halving note-values and eliminating barlines, but this proved unsatisfactory and he crossed out the whole thing. Starting over again, he changed Fasolt's lead-in to 'folge uns!', and composed a different four-bar dominant preparation, incorporating Freia's line 'Helft! Helft vor den Harten!' While scoring, however, Wagner sketched out yet a third version of the introductory four bars (Ex. 8.9) on a separate sheet,[13] then orchestrated *this* version in the *Partiturerstschrift*.

The fact that Froh's theme (mm. 1138–45; 75/4/2–76/1/5) is merely an optimistic variant of the Apples motif allowed Wagner to draft it immediately in its definitive form. The blustery figure representing Donner's wrath (mm. 1145–6; 76/1/5–6) was first lightly sketched on

---

[13] WWV 86A Musik Ic. This is the manuscript which, as mentioned in Chapter 2, has been filed by the Bayreuth archivist with the *Tristan* sketches.

a page of the 1853 printing (Ex. 2.2*d*), then entered into the complete draft. However, Donner's vocal line 'Hammers harten Schlag?' (mm. 1149–50; 76/2/3–4) was changed twice in the *Partiturerstschrift* (Ex. 8.10). Donner's challenge to the giants ('Schon oft zahlt' ich . . . mit gutem Gewicht!' (mm. 1157 ff.; 76/3/5 ff.) was revised considerably while scoring, eliminating the lines 'schuldig blieb ich | Schächern nie'; Wagner sketched the new version into the instrumentation draft,[14] scored it, then crossed out the sketch. Finally, the last bar of the complete draft version ('Mann?') was expanded to two while scoring.

Ex. 8.10

a. Complete Draft [Donner]

ham-mers har - ten schlag?

b. Partiturerstschrift (A) [Donner]

hammers har - ten schlag?

c. Partiturerstschrift (B) [Donner]

hammers har - ten schlag?

The episode is framed by a dominant preparation on V/D (mm. 1134–7 and 1175–82; 75/3/1–75/4/1 and 77/2/8–77/3/7). Within this frame, the tonal progression traces a clear path from an expanded tonic to a prolonged dominant (Ex. 8.11). Particularly interesting is the manner in which the Donner/Wotan clash outlines a descending arpeggiation of V^7, the dissonant seventh G articulated by the onset of the Spear scale. The episode is thus tonally closed but harmonically

Ex. 8.11

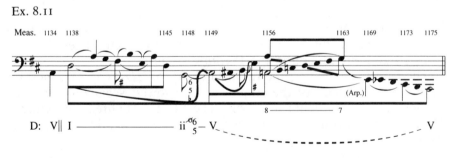

Meas. 1134 1138   1145 1148 1149   1156   1163 1169   1173 1175

D: V‖ I ——————————— ii⁰⁶₅ – V —————————————————— V

---

[14] See WWV 86A Musik III, p. 86.

open, as was also true of Episode 2. No formal archetype is discernable; it is as if formal coherence itself has collapsed in the face of an insoluble dramatic crisis.

6. *Episode 8 (mm. 1184–1313; 77/4/2–84/2/7)*

Chapter 3 detailed the gradual emergence of the god Loge in the *Rheingold* manuscripts. As regards the action of Episode 8, a supplementary prose sketch states merely that 'during the dispute over Freia, Loke finally arrives,' whereas the prose draft outlines in some detail Loge's initial words with Wotan as well as the reactions of the other deities. We recall that Wagner had not yet decided to make Loge a god of fire.[15]

By the time the actual composition got under way, Loge's status as fire god had clearly become central to the entire tetralogy; yet the text of Scene 2 still contained nothing which called attention to this status. Instead of revising the text, Wagner elected to express Loge's fiery nature exclusively through the music. His method, of course, was to represent Loge by means of several extremely chromatic motifs; however, these chromatic fragments serve to expand and prolong a diatonic substructure (one might almost speak of a 'chromaticized diatony'). For most of Episode 8, Wagner worked out a rather self-sufficient orchestral background, adding the vocal lines later; this is evident from the extremely crowded appearance of the text in the complete draft. The vocal lines themselves underwent frequent revision.

The beginning of the complete draft version of this episode (mm. 1184–96) is transcribed in the Appendix, to give the reader an idea of how Wagner first notated Loge's music. The initial ascending figure of chromatically interlocked perfect fourths (mm. 1184–7; 77/4/2–5) appears only in the top voice of the draft, while the two lower voices follow in parallel thirds; in the full score, all three parts (violas and divided cellos) play the semiquaver figure, and the continuous overlapping produces an extraordinary sonic effect. The chromatic runs and trills in mm. 1188–91 (77/4/6–78/1/3) are parallel sixths in the draft, full $^6_3$ chords in the score. Finally, the descending figure of interlocked perfect fifths (mm. 1195 ff.; 78/2/3 ff. and elsewhere) was revised in the complete draft so that in its final form it represents a rhythmic diminution of two previous vocal lines: mm.

---

[15] The verse draft exhibits one interesting point: Loge's lines 'Donner und Froh, | die denken an Dach und Fach' began as 'Donner und Froh, | die denken freilich anders', the second line of which was soon changed to 'die denken an frau und kind'. Wagner contemplated substituting 'fried' for 'frau' and 'dach' for 'kind', before entering the final version into the fair copy.

950–3 (65/3/6–65/4/3: Wotan: 'lehrt nur Schlauheit und List . . .')
and mm. 1038–40 (70/4/5–71/1/2: Fafner: 'Getreu'ster Bruder . . .').
In performance, of course, the vocal lines (both of which refer to
cunning and deception) *anticipate* the Loge music.

The episode is organized as an ABA′ ternary form; a developmental
transition leads from A to B, while a recitative separates B from A′.
Both A (mm. 1184–1206; 77/4/2–78/4/5) and A′ (mm. 1274–1302;
82/3/2–84/1/2) are based upon the chromatic Loge/Magic Fire music,
while B (mm. 1225–37; 79/4/5–80/4/1) reprises the diatonic Valhalla
theme (in its original key of Db) from Episode 3. The transition
(mm. 1206–24; 78/4/5–79/4/4) fragments and juxtaposes both ideas;
the recitative (mm. 1237–73; 80/4/1–82/3/1) is shot through with
Loge's motifs, but also contains a reminiscence of the Spear scale in
its associative D minor. During the reprise (A′), the Loge music from
A is interrupted by brief snatches of recitative; it breaks off on a
dissonance (m. 1302; 84/1/2), whereupon a transition (mm. 1303–21;
84/1/3–84/4/4) prepares the key of Episode 9.

Tonally the episode is centred around Loge's key of F♯, although
this sometimes sounds as slippery and elusive as the fire god himself.
Section A comprises two parallel units: in each, an eight-bar anacrusis
leads to a four-bar statement of the relatively diatonic Magic Fire
motif, the first on F♯ (mm. 1192–5; 78/1/4–78/2/3), the second on its
dominant C♯ (mm. 1203–6; 78/4/2–5). Both anacruses (mm. 1184 ff.
and 1195 ff.; 77/4/2 ff. and 78/2/3 ff.) are based upon parallel $\frac{6}{3}$
motion, and employ four bars of the interlocked perfect fourth figure
(replaced in the second anacrusis by descending fifths), two bars of
chromatic scales, and two bars of chromatic trills. The Magic Fire
motif expands its initial $\frac{5}{3}$ triad through 5–6–5 neighbouring motion,
then clinches the pitch level with a dominant–tonic progression.
Section A thus moves from I to V of F♯ major (Ex. 8.12).

As Loge jibes at the gods' desire for a new home, the transition
couples a rather flippant version of the Valhalla motif with the

Ex. 8.12

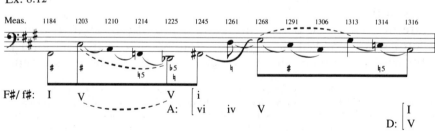

chromatic descending Loge music; this four-bar combination is sequenced from C♯ (m. 1206; 78/4/5) through A (m. 1210; 79/1/4) to F (m. 1214; 79/2/4), whereupon a brief recitative (mm. 1221–4; 79/4/1–4) leads to D♭. The transition thus prolongs the tonicized V/F♯ through equal division of the octave, respelling the dominant enharmonically as D♭ (Ex. 8.12).

The reprise of the Valhalla theme represents both 'associative' and 'classical' tonality: D♭ major has already been linked to the fortress (Episode 3), but as C♯ it also functions as dominant of the controlling F♯ major. The most chromatic theme of the entire opera has imperceptibly yielded to the most diatonic. Structurally Section B recalls the A′ section of Episode 3; the sequences on G♭ and B♭ as well as the restatement on F are omitted, so that the initial tonic passes immediately to an expanded subdominant (mm. 1231–4; 80/2/3–80/3/2) and then to the concluding V–I cadence. It is likely that Wagner's recomposition of the conclusion of Episode 3 resulted from his drafting of this section. In any case, the quicker tempo and far less majestic orchestration of the theme pointedly express Loge's contempt for the entire godly enterprise.

The following recitative begins to undermine this diatonic stability. Loge's chromatic figures reappear, cadencing twice on the tonic F♯ (mm. 1245 and 1253; 81/1/5 and 81/3/2), then moving to D minor (m. 1261; 81/4/4) for a recall of the Spear theme, which in turn leads to E as V/A (mm. 1268–74; 82/2/1–82/3/2). This tonal progression (F♯–D–E) could be read as vi–iv–V in A; Wagner is already preparing the dominant of the next episode (Ex. 8.12).

All the elements of the first section return in the reprise, but the F♯ tonality has by now almost completely disintegrated; even the Magic Fire motif is distorted by harmonic dissonances (mm. 1285–9 and 1299–1302; 83/1/1–5 and 83/3/4–84/1/2). Interjected snatches of recitative imply G♯ (mm. 1277–82; 82/3/5–82/4/4) and a dominant on C♯ (mm. 1290–1; 83/1/6–83/2/1), but the apparent II–V–I progression (G♯–C♯–F♯) is exploded by a final harmonic dissonance (m. 1302; 84/1/2). This tonal breakdown parallels the dramatic situation: the angry gods heap abuse upon Loge, and even physically threaten him.

Wotan steps forward to restore both peace and tonal equilibrium, leading from A to a cadence on E (m. 1313; 84/2/7); the giants demand their wages on C (mm. 314–15; 84/2/8–84/3/1); and Wotan in turn demands satisfaction from Loge over A as V/D (mm. 1316–21; 84/3/2–84/4/4). This transition thus arpeggiates a descending A minor triad, continuing earlier tonal implications and preparing the dominant of Episode 9.

7. *Episode 9 (mm. 1321–1584; 84/4/4–97/5/3)*

Chapter 3 outlined Wagner's different strategies for informing Wotan about Alberich's theft of the gold. As we saw, he finally decided to make Loge the agent of Wotan's enlightenment. The last supplementary prose sketch reads:

During the dispute over Freia, Loke finally arrives: in answer to Wodan's reproaches over his absence (since he promised to get rid of the giants) he informs them about the lament of the Rhinedaughters, who have complained to him about Alberich's theft. The giants stop short when they hear about the gold; Loke finally offers them the gold in exchange for Freia (more argument—finally resolution).

The prose draft expands this sketch into a rather detailed outline. The manuscript suggests that Fricka's lust for the gold did not form part of Wagner's original plan. Towards the end of the passage describing the various characters' reactions to Loge's tale, Wagner jotted in the margin: 'Das geschmeide, | das durch den reif | zu gewinnen, reizt | au[ch]' ('The jewellery which may be won through the ring also entices [Fricka]'). Crossing out this sketch, he entered a variant of it into the body of the draft: 'Fricka, von der schilderung ebenfalls gereizt, frägt Loke nach dem Geschmeide das durch das Gold zu gewinnen?' ('Fricka, likewise enticed by the description, questions Loke about the jewellery which might be won through the gold'). He continued with Loge's response, then framed the entire exchange with special markings to remind himself that it was to be inserted *before* Wotan's question as to how the ring might be forged.[16] This is the place where it appears in the poem; nevertheless, its versification caused Wagner some trouble, and Fricka's question went through three versions in the verse draft:

Verse Draft (A)	*Verse Draft (B)*	*Verse Draft (C)*
Taugte wohl auch	Taugte wohl auch	Taugte wohl auch
der gold'ne tand	des gold'nen tandes	des gold'nen tandes
zu holden	gleissend geschmeid	gleissend geschmeid
	schönen frauen	frauen zu schönen Schmuck?

The last part of Loge's response (after 'Des Gatten Treu' | ertrotzte die Frau') also needed reworking:

Verse Draft	*Fair Copy*
trüge sie ~~frei~~ hold	trüge sie hold
den schimmernden schmuck	den hellen Schmuck,

---

[16] This is not apparent from Otto Strobel's transcription, which omits the special markings. See *Skizzen und Entwürfe*, 219–20.

| den zwerge schmieden, | den schimmernd Zwerge schmieden, |
| rastlos im zwange des reifs! | ~~rastlos~~ rührig im Zwange des Reifs. |

In general, the verse draft of Episode 9 contains a sizeable number of alterations, and is one of the few sections of that manuscript which deviate slightly from the fair copy. The complete musical draft also contains revisions, and at least one segment was significantly recomposed while scoring; these variants are discussed within the context of the following analysis.

Episode 9 is extremely important from at least one point of view: it represents the first instance in the *Ring* of a verbal/musical *narrative*. Actually, it would be more accurate to speak of a narrative-within-a-narrative. The *Ring* itself is, of course, the primary or 'diegetic' narrative, while Loge's tale is a second-degree narrative. Loge did not witness Alberich's theft directly, but learned about it from the Rhinedaughters; this implies yet a third-level narrative, that recounted by the mermaids.

An embedded or second-degree narrative may fulfil various functions: it might advance the action of the primary narrative (actional function), offer an explanation of the diegetic level (explicative function), or establish an analogy between the primary and secondary levels (thematic function).[17] Loge's narrative is not really explicative, because the events it recounts are already known to the *Ring* audience (in contrast, say, to Siegmund's narrative in Act I of *Die Walküre*). On the other hand, by informing the gods and giants of Alberich's deed, and casting the spell of the ring over one and all, Loge's narrative triggers the subsequent turn of events, and thus possesses a strong actional function. The tale is also thematic in function, for it implies an analogy between Alberich, who renounced love in favour of power, and Wotan, who in his pursuit of power appears willing to place the goddess of love herself in jeopardy.

Episode 9 as a whole is binary in structure: Part 1 is the actual narrative, while Part 2 surveys the reactions of Loge's listeners (Table 8.5). Neither part is tonally centric: the first moves from D major to C major, while the second focuses upon E major before returning to D. The episode is framed by an introduction (dominant preparation) and a coda (tonic pedal), and features a recurrent textual/musical refrain ('Weibes Wonne und Werth').

The introduction (mm. 1321–40; 84/4/4–85/4/3) is a recitative for Loge, supported largely by detached string chords. It contains two phrases which relate dialectically: in the thesis (arco accompaniment)

---

[17] See Shlomith Rimmon-Kenan, *Narrative Fiction: Contemporary Poetics* (London and New York, 1983), 92–3. Her description of narrative functions basically follows that of Gérard Genette in *Narrative Discourse: An Essay in Method* (Ithaca, NY, 1980), 231–4.

TABLE 8.5 Episode 9: Structural outline

Meas.	Section and Content
	INTRODUCTION (Dominant Preparation)
1321	1. Loge searched everywhere for Freia's ransom.
1332	2. He searched in vain.
	PART I: LOGE'S NARRATIVE (Bipartite: D major → C major)
	Part 1: Loge's failure
1340	Prelude (Orchestra)
1348	1. Loge sought everywhere for something more valuable than love.
1362	2. No man would forgo the delights of love.
1370	Postlude (Orchestra)
	Part 2: Loge's success
1376	Introduction: There *was* one who forswore love.
1382	1. The Rhinedaughters complained to Loge about Alberich's theft.
1400	2. The sisters implore Wotan to restore their gold to them.
1415	Postlude (Orchestra)
	PART II: REACTIONS TO LOGE'S NARRATIVE (Four Cycles: E major → D major)
	Each cycle contains a reaction (R), a question (Q), and an answer (A):
1426	R1: Wotan cannot help the Rhinedaughters.
1441	Q1: Fafner: Why is the gold so valuable?
1447	A1: Loge: Forge it into a ring and rule the world!
1459	R2: Wotan has heard of the gold.
1469	Q2: Fricka: Would the gold serve to adorn a woman?
1473	A2: Loge: It would keep her husband faithful!
1481	R3: Fricka wishes her husband could win the gold.
1491	Q3: Wotan: How could *I* forge the ring?
1501	A3: Loge: You would have to forswear love, which Alberich has already done.
1520	R4: Donner, Wotan, and Froh realize they must obtain the ring.
1533	Q4: They ask Loge how this may be done.
1534	A4: Loge: Steal it from Alberich, then return it to the Rhine!
	CODA (Tonic Pedal)
1555	1. Wotan and Fricka have no use for the Rhinedaughters.
1567	2. Fafner convinces Fasolt to accept the gold.

Loge tells that he sought everywhere for a substitute for Freia, while in the antithesis (pizzicato accompaniment) he claims that he searched in vain. This last point is, of course, not strictly true, and to that extent Loge is an 'unreliable narrator'. The introduction establishes

Ex. 8.13

A minor, then transforms A into the dominant of D: both phrases terminate in half cadences, the first on V/A minor (m. 1331; 85/2/4), the second on V/D minor (m. 1340; 85/4/3). Each cadence is emphasized through sustained chords: in the first phrase, these are prefaced by Loge's chromatic scale; in the second, they support his descending vocal line 'Weibes Wonne und Werth' with a harmonization derived from the Renunciation theme. The introduction thus outlines the story that Loge intends to tell.

The narrative itself replicates the binary structure of the introduction: Loge first describes the failure of his quest, then relates the story of Alberich (without, however, suggesting that this tale might provide a solution to Wotan's problem). Part 1 (mm. 1340–75; 85/4/3–87/2/2) begins with an orchestral prelude, which was sketched in the complete draft as four bars of dominant harmony followed by four bars of Freia's motif (Ex. 8.13). While scoring, Wagner recomposed this prelude, replacing the rather colourless triadic arpeggiation with a slowed-down version of the new Nature in Motion figure from Scene 1; the canonic imitations in divided strings, ascending through the triad, recall the horn canon of the revised Prelude. The triplet rhythm of this new figure motivated an alteration of the Freia motif, replacing its three semiquavers with triplet quavers; all subsequent statements were changed as well.

Loge's two vocal phrases relate as antecedent–consequent, the first ('So weit Leben und Weben...') terminating in an imperfect cadence on A (and utilizing the 'Weibes Wonne und Werth' refrain), the second ('Doch so weit Leben und Weben . . .') in an authentic cadence on D followed by a brief postlude. Westernhagen has pointed out Wagner's revision of Loge's vocal line at 'verlacht nur ward | meine fragende List' (mm. 1364–5; 86/4/2–3);[18] the accompanying wind parts also underwent changes as Wagner scored. The Freia motif recurs to articulate the phrase structure, and also functions as a musical sign signifying the love which men refuse to renounce. During Part 1, Loge repeats in varied form the facts he outlined in the introduction: this section may thus be regarded as an enriched synthesis of that passage, which in turn leads, as a higher level thesis, to a new antithesis: there *was* one who renounced love.

This antithesis (Part 2 of the narrative: mm. 1376–1419; 87/2/3–89/3/2) is also an antecedent–consequent structure; as in Part 1, the antecedent terminates in a half-cadence utilizing the refrain (now in a distorted form: 'hehrer als Weibes Huld'). However, the phrases are longer, the period is tonally progressive, and the orchestral texture is heavy with leitmotifs.

The tonal move of this section might be interpreted as an 'expressive' semitone descent from the previous D major through C♯ minor to C major. However, C♯ minor is represented primarily through its dominant G♯ (mm. 1396–9, the cadence of the antecedent phrase; 88/2/4–7). The complete draft shows that Wagner originally composed mm. 1388–99 (87/4/4–88/2/7: 'buhlte vergebens . . . Weibes Huld') a semitone lower; this enabled the 'Weia! Waga!' melody (mm. 1388–9; 87/4/4–88/1/1) to appear at its original pitch level (a ⁶₄ chord on E♭), and ended the antecedent phrase on V/C minor (Ex. 8.14a). Thus Wagner originally planned to move from D to C by descending fifths; his transposition, apparently motivated by a desire to avoid C until the end of the consequent, altered D–G–C to D–G♯–C. As Ex. 8.14b shows, the original D–(B–G–E♭–C)–G bass move became D–(B–G–E–C♯)–G♯; after unfolding the C♯ minor triad, the consequent reaches C by descending major thirds (G♯–E–C), then clinches C with an authentic cadence and an orchestral postlude.

It is interesting to note that the orchestral leitmotifs appear only at the point where Loge changes diegetic levels; that is, where he moves from his own second-level narrative to the Rhinedaughters' third-level narrative. The transition begins in the introductory recitative 'Nur einen sah ich . . . Gunst' (mm. 1376–81; 87/2/3–87/3/2), which recalls the Gold fanfare; the motif's original bright C major is now absorbed into the key of B minor as its dark Neapolitan. This initiates

[18] *The Forging of the Ring*, 33.

Ex. 8.14

a

b

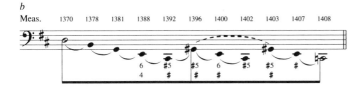

a chain of descending thirds in the bass (D–B–G–E–C♯), above
which themes from Scene 1 reappear (including the original semiquaver figure from the complete draft); it is as if a descent in diegetic
levels evokes a corresponding tonal descent, and opens the motivic
floodgates (see again Ex. 8.14*b*). The consequent phrase finally
reaches the C major of Scene 1 and celebrates it with an orchestral
reprise of the 'Rheingold!' cry over a tonic pedal; not until Loge
returns to his own diegetic level, sealing off his narrative with a
verbal 'coda' (mm. 1420–4; 89/3/3–89/4/2: 'Dir's zu melden . . . sein
Wort') does his original D major return. However, this tonal return
cannot compete with the preceding C major cadence: having once
been opened, the narrative gateway to Scene 1 cannot be closed.

Part 2 of the Episode is cyclical in structure: each of its four cycles
contains a reaction, a question, and a response (see Table 8.5). As
was the case with Episodes 1 and 2, the cyclical structure is clearly
outlined in the prose draft, although as noted above, Fricka's query
and Loge's reply (Cycle 2) were apparently an afterthought. The
orchestral flood of reminiscences from Scene 1 continues unabated:
those which have already appeared are joined by the Ring and
Renunciation motifs (mm. 1451 and 1505 respectively; 91/1/4 and
93/4/5), both at their original pitch levels. In addition, Fricka's
question initiates a reprise of her 'wonniger Hausrath' verse-melody
from Episode 4 (mm. 1475–7; 92/2/4–92/3/1), while her 'caressing'
words to Wotan are underlined by a seductive form of Freia's motif
on solo violin (mm. 1481 ff.; 92/4/1 ff.). Loge's announcement that

Ex. 8.15

a

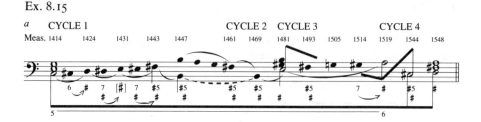

b

Alberich has already forged the ring (mm. 1517–19; 94/3/3–5: 'gerathen ist ihm der Ring!') is set to a harsh form of the 'Weibes Wonne und Werth' refrain, while his final admonishment to Wotan reprises the cadence of his narrative a whole tone higher, restoring the original key of D major (mm. 1548–54; 96/2/1–96/3/3).

Tonally Part 2 is more complex than Part 1 (Ex. 8.15*a*). Cycles 1 and 2 move from C to E, and the latter is maintained through the beginning of Cycle 3; E itself is invoked because it is the key in which the Rhinedaughters first discussed the gold's *potential* for being forged into a ring (cf. Episode 2). As Ex. 8.15*a* shows, the move from C to E is made by falling fifths (C–F♯–B–E); the first interval is filled in stepwise (C–D–E–F♯) and the resolution of the last fifth is delayed. During Cycle 3, the bass rises from E (m. 1481; 92/4/1) through F♯ (m. 1493; 93/2/3), G (m. 1505; 93/4/5), and G♯ (m. 1514; 94/2/5) to A as V/D minor (m. 1519; 94/3/5), while in Cycle 4 it descends linearly from A to C♯ (m. 1544; 96/1/1) before resolving to D (m. 1548; 96/2/1). This E–A–C♯ motion outlines V/D; the initial E major is thus absorbed into an unfolding of the dominant triad. In fact, the entire episode could be reduced to the progression shown in Ex. 8.15*b*, although such a reduction obviously entails a high degree of abstraction.

The long tonic pedal of the Coda (mm. 1555–86; 96/3/4–97/5/3) allows the tonal/rhythmic momentum generated during Part 2 to coast to a standstill. Wotan and Fricka's references to the Rhine-daughters are accompanied by three verse-melodies from Scene 1:

'Rheingold!', 'Weia! Waga!', and 'Heia, du Holder!' Fafner's confer-
ence with his brother evokes three motifs which now function as
musical signs: the first (Freia) originally accompanied a gesture
(the goddess's flight from the giants), the second (Golden Apples)
originated as a verse-melody, and the third (Gold) was once a motif
of 'foreshadowing' accompanying a visual spectacle. The moment
when 'Fasolt's demeanour shows that he feels himself convinced
against his will' is marked by a dissonance (m. 1581; 97/4/7) created
by the simultaneous sounding of two pitches of the tonic chord (F♯
and A) against their upper neighbours (G and B♭).

8. Episode 10 (mm. 1587–1668; 98/1/1–102/4/5)

As mentioned earlier, the 'expressive' tonal rise which governs the
first part of Scene 2 reaches its climax on the F♯ of Loge's entrance
(Episode 8), which also constitutes an axis of symmetry for the scene
as a whole. The tonal centres that follow F♯ symmetrically reflect
those which precede it. The D major of Episode 9 mirrors that of
Episode 7 and the second half of Episode 6; poetic and thematic
references to Freia strengthen this relationship. Episode 10 reflects
the *first* half of Episode 6, during which the giants entered in the key
of F major/minor; they now exit in the same key, to the strains of
their original motif. Two subordinate cadences on D minor (mm.
1598 and 1619; 98/3/3 and 100/1/1) recall the latent implications of
this key embedded within the first part of Episode 6.

  Although through-composed, Episode 10 falls into three distinct
sections. Part 1 (mm. 1587–1611; 98/1/1–99/3/1) contains two exchanges between Fafner and Wotan, during which the former demands
the gold as ransom and the latter angrily refuses; declamatory
recitative is punctuated by various motifs, especially that of the
Giants. In Part 2 (mm. 1612–47; 99/3/2–101/3/3), two agitated
upward-rushing passages depicting Fasolt's seizure of Freia frame a
central segment in which the giants warn the gods to have the ransom
ready when they return. Part 3, a solo for Loge (mm. 1648–68;
101/3/4–102/4/5), vividly depicts the giants' journey to Riesenheim:
sequential treatment of a fragment of the Giants motif articulates a
chromatic bass descent from F to C (i to V), above which plaintive
woodwinds suggest Freia's misery.

  Neither the complete draft nor the *Partiturerstschrift* exhibit any
significant deviations from the final version. However, the versification
of Loge's solo did not come easily to Wagner. He first wrote: 'Ueber
das thal | tappen sie schon: | durch das wasser des Rheines | waten sie

rasch.' Crossing this out, he wrote the next version in the left margin, altering it as indicated below:

> Ueber stock und Stein ~~in's~~ zu thal
>   stapfen sie hin;
> durch des Rheines Wasserfurth
>   ~~wass~~ waten die riesen:
>   ~~nicht froh hängt Froia~~
>   fröhlich nicht
>   hängt Freia
> den Rauhen über dem Rücken!
>   Heia! hei!
> Wie taumeln die tölpel dahin!
> [*insert*: durch das thal talpen sie schon!]
>   An Riesenheim's mark
>   [*A*: wohl rasten sie]
>   [*B*: wohl erst halten sie rast:—]

In the fair copy, Wagner changed the last two lines to 'wohl an Riesenheim's Mark | erst halten sie Rast'.

9. *Episode 11 (mm. 1669–1803; 103/1/1–110/2/3)*

The second paragraph of the prose sketch concludes with the statement 'Theft of the Nibelung hoard resolved upon.' One of the supplementary notes expands this into: 'as [the giants] depart with Freia, loud wailing breaks out among the gods: mists envelop them, Valhalla darkens; Wodan and Loke disappear into the twilight to go to the Rhine'. The prose draft outlines the episode in detail: the sky darkens and the air fills with mist, while the gods grow pale and begin to age. Loge taunts them with the fact that 'Holda possesses the magic of youth, which she pours out over all those with whom she stays; now they must grow old, gloomy, and sick: this was known full well by the giants, who aimed at the gods' destruction; if they do not win back Freia, they must miserably age and pass away, the laughing stock of the world.' The reader will again notice the absence of any reference to Freia's golden apples, which of course are mentioned in the verse draft.

Apart from a few changes in the vocal line, the complete draft version of this episode essentially parallels its final form. Wagner originally prefaced Loge's 'Doch ihr setztet alles ...' (mm. 1742 ff.; 107/1/1 ff.) with the marking 'Recit.', but replaced this in the score by 'frei, doch lebhaft und grell'. Loge's chromatic scales are generally notated as single lines, with an indication that they are to be doubled at the lower sixth. Folio 16ᵛ concludes with two bars of the descending interlocked fourth motif (following 'bald fällt faul es herab': mm. 1731–2; 106/1/5–106/2/1); on a free staff at the bottom of the page, Wagner sketched an ascending chromatic bass-line to this music, but did not use it in the score. However, he *did* employ this bass-line during the initial part of the Second Transformation.

Essentially a solo for Loge, the episode is structured as a five-part ABA^{1}CA^2 form followed by a coda. The two reprises are articulated primarily by the return of the Golden Apples motif; the tonal progression delineates a i–III–V–i arpeggiation in E minor.

In Section A (mm. 1669–86; 103/1/1–103/4/3), Loge comments upon the gods' wan demeanour, feigning ignorance as to its cause. Tremolo diminished seventh chords representing the gathering mists are underpinned by a dominant pedal, which resolves first to E major (m. 1679; 103/3/1), then to E minor (m. 1685; 103/4/2) for statements of the Golden Apples motif. Wagner originally scored the second statement for horns doubled by clarinets; he then crossed out the clarinets, reserving the combined sonority for section A^1.

In Section B (mm. 1687–1716; 103/4/4–105/2/5), Loge taunts each of the gods in turn, then pretends suddenly to grasp the truth of the matter. Towards the end of this section, the deliberately ambiguous harmonies gradually crystallize on vii$^{\varnothing6}_5$ of G major; this harmonic 'clarification' reflects the manner in which Loge feigns to 'see the light'.

Section A^1 (mm. 1717–31; 105/3/1–106/1/5) reprises the entire Golden Apples theme from Episode 6 (cf. mm. 1111–24; 74/2/1–74/5/2), as Loge paraphrases Fafner's earlier solo; the theme is transposed to G major, although pedals on D hint at its original tonality. The chromatically descending 'Twilight chords' (mm. 1727 ff.; 106/1/1 ff.) are extended past the expected Neapolitan A♭ to end on E♭, thus forgoing tonal closure.

Section C (mm. 1731–46; 106/1/5–107/2/2) contains the afore-mentioned recitative, a vehicle for Loge's expression of his own equanimity over the whole affair. Tonal centricity deteriorates still further, only to be abruptly restored by a concluding cadential jolt on G.

During Section A^2 (mm. 1747–55; 107/2/3–107/3/6), the Golden Apples motif returns in bar form (2 + 2 + 5 measures) and leads to a ♭II^6–V–i cadence in G minor. The progression by rising minor thirds G–B♭–D♭ (mm. 1746–50; 107/2/2–107/3/1) is striking, as is the expansion of the minor Neapolitan (mm. 1751–2; 107/3/2–3); these devices, exploring as they do rather 'dark' harmonic relationships, chillingly underscore Loge's prophecy of the gods' extinction.

Although the formal design is now complete, the tonal progression has only reached the mediant G; the succeeding Coda gains the structural dominant and resolves to the tonic E at mm. 1779–80 (108/4/2–3), then repeats this V–I progression twice (mm. 1786–7 and 1798–9; 109/2/1–2 and 109/4/6–110/1/1). These decisive cadences articulate Wotan's resolve to journey to Nibelheim in search of a ransom. Thematic reprise and tonal return are thus out of phase, a not uncommon situation in Wagner's later works.

9 *Second Transformation and Scene Three*

I am spinning a cocoon round myself like a silkworm, but at the same time I am spinning the thread out of myself. I have written no music for five years. Now I am in 'Nibelheim'; today Mime was bewailing his fate.

(Wagner to Franz Liszt, 17 December 1853)

I. THE SECOND TRANSFORMATION

Although the prose sketch is mute concerning this second scenic transformation, a supplementary note informs us that 'Wodan and Loke disappear into the twilight to go to the Rhine.' The account in the prose draft is much fuller:

The entire scene is now enveloped in sulphurous mist: Loke and Wodan disappear into the cleft: the other gods become invisible, after Fricka has anxiously called out 'Farewell' to the departing ones. Then the sulphurous clouds rise: dark vapours climb to the top [of the scene], which then changes into a dark chasm; this continues to ascend, so that it appears as if the scene is sinking ever deeper into the earth. Finally a dark red glow shines: there appears an immense subterranean chasm, stretching out in all directions.

The description in the verse draft approaches its final wording, although Wagner did make a few additions while writing out the fair copy. However, none of the textual manuscripts mention what is arguably the most memorable aspect of this orchestral transition—the clang of the Nibelungs' anvils.

The complete draft differs only in a few respects from the final version. Measures 1807–8 (110/4/1–2) were originally sequenced at the lower minor third instead of the tritone (mm. 1809–10); Wagner simply crossed out the first version and continued with the second. The semiquaver Loge figurations (mm. 1810 ff.; 111/1/1 ff.) also underwent some revision. The final statement of the Ring motif (mm. 1892–3; 114/4/3–4) originally continued the $A^{\circ 7}$ harmony of the preceding two measures; after Wagner had composed at least some of Scene 3, he changed these bars so that they outlined an $E^{\circ 7}$ chord (a key sonority in Episode 12), writing the second version over the first. Finally, Wagner's sketch for the a capella anvils (marked

Ex. 9.1

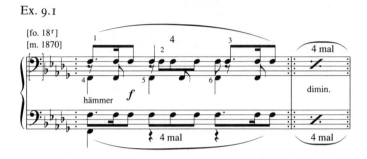

Ex. 9.2

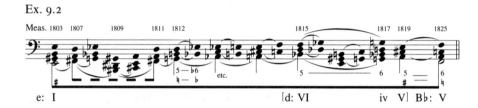

'hämmer') is interesting (Ex. 9.1): he first notated the additive rhythm on the lower staff, then 'scored' it on the upper.

Musically the Second Transformation falls into two parts: a Postlude to Scene 2 (mm. 1803–30; 110/2/3–111/5/4) and a Prelude to Scene 3 (mm. 1831–93; 111/5/5–114/4/4). Part 1 begins on E major, the concluding sonority of Episode 11, and moves to the dominant of Bb minor, the key of Episode 12; Part 2 prolongs V/Bb minor with an extended dominant pedal. The bass thus ascends a semitone (E to F), while the tonal move spans a tritone (E to Bb).

The overall harmonic progression can best be understood by reference to Ex. 9.2. Measures 1803–15 (110/2/3–111/2/3) feature a bass ascent from E to Bb, utilizing parallel $^6_3$ motion (mm. 1807–11; 110/4/1–111/1/2) and the chromatic 5–6 technique (mm. 1812–16; 111/1/3–111/3/1). Bb is absorbed into a half-cadence in D minor (mm. 1817–24; 111/3/2–111/4/4), whose dominant is then transformed into V/Bb through a 5–6 shift (m. 1825; 111/4/5). The remainder of the Transformation (almost 70 bars) comprises an enormous expansion of this dominant.

The reader will recall that the First Transformation employed a fourfold repetition of the Ring motif, a sort of developing variation procedure during which that theme was gradually transformed into the Valhalla motif. The Second Transformation utilizes multiple

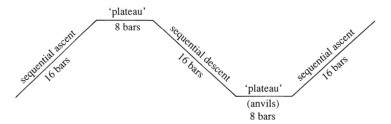

FIG. 9.1. Second Transformation: Contour of Part 2

repetition as well, but this time in the form of ascending and descending sequences. Motivic reiteration is here carried to an almost unprecedented extreme.

Part 1 looks back motivically over the latter portion of Scene 2. After Loge's chromatic trills have undermined the stability of E major (a process begun during the final bars of Episode 11), a new ascending bass line first alternates with the descending Loge motif, then is contrapuntally combined with it (mm. 1807–14; 110/4/1–111/2/2).[1] As winds and strings fill the entire tonal space with chromatic fire, the sequential units decrease in length from two bars to one. Tubas then alternate descending octaves on B♭ and E every half-bar, simultaneously summarizing the preceding bass move (E to B♭) and providing a thematic/instrumental 'preview' of the Dragon theme. The change to triple metre (m. 1817) ushers in the 'Weibes Wonne und Werth' refrain from Episode 9; this verse-melody is played twice by low brass in its original key of D minor, then by horns in the new tonality of B♭. Meanwhile, strings gradually transform the swirling Loge music into Alberich's semitonal 'Wehe!' motif. Measures 1817–28 (111/3/2–111/5/2) thus retard the forward motion through a lengthening of the repetition-unit to four bars.

Part 2 of the Transformation is Janus-faced: it first looks back to Scene 1, then points ahead to Scene 3. Its overall shape is schematized in Fig. 9.1.[2]

Part 2 begins (m. 1831, marked 'B-moll accel.' in the complete draft, 'Beschleunigend' in the score) by indulging in a rather bold analeptic leap: it hearkens all the way back to Alberich's cry of despair preceding the recapitulation of Episode 1 (cf. mm. 408–13;

---

[1] This is the bass-line which Wagner sketched into the complete draft at the bottom of fo. 16ᵛ. In that draft, the rhythm of the first two beats is ♫♫♫; Wagner changed this to ♩ ♪♫♫ while scoring.

[2] The end of the first eight-bar 'plateau' (m. 1854; 112/5/2) is elided with the following sequential unit.

24/1/3–24/2/3). Alberich originally sang 'Wehe! ach wehe!' over V^9/V in E♭ minor, resolving to $\bar{V}^9/E♭$ for his cry 'Die dritte, so traut, | betrog sie mich auch?' Both verse melodies now return at their original pitch levels, energized into a series of ascending sequences; however, the bass pedal on F implies V/B♭ minor throughout. This sixteen-bar sequential ascent (mm. 1831–46; 111/5/5–112/3/2) leads to an eight-bar 'plateau', during which the Gold motif is twice trumpeted forth with shattering effect (mm. 1847–54; 112/3/3–112/5/2); the fortissimo climax (m. 1853) is marked by the *Durchbruch* of the Nibelungs motif, whose incessantly repeated one-bar rhythm seems literally to whip the music along. The elided sixteen-bar sequential descent (mm. 1854–69; 112/5/2–113/2/4) is based upon an agonized augmentation, in unison brass, of 'Die dritte, so traut', which Cooke equates with the second part of Freia's motif.[3] At m. 1862 (113/1/1), eighteen anvils begin their noisy rendition of the Nibelungs rhythm; an eight-bar 'plateau' of a capella hammering (mm. 1870–7) leads to the return of the orchestra, beneath which the anvils gradually retreat.[4] During the final sixteen-bar sequential ascent (mm. 1878–93; 114/1/1–114/4/4), a rising version of the 'dritte so traut' augmentation leads to another fortissimo climax, and the Second Transformation ends with four bars of the downward-plunging Ring motif.

II. EPISODE 12 (MM. 1878–2319; 114/1/1–134/4/6)

Like the first scene, the third comprises only two long episodes. The B♭ minor tonality of Episode 12 is henceforth associated with Alberich and the Nibelungs, while an 'expressive' semitonal descent to the A major of Episode 13 suggests the dwarf's downfall. Both keys are represented primarily by their dominants, producing a large-scale F–E bass descent which effectively reverses the E–F ascent of the Second Transformation.

The third paragraph of the prose sketch begins:

III. Alberich as lord of the Nibelungs. Mime has just been forced to forge the tarncap for him. He puts it on and immediately disappears: from afar he is heard scolding and driving: from all sides the Nibelungs bring out the hoard.—Wodan and Loke (?) call upon Alberich.

A supplementary note reads:

Only now do [Wodan and Loke] go to the Nibelungs.—Alberich receives

---

[3] *I Saw the World End*, 22.
[4] At this point in the complete draft, Wagner wrote 'Die hämmer verlieren sich ganz.'

the tarnhelm from Mime, and then goes into the depths, swinging the whip.—They learn about the power of the ring; Wodan desires to win it for himself.

In both sketches, Mime is present solely to provide Alberich with the tarnhelm. However, in the prose draft, which outlines the action in considerable detail, Wagner uses Mime for two additional purposes: to demonstrate Alberich's cruelty, and to inform the two gods (and the audience) about what transpired after the close of Scene 1. Thus the prose draft contains Mime's narrative about Alberich and the ring.

In its final form, Episode 12 contains three main sections: (1) the Alberich/Mime dialogue, (2) Mime's narrative, and (3) Alberich's return. In the prose draft, Alberich's spell (Section 1) originally ran: 'Nebel und dunst will ich sein!'; above this, in the top margin, Wagner wrote the final version ('Nacht und Nebel | Niemand gleich'). Mime's narrative (Section 2) is outlined in detail; however, this prose version contains no reference to the dwarfs' happier times before Alberich forged the ring. In Section 3, Alberich was originally to have reappeared alone; Wagner soon decided to bring the Nibelungs on stage *en masse* (as he had originally planned for Act II of *Der junge Siegfried*), and he made a marginal note to that effect. Perhaps he suddenly remembered that the Nibelungs were required to carry the hoard on stage! As a result, Part 3 enlarges the scope of Alberich's cruelty by demonstrating the dwarf's barbarous treatment of his own people.

The most significant alteration in the verse draft involves the beginning of Mime's narrative. Wagner crossed out the original version and wrote the revision in the right margin:

Verse Draft (Version A)	*Verse Draft (Version B)*
Wonnig geschmeid,	Sorglose schmiede,
unsre weiber zu schmieden,	schufen wir sonst
schufen wir sonst;	schmuck unsren weibern,
sorglose schmiede	wonnig geschmeid,
niedlichen tand	niedlichen Niblungentand,
nach niblungen art	wir lachten lustig der müh'!

In addition, Mime's final summarizing line 'Das schuf ich mir Dummen | schön zu Dank!' was apparently an afterthought, jotted first in the right margin as 'das schuf ich mir dummen zum dank!', then in the left as 'das schuf ich mir dummen | zum schönen dank!' The climax of the episode, Alberich's terrible demonstration of the power of the ring, was altered when Wagner wrote out the fair copy:

Verse Draft	Fair Copy
Zagen fasse	Zitt're und zage,
und zähme' eu'r heer!	gezähmtes Heer:
Rasch gehorcht	rasch gehorcht
des ringes herrn!	des Ringes Herrn!

The 1853 printing contains essentially the version found in the score, although Wagner did make minor changes while setting the text.[5]

Westernhagen correctly points out that Scene 3 inhabits a most unusual sound world.[6] Although our discussion of the scene's 'tone' or 'tinta' must necessarily be brief, a few general observations are in order.

Westernhagen has drawn attention to Wagner's 'orchestration' of the four male voices: 'Wotan's bel canto', 'Alberich's declamatory delivery', 'Mime's wails', and 'Loge's ironic hauteur'.[7] To this may be added the orchestra's insistence upon dark double-reed sonorities, mysterious muted horns, and snarling trombones. Harmonically, Episode 12 makes extensive use of unresolved dominant pedals: B♭ minor is represented largely through a continuation of the F pedal from the Second Transformation, now neighboured by both E and either G♭ or G. In addition, the diminished seventh chord attains the status of a referential sonority, especially at the pitch level E–G–B♭–D♭ (vii°⁷/V). Finally, rhythmic repetition (usually of the one-bar Nibelung motif) becomes the order of the day.

The 'controlling' diminished seventh chord E–G–B♭–D♭ (first heard in the final two bars of the Second Transformation) is often expanded through the voice-exchange techniques shown in Ex. 9.3.

Ex. 9.3

This may result either in the exchange of G and G♭ (perhaps turning vii°⁷/V into a German augmented sixth chord) or in the dissonant clash of F and G♭. Locally, the chord might resolve directly to V/B♭, or be absorbed first into V⁷/V or V⁹/V. Even when prolonged across long stretches of time, it never loses its inherent tension.

As suggested earlier, Episode 12 is essentially a large ABA' ternary

[5] For example, Mime's 'schufen wir sonst' became 'schufen wir sonst wohl', while his 'den Hort zu häufen dem Herrn' became 'dem Herrn zu häufen den Hort'.

[6] *The Forging of the 'Ring'*, 43.

[7] Ibid.

TABLE 9.1 Episode 12: Structural outline

Meas.	Section and Content
	PART 1 (A): ALBERICH AND MIME QUARREL (Ternary Form: B♭ minor)
1878	Refrain: Nibelung music
1894	a: Alberich upbraids Mime for withholding the tarnhelm.
1930	b: Alberich examines the Tarnhelm and uses it to become invisible.
1969	Retransition: Alberich beats Mime.
1984	a': Alberich warns the Nibelungs to bow before his might, in a symmetrical arch form:

$$3 + 2 + 4 + 8 + 3 + 7 + 3 \text{ bars}$$
$$a \quad b \quad c \quad d \quad c' \quad b' \quad a'$$

Meas.	Section and Content
2014	Refrain: Nibelung music
2035	TRANSITION: WOTAN AND LOGE ARRIVE
	PART 2 (B): MIME'S NARRATIVE (Strophic Form: G minor)
	Introduction:
2053	1. Mime must obey Alberich.
2066	2. The Nibelungs tremble before Alberich's ring.
	Strophe 1:
2084	1. Once the Nibelungs were happy smiths.
2099	2. Now they toil incessantly, mining gold for Alberich.
2130	Transition: Loge asks about Mime's recent affliction.
	Strophe 2:
2136	1. Mime made the tarnhelm for Alberich.
2156	2. Mime hoped to use it himself.
2170	Transition: Loge asks why Mime's plan failed.
	Strophe 3:
2175	1. Mime did not correctly grasp the tarnhelm's spell.
2191	2. Alberich became invisible and beat him.
2207	RETRANSITION: MIME IS WARY OF THE STRANGERS
	A': ALBERICH RETURNS (Ternary Form: B♭ minor)
2221	Refrain: Nibelung music
2234	a: Alberich upbraids the Nibelungs.
2252	b: Alberich notices the visitors.
2264	Retransition: Alberich whips Mime.
2267	a': Alberich warns the Nibelungs to obey him.
2288	Coda: Alberich demonstrates the power of the ring.
2296	Refrain: Nibelung music

form (see Table 9.1). The outer sections depict Alberich's power and cruelty, and are themselves ternary (aba'); each is framed by an orchestral refrain. This refrain (marked 'Nibelung music' in Table 9.1) is characterized by rising or falling sequences on the material

Ex. 9.4

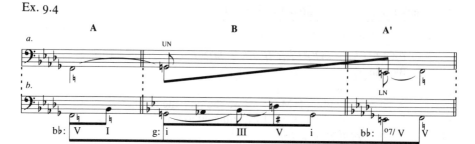

which concluded the Second Transformation; in fact, the final section of the latter (mm. 1878–93; 114/1/1–114/4/4) functions simultaneously as the first refrain, thus effecting a structural overlap. The middle section, Mime's narrative, loosely suggests a tri-strophic form, and is separated from the outer sections by transitional passages focusing upon Wotan and Loge. Sections 1 and 3 articulate Bb minor through unresolved dominants, while Section 2 effects strong harmonic closure in G minor.

This ternary form correlates with the episode's macro-tonal design as shown in Ex. 9.4. At the deepest structural level (Ex. 9.4a), F as dominant of Bb minor is neighboured by G and E (two members of the 'controlling' diminished seventh chord). At a somewhat later level (Ex. 9.4b), Section A resolves its dominant locally to Bb major; Section B expands G minor through a i–III–V–i arpeggiation; and Section A' leads vii°⁷/V to the final unresolved dominant. Episode 12 is thus tonally closed but harmonically open.

Although the complete draft of Section A differs little from its final version, a few words are in order concerning the all-important Tarnhelm theme. Wagner sketched both appearances of this motif (mm. 1930 ff. and mm. 1953 ff.; 117/2/6 ff. and 118/3/2 ff.) in Ab minor;[8] however, as Ex. 9.5 shows, he sometimes notated the Fb triads (bvi) as E minor chords. He marked the theme for 'winds' ('Bl[äser]') in the draft, and actually began to score it for three clarinets and bass clarinet. However, no sooner had he written out the first eight bars for Clarinets 1 and 2 than he crossed out the parts and rescored the motif for four muted horns in E. Wagner then went back to the F minor chord at 'Her das Geschmeid!' (mm. 1927–8; 117/2/3–4), which he had originally given to four horns; in order not to anticipate the scoring of the Tarnhelm theme, he reassigned this chord to low woodwinds.

---

[8] The Schirmer vocal score (p. 118) notates the second statement in G♯ minor.

Ex. 9.5

Ex. 9.6

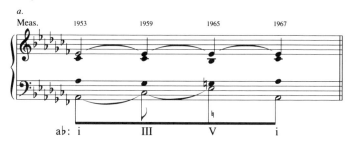

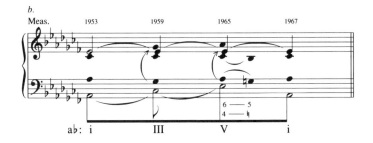

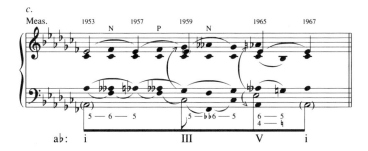

It is unlikely that Wagner's rescoring of the Tarnhelm motif was motivated, as Knapp feels, by a conviction that 'the winds would not have the necessary carrying power'.[9] Surely Wagner was searching for a timbre which, in combination with the theme's prominent open fifths, would convey an aural sense of the eerie power residing in the Tarnhelm. He certainly succeeded—this theme sounds invisible! In fact, its first appearance creates such a radical disjunction with its musical surroundings that the motif seems almost to have fallen in from another world. The following discussion explores the process by which Wagner gradually integrates this alien entity into the musical texture.

As shown in Ex. 9.6, the Tarnhelm theme arpeggiates i–III–V–i in A♭ minor; the tonic and mediant are expanded by 5–6–5 neighbouring motion and connected by a passing tone, while the cadential $^6_4$ is represented by an 'apparent tonic'. The antecedent phrase moves from i to III (represented at the surface level by an open fifth on C♭); the consequent phrase neighbours III before progressing to V–i. In the later stages of the Ring (especially Götterdämmerung), only the first phrase is used, throwing the theme's harmonic/tonal weight upon C♭ (or B).

To understand Section A.b, in which the Tarnhelm theme first appears, it is necessary first to consider Section A.a, the initial quarrel between Alberich and Mime (mm. 1894–1929; 115/1/1–117/2/5). As shown in Ex. 9.7a, this section prolongs the dominant of B♭ minor through an expansion of vii°⁷/V; the latter is unfolded into V⁷/V, which then resolves to F minor. The first statement of the Tarnhelm theme (antecedent phrase only) thus follows an F minor triad (mm. 1927–9; 117/2/3–5), while the second (complete) statement is succeeded by an F major triad (m. 1969; 119/1/1). As Ex. 9.7b suggests, this theme's A♭ minor could be interpreted as an unfolded upper third of the minor dominant of B♭.[10] However, the disjunction in tone colour, range, and modality at m. 1930 (117/2/6) makes this relationship initially very difficult to hear. Wagner gradually draws the connection by means of a rising bass-line which connects the previous F (m. 1927; 117/2/3) through G♭ (mm. 1944; 118/1/5) and G (m. 1951; 118/2/6) with the A♭ of the second Tarnhelm statement (mm. 1953–68; 118/3/2–118/4/8). After A♭ has unfolded back into an active V/B♭ minor (m. 1969; 119/1/1), the latter is intensified through another expansion of vii°⁷/V (mm. 1974–83; 119/2/1–119/3/6); this

---

[9] 'The Instrumentation Draft', 292.
[10] The appearances of the Tarnhelm motif are represented by the abbreviation 'TH' in Exx. 9.7, 9.9, and 9.11.

Ex. 9.7

a.

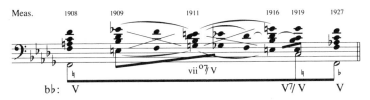

b.

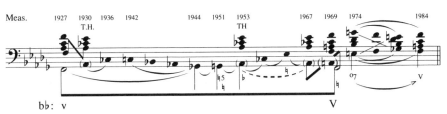

c.

d.

Ex. 9.8

Meas.   2014   2026   2038   2049 2051   2061   2084

retransition, during which the invisible Alberich beats Mime, prepares for section A.*a'*.

As outlined in Table 9.1, Alberich warns the Nibelungs to bow
before his might in a symmetrical seven-part arch (mm. 1984–2013;
120/1/1–121/2/3). The bass-line delineates the dominant expansion
graphed in Ex. 9.7c; this resolves to Bb *major* at m. 2004 (120/4/6).
Suddenly (m. 2008; 121/1/4) woodwinds and stopped horns blare out
the Ab minor triad of the Tarnhelm, which now resolves as iv/iv
through iv (m. 2011; 121/2/1) to I (m. 2014; 121/2/4). This gigantic
plagal cadence sets a terrible seal upon Alberich's declaration
of power, and represents a further integration of the key of the
Tarnhelm motif into the governing Bb minor. Section A as a whole
may be interpreted as an enormous auxiliary cadence in that key (Ex.
9.7d).

The two worlds of the drama finally meet. The transition between
A and B (mm. 2035–52; 122/2/1–123/2/2) ushers in Wotan and Loge
with one bar of chromatic fire; then Loge's recitative-like declamation
alternates with Mime's groans, the latter supported by various
Nibelung motifs. The chromatic bass descent from F (m. 2026;
121/5/2) through C (m. 2038; 122/3/1) to A (m. 2049; 123/1/3) is
followed by a Neapolitan half-cadence in A minor (mm. 2050–2;
123/1/4–123/2/2); however, this key is passing between the previous
Bb and the upcoming G minor (Ex. 9.8). The overall Bb–A–G
descent recalls the similar tonal move which introduced Alberich in
Episode 1 (cf. mm. 166–82; 7/3/2–8/3/2).

Mime's narrative loosely suggests strophic form, a procedure
commonly used for operatic narrative songs.[11] Each of its three
strophes comprises two contrasting segments which relate dialectically
as thesis–antithesis; thus the form could be represented as: ab–
a^1b^1–a^2b^2.

The narrative proper is preceded by a two-phrase introduction
(mm. 2053–84; 123/2/3–124/2/5) which establishes G minor through

---

[11] Carolyn Abbate, *Unsung Voices: Opera and Musical Narrative in the Nineteenth Century*
(Princeton, NJ, 1991), 69–87.

Ex. 9.9

a.

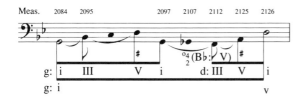

b.

an antecedent–consequent relationship. Wagner began this introduction in 4/4 metre, then changed it to 2/4 by cutting each bar in
half. The conclusion of Phrase 2 (mm. 2076–84; 124/1/4–124/2/5)
also caused him some difficulty; he tried and rejected more than one
version.

Example 9.9 outlines the tonal structure of the narrative. Strophe I
contrasts the Nibelungs' happier days with their present oppression;
the first part (mm. 2084–98; 124/2/5–124/4/6) arpeggiates i–III–V–i
in G minor, the second (mm. 2099–2129; 125/1/1–126/2/2) suggests

Ex. 9.10

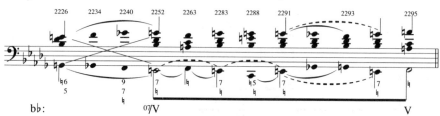

Alberich's key of Bb before modulating to D minor.[12] Strophe 2 begins by transposing the Tarnhelm theme (still in muted horns) to Mime's key of G minor (mm. 2136 ff.; 126/3/4 ff.), then continues with Mime's pathetic plan for using the device.[13] After unfolding the upper third of G minor, this strophe executes a double neighbour around G, recalling the Ring theme at the same pitch level at which it had appeared to initiate the First Transformation (cf. mm. 2161 ff. (127/3/4 ff.) with mm. 749 ff. (53/6/3 ff.)). Strophe 3 suggests the failure of Mime's plan by sounding the Tarnhelm theme in its original key of Ab minor (but played now by low double reeds: mm. 2175 ff.; 128/2/1 ff.). Alberich's ill-treatment of his brother is marked by a return of the Bb minor 'whipping music' (m. 2191; 128/4/3); Bb then moves as III/G minor to an authentic cadence in that key (mm. 2198–2201; 129/2/1–4). Strophes 2 and 3 together thus expand the i–III–V–i arpeggiation which began Strophe 1; the Tarnhelm's Ab minor is a composed-out passing tone (bii) between i and III (Ex. 9.9b). This marks the final integration of the Tarnhelm motif into the musical texture of Episode 12.

A brief retransition focusing upon Loge (mm. 2207–20; 129/3/3–130/1/4) prepares for a cadence in Bb major; however, this is interrupted by the sounds of Alberich's return. The E^{o6}_5 chord at 'Schneller im Zeitmass' (m. 2226; 130/3/1) initiates a long expansion of vii°7/V which overlaps the beginning of Section A'.a (m. 2234; 130/4/5) and terminates at the beginning of Section A'.b (m. 2252; 131/4/1); this expansion contains the dissonant voice-exchange $^{F\ -Gb}_{Gb-F}$ (see Ex. 9.10). During Section A'.b the E°7 chord, reverberating in syncopated clarinets, is led chromatically to V9/Bb. A brief dominant preparation (mm. 2263–66; 132/2/3–132/3/2) leads into Section A'.a', which features a return of Alberich's 'Schein ich nicht schön dir' verse-melody in the form it assumed during the orchestral transition between Episodes 1 and 2 (mm. 2267 ff. (132/3/3 ff.); cf. mm. 461 ff. (28/3/4 ff.)). A final cadence in Bb minor is evaded through a deceptive resolution to the controlling E°7 chord (m. 2283; 133/2/1). This ushers in the climactic coda (mm. 2288–95; 133/3/2–133/4/3), during which Alberich demonstrates the terrible power of the ring. A statement of the Ring motif over V/F minor announces the transformation of the Rhinedaughters' joyous song ('Rheingold! Rheingold! Heiajaheia!') into the baleful Power of the Ring theme. The latter (mm. 2291–5; 133/3/5–133/4/3) alternates E°7 and Gb major chords before resolving to a chilling F major triad; it thus encapsulates the most important tonal relationships of the episode.[14] The concluding refrain (mm. 2296–2319; 133/4/4–134/4/6) restores the F dominant pedal which introduced the episode.

III. EPISODE 13 (MM. 2320–2766; 134/5/1–155/4/5)

The prose sketch outlines the action of this episode quite succinctly:

[Alberich] boasts about the hoard and about his power: L. persuades him to demonstrate the power of the tarnhelm also: A. transforms himself into a toad; L. captures him in this state, and tears the tarnhelm off him. Alberich in his natural form is dragged as a prisoner through the ravines to the rocky heights.

The prose draft fleshes out this sketch in great detail, including Alberich's transformation into a serpent. The versification caused Wagner little difficulty, and the wording of the verse draft generally matches that of the fair copy and 1853 printing; as always, he made a few minor changes while setting the text to music.

In composing this episode, Wagner faced the challenge of integrating into a coherent musical structure a great deal of dramatic incident: the contest of wits between Loge and Alberich, the latter's plan to rule the world, Loge's clever taunting of the dwarf, Alberich's successive transformations into a serpent and a toad, and the gods' climactic capture of the Nibelung. Wagner's solution—a most imaginative one—was to organize the episode as a nine-part rondo in which a recurrent musical refrain (A) alternates with four contrasting episodes: ABA¹CA²DA³EA⁴ (Table 9.2). The refrain recurs each time in the controlling key of A major, while the episodes explore different tonalities and thematic material.

---

[14] In the complete draft, Wagner first preceded 'Zitt're und zage' with a loud statement of the Gold fanfare in Bb minor and cadenced on an F *minor* triad; he later inserted the Ring motif, then later still deleted the Gold theme and changed the final chord to major.

TABLE 9.2 Episode 13: Structural outline

Meas.	Section and Content
	INTRODUCTION: PREPARATIONS FOR THE CONTEST OF WITS
2320	1. Wotan informs Alberich why they have come.
2333	2. Loge reminds Alberich how he once served him.
2343	3. Alberich remembers well how Loge served him!
	REFRAIN 1 (A): THE CONTEST BEGINS (A major)
2354	1. Loge admires Alberich's treasure.
2380	2. Wotan learns that Alberich plans to use it to conquer the world.
	EPISODE 1 (B): ALBERICH'S PLAN (D♭ major → B♭ minor)
2421	1(a). The gods will be snared by Alberich's gold.
2446	2(a′). Like Alberich, they will renounce love for wealth.
2476	3(b). At present the gods despise the Nibelungs.
2488	*Recitative*: But beware! All will succumb to his gold!
2502	4(c). Fear the day when the hoard rises from the depths!
	REFRAIN 2 (A¹): THE CONTEST CONTINUES (A major)
2522	Loge pretends to marvel at Alberich's might (bar: 8 + 8 + 16 bars).
	EPISODE 2 (C): ALBERICH'S SAFEGUARD (D minor)
2554	1a. *Loge*: The Nibelungs must continue to obey Alberich.
2567	b. Yet what if someone were to steal the ring?
2587	2a. *Alberich*: Loge thinks he is so smart!
2603	b. The tarnhelm renders the dwarf invisible.
2613	c. He is safe even from Loge!
	REFRAIN 3 (A²): THE CONTEST CONTINUES (A minor → G♯ minor)
2624	1. Loge has never seen such a wonder; he can't believe it!
2643	2. Alberich is ready. Into what should he transform himself?
	EPISODE 3 (D): THE SERPENT (G♯ minor)
2656	1. Alberich murmurs a spell and disappears.
2664	2. A huge serpent appears; Loge feigns fright.
2679	3. Alberich reappears; Loge compliments him.
	REFRAIN 4 (A³): THE CONTEST CONTINUES (A minor → G♯ minor)
2692	1. Loge wonders if Alberich could become very small.
2707	2. Alberich is ready for this challenge also.
	EPISODE 4 (E): THE TOAD (G♯ minor)
2717	1. Alberich murmurs a spell and disappears.
2723	2. A small toad appears; the gods capture it.
2735	3. Alberich reappears; Loge binds him.
	REFRAIN 5 (A⁴): THE CONTEST CONCLUDES (A major)
2745	Alberich's captors drag him into the shaft.

The rondo proper is preceded by an introduction (mm. 2320–53; 134/5/1–137/1/3), during which Loge and Alberich prepare for their contest of wits. This section is marked by the gradual diatonicization of the Loge music, as it quickly flits from one tonal level to another, almost as if the two protagonists were disputing over the key in which their duel should be fought. Ironically, Loge allows Alberich himself to choose A major (mm. 2350–4; 136/4/4–137/2/1), an unfortunate choice for the dwarf: while closely related (through modal mixture) to Loge's F♯, the key of A represents a semitone depression of Alberich's B♭.

The 'rondo theme' does not remain static, but continuously evolves from one refrain to the next. In Section A, it comprises a two-bar scalar ascent representing Alberich's aspirations (mm. 2354–5; 137/2/1–2) checked by a six-bar descent based upon the diatonicized Loge motif (mm. 2356–61; 137/2/3–137/3/2); this complex is immediately repeated (mm. 2362–9; 137/3/3–137/4/4), after which the scalar ascent evolves into the theme of the Rising Hoard (mm. 2370 ff. and mm. 2399 ff.; 137/4/5 ff. and 139/1/1 ff.). Section A^1 begins with a varied statement of the rondo theme (mm. 2522 ff.; 144/1/1 ff.), and after repeating it moves on to a rather flippant idea which combines an accelerated version of the fifth bar of the Valhalla motif with the diatonic Loge figure (mm. 2538 ff.; 144/3/6 ff.). Often dubbed the 'Arrogance of Power' theme, this motivic combination signifies Loge's mockery of Alberich's plan to storm Valhalla. It initiates each of the final three refrains (Sections A^2, A^3, and A^4; see mm. 2624 ff., mm. 2692 ff., and mm. 2745 ff.; 148/2/5 ff., 152/1/5 ff., and 154/4/3 ff.), replacing the original scale/Loge complex and thereby suggesting that Alberich has fallen victim to his own ambition.

Section B recounts Alberich's plan to snare the immortals through his gold; based upon both associative and directional tonality, it progresses from the Valhalla key of D♭ major (cf. especially mm. 2476 ff.; 142/1/1 ff.) to the B♭ minor of Alberich and the hoard (mm. 2502 ff.; 143/1/5 ff.). In Section C, Alberich explains to Loge how he is protected by the magic of the tarnhelm; the latter motif appears in its associative key (now respelled as G♯ minor: mm. 2603 ff.; 147/2/4 ff.), but this is embedded within an overall arpeggiation of D minor (iv/A). Sections D and E contain the two transformations; they introduce the Dragon and Toad themes respectively, each in the tarnhelm's key of G♯ minor (mm. 2664 ff. and mm. 2723 ff.; 150/3/1 ff. and 153/4/3 ff.). It should also be noted that the refrains themselves become tonally more fluid as the episode proceeds: the first is securely framed by A major, but the second progresses by ascending thirds from B minor to A, and the next two modulate from

Ex. 9.11

a.   *b.*

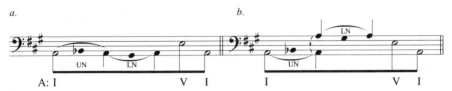

c.

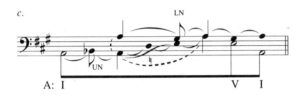

d.

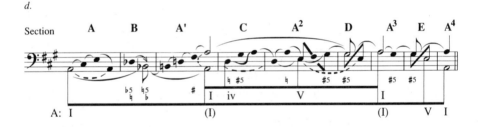

A to G♯. The fifth (depicting the gods' triumph) restores tonal emphasis upon A major, but energizes it through an unresolved dominant pedal.

The remarkable tonal coherence of this extended episode may be demonstrated by a series of four graphs (Ex. 9.11). The first (Ex. 9.11*a*) shows that the initial tonic of a fundamental I–V–I progression in A major is neighboured by both B♭ and G♯ (the keys of Alberich and the Tarnhelm). The second graph (Ex. 9.11*b*) displays this neighbouring motion as occuring in two different registers. The third (Ex. 9.11*c*) reveals that the A–G♯–A motion is supported by a subordinate I–iv–V–I progression, and that the fundamental V–I resolution itself supports a less important G♯–A motion. Finally, the fourth graph (Ex. 9.11*d*) suggests how this structure is elaborated at a later level. Although the G♯ minor or Sections D and E is both times understood as the unfolded upper third of V/A, the first G♯ is structurally more important than the root of V, while the second is clearly subordinate to it. This distinction corresponds to the difference in tonal weight between the dragon and toad transformations.

Although both the complete draft and the instrumentation draft contain several interesting deviations from the final score, the most intriguing cases concern Section B (Alberich's plan to storm Valhalla) and Section D (the dwarf's transformation into a serpent).

In its final form, Section B begins with two parallel statements: the first ('Die in linder Lüfte Weh'n': mm. 2424 ff.; 139/4/7 ff.) begins in C♯ major and leads to a half-cadence in C minor ('euch Göttliche fang' ich mir alle!'), while the second ('Wie ich der Liebe abgesagt': mm. 2446 ff.; 140/4/3 ff.) begins in C minor and ends with a half-cadence in D♭ ('nach Gold, nur sollt ihr noch gieren!'). D♭ major is then confirmed by the Valhalla theme (mm. 2476 ff.; 142/1/1 ff.). However, the complete draft reveals that the keys of these two half-cadences were originally reversed: the first occurred in C♯ minor, in which key the Renunciation theme soon followed, while the second occurred in C minor (soon 'corrected' by a turn to V⁷/D♭). While scoring, Wagner apparently decided that the Renunciation motif should return in its 'proper' key of C minor. After he had copied out the vocal line, he overwrote it in both the complete draft and the instrumentation draft, exchanging the keys of the half-cadences. He then orchestrated the accompaniment, making tonal adjustments as needed, but not bothering to write out these changes in the complete draft. In the final version, the C–D♭ relationship of the two half-cadences represents an 'expressive' tonal intensification as well as an 'associative' juxtaposition of the Renunciation and Valhalla keys.

Apropos the appearance of the Dragon theme in the complete draft, Westernhagen wrote: 'The ponderous motive of the giant serpent, identified in the sketch by the word "snake" above it, is another to be altered: the quavers in the sketch, to which it uncoils in the last three bars, became crotchets in the score.'[15] Deathridge transcribed the first eight bars of the theme, then chastised Westernhagen for misreading the draft: 'It is not clear why Westernhagen refers to "quavers" in the last three bars. Perhaps he mistook the crescendo signs, which are sometimes written close to the stems of the crotchets, for beams.'[16] However, Westernhagen was correct. The Appendix transcribes the complete draft version of mm. 2664–78 (150/3/1–151/3/1), some of which is heavily overwritten and extremely

---

[15] *The Forging of the 'Ring'*, 46.
[16] 'Wagner's Sketches for the "Ring"', 389.

difficult to read. It seems clear that Westernhagen was referring not to the crotchets three bars before Loge's 'Ohe! Ohe!', but to the quavers at Wotan's 'wie wuchs so rasch . . .', which Wagner *did* augment to crotchets while scoring.

However, the situation is somewhat more complex than either Westernhagen or Deathridge imply. In the complete draft (see transcription), seven measures of the unison Dragon theme lead to a climactic G minor chord; the theme is absent from the next three bars ('Ohe! ohe! . . . Schone Loge das Leben!'), then reappears in the bass as a sequential two-bar quaver pattern leading to $V^7/G\sharp$ minor. Wagner scored the first seven measures for two bass tubas in B♭ doubled an octave lower by contrabass tuba in E♭.[17] He then filled in the next three bars with a new continuation of the Dragon theme; this continuation originally featured descending octaves, later changed to tenths. Wagner first scored the concluding two bars of quavers as drafted, then expanded them to four bars of crotchets, doubling the original note-values in the vocal part.

[17] Changed for the 1872 printing to F and C respectively.

10 Third Transformation and Scene Four

> *Das Rheingold* is finished—: but *I* am finished as well!!! ...
> Believe me, no work has ever been composed like this before: I
> imagine my music must be terrible; it is a morass of horrors and
> sublimities!
>
> (Wagner to Franz Liszt, 15 January 1854)

I. THE THIRD TRANSFORMATION

As mentioned earlier, the third paragraph of the prose sketch outlines the events of both Scenes 3 and 4 of the completed opera;
the sentence 'Alberich in his natural form is dragged as a prisoner
through the ravines to the rocky heights' implies some sort of transition. This suggests that Wagner originally conceived *Das Rheingold*
in his usual three-act format, with Act III containing two scenes
(Nibelheim–Valhalla) separated by an orchestral interlude. By the
time he wrote the prose draft, he had of course decided upon a
continuous four-scene structure, and he elaborated the transition
between the last two scenes as follows:

The scene appears to sink from top to bottom, so that we now seem to
ascend. The transformation occurs in exactly the reverse manner as the
previous one: finally the rocky region of the second scene reappears: only it
is still enveloped in a yellowish dark haze, as at the conclusion of the second
scene after Freia was carried off.

The description in the verse draft approaches that of the 1853 printing,
although Wagner did make a few changes while writing out the fair
copy; for example, the 'yellowish dark haze' became a 'pale mist'.
Again, none of the textual manuscripts mention the Nibelung anvils.
The stage directions in the score do not specify the 'retrograde' effect
('in exactly the reverse manner as the previous one'), as this is
obvious from the music; at one point however, the score does read:
'the transformation leads again past the smithies'.
 Westernhagen has pointed out that the complete draft contains a
revision of the Loge figurations at m. 2799 (157/1/1);[1] he might also

---

[1] *The Forging of the 'Ring'*, 47.

Ex. 10.1

a.

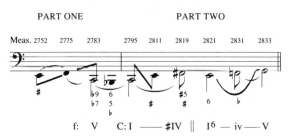

b.

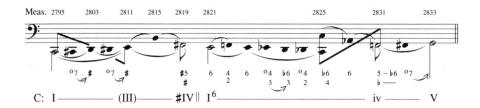

have mentioned a similar revision at m. 2807 (157/3/2). The change to 6/4 metre at m. 2833 (158/5/1) occurs four bars later in the complete draft than in the *Partiturerstschrift*; otherwise, the two manuscripts basically agree.

Like the Second Transformation, the Third comprises two parts: a Postlude to Scene 3 (mm. 2752–94; 155/2/1–156/3/8) followed by a Prelude to Scene 4 (mm. 2795–856; 156/4/1–159/5/4). In keeping with its 'retrograde' effect, this interlude relates musically to its predecessor as follows:

Second Transformation	*Third Transformation*
Part 1 (Postlude): Loge music	Part 1 (Postlude): Nibelung music
Part 2 (Prelude): Nibelung music	Part 2 (Prelude): Loge music

Part 1 of the Third Transformation overlaps with the end of Episode 13 (just as Part 2 of the Second Transformation overlapped with the beginning of Episode 12): it starts with the downward-plunging Ring

motif over E as V/A (mm. 2752 ff.; 155/2/1 ff.). Eight bars of the
Nibelung/'Wehe!' combination (mm. 2767 ff.; 155/5/1 ff.) prolong this
dominant, which rises quietly to F at the entrance of the a capella
anvils (m. 2775; 156/1/1). The brass soon let out a fortissimo howl of
anguish (the 'dritte so traut' augmentation: m. 2783; 156/2/3) over C
as V/F minor; this leads, diminuendo, to a half-cadence at m. 2795
(156/4/1). Thus Part 1 absorbs its initial E (V/A) into a dominant on
C; this C is then reinterpreted as a tonic to begin Part 2 (Ex. 10.1a).

Tonally, Part 2 moves from I to V in C major, ending on an
extensive dominant preparation (mm. 2833 ff.; 158/5/1 ff.). As Ex.
10.1a suggests, it also displays a rather unorthodox interruption structure: the interruption occurs after the pre-dominant harmony (♯IV)
rather than the usual dominant. This tonal design emphasizes the
C/F♯ tritone, a crucial sonority in Scene 4, and focuses attention
upon Loge's original pitch level (F♯).

Thematically, Part 2 comprises three subsections, each alternating
or combining the Loge figurations with other motifs or verse-melodies:
Giants and Arrogance of Power in the first (mm. 2795–820; 156/4/1–
158/1/3), 'siech und bleich' and 'gold'ne Äpfel' in the second (mm.
2821–32; 158/1/4–158/4/3), 'Rheingold!' and 'Wehe!' in the third
(mm. 2833–56; 158/5/1–159/5/4). The essentially proleptic semantic
references are clear: even as Loge and Wotan bear Alberich and the
ring to Valhalla, the giants are returning with Freia; if she is not
ransomed with the Rhinegold, the gods will wither and die. The first
subsection is shaped as a clear bar form of 8 + 8 + 10 measures; as
Ex. 10.1b shows, it moves sequentially by step from C to E (III),
then by ascending fifths to F♯ (♯IV). The second subsection 'starts
over again' harmonically on I⁶; it first recalls Fafner's verse-melody
'siech und bleich | doch sinkt ihre Blüthe . . .' from Episode 6 (cf.
mm. 1119–22; 74/4/1–4), then sequences the one-bar Golden Apples
motive through the F minor triad (iv). The third subsection marks the
arrival at the dominant G, and frames a staccato variant of the Loge
motif (mm. 2839 ff.; 159/1/2 ff.) with the closely related 'Rheingold!'
and 'Wehe!' verse-melodies (mm. 2833 and 2849 respectively; 158/5/1
and 159/4/1).

Although the sequential repetitions of this final transformation
sometimes sound rather mechanical—similar in this regard to those
Liszt was writing at the time[2]—the danger of aural tedium is miti-
gated to a great extent by the continual brilliance and ingenuity
of the orchestration. This is particularly true of Loge's motif, which
Wagner treats to all manner of variation, culminating in the spiky

[2] See especially the Piano Sonata in B minor, composed in 1852–3 and published in 1854.

Ex. 10.2

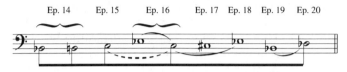

woodwind staccatos suggesting the god's mocking laughter (mm. 2839 ff.; 159/1/2 ff.). Westernhagen displayed great insight when he remarked that 'unlike other characters, Loge reveals his true nature only in the two symphonic interludes'.[3] Certainly the Loge who will ultimately engulf the world in flames appears only in the music of the Second and Third Transformations.

II. SCENE FOUR AS A WHOLE

As shown in the Structural Outline, Scene 4 comprises seven dramatic/musical episodes (Nos. 14–20). Episodes 14 and 16 exhibit directional tonality: each of the remaining five is controlled by a single key. The tonal background of the scene is displayed in Ex. 10.2.

Overall, the scene returns from the Nibelheim key of B♭ minor to the Valhalla key of D♭ major; this ascending minor third is filled in chromatically (B♭–B–C–D♭), and is ultimately encapsulated by the keys of the last two episodes (B♭–D♭). During the chromatic ascent, C is twice prolonged by motion to its upper minor third E♭; the second time, this move is filled in by the passing C♯ minor of Episode 17.

Associative tonality continues to reign. In addition to the Nibelheim/ Valhalla keys (B♭ minor/D♭ major), B minor becomes linked to Alberich's curse, while C♯ minor, the enharmonic parallel of Wotan's D♭, symbolizes the mysterious earth goddess Erda. The giants now enter in the key of E♭ major; this tonality was associated in Episode 6 with Wotan's treaty with the giants (through the verse-melody 'weisst du nicht offen, | ehrlich und frei . . .'; cf. mm. 1061–5; 72/1/2–6). In addition, the progression in Episode 16 from E♭ major to C minor rather subtly recalls the tonal move of Scene 1. Finally, when Donner clears the air in Episode 19, he turns the B♭ minor of Alberich's power over the Nibelungs into a B♭ *major* symbolizing his own power over the storm.

---

[3] *The Forging of the 'Ring'*, 48.

Exactly how the tonal scheme of Scene 4 fits into that of *Das Rheingold* as a whole will be demonstrated in Chapter 11. Yet before examining the individual episodes, one further aspect of Scene 4 should be noted. Up to now, Wagner has kept fairly separate the two worlds of the drama (Valhalla representing civilization, Nibelheim the wilderness). During Scene 4, however, the world of the Nibelungs begins gradually to penetrate and contaminate that of the gods, and this invasion of one world by another results in some extraordinary musical effects.

III. THE SEVEN EPISODES

1. Episode 14 (mm. 2857–3203; 160/1/1–178/5/1)

The prose sketch reads: '[Alberich] pays as ransom the hoard and finally also the ring—which he curses.' The prose draft outlines this episode in detail, largely through prose dialogue; there are few crossings-out or alterations.

Although the verse draft exhibits a number of interesting variants, the most reworked part concerns the climax of the episode, the moment when Alberich pronounces his curse. The first portion, from 'Bin ich nun frei?' through 'doch den Würger zieh' er ihm zu' came fairly easily to Wagner. He began the next part with 'furcht vor dem tode | fessle den feigen,' changed this to 'Dem tode verfallen, | furcht fessle den feigen,' then altered it once more to the familiar 'Dem tode verfallen, | fessle den feigen die furcht.' He continued with 'des ringes tugend | dazu tauge sie ihm', then changed the second line successively to 'nur dazu tauge sie ihm' and 'taug' ihm dazu allein!' He then crossed out these two lines entirely and substituted 'So lang er lebt | sterb' er lechzend dahin!' The remainder of the curse does not differ from its definitive version, although some of the lines do appear in the left margin as second thoughts. Also in the margin are three concluding lines which Wagner omitted in subsequent manuscripts: 'hör es, du gott! | des neidlichen goldes | geniess' nur nach herzensgier!'

In his discussion of this section, Lorenz grumbled that it was 'the only period in the *Ring* which, it must be admitted, is still governed by the recitative-style'.[4] Certainly large portions of Episode 14 *are* set in a declamatory mode, but this represents neither a compositional defect nor a return to an outmoded convention. The recitatives serve

---

[4] *Der musikalische Aufbau*, 279. We recall from Chapter 5 that Lorenz's 'Period 16' comprises Episodes 14 and 15 of the present analysis.

TABLE 10.1 Episode 14: Structural outline

Meas.	Section and Content
	RECITATIVE: THE GODS' FIRST DEMAND (Bipartite)
2857	*Part 1*: Alberich and the gods trade insults.
2899	*Part 2*: Wotan demands the hoard.
	SOLO NO. 1 (ALBERICH): THE HOARD RISES (Bar form: B♭ minor)
2917	*Introduction*: Alberich summons the Nibelungs.
2926	*False beginning*: Wotan refuses to liberate Alberich until all has been paid.
2942	*a*: Alberich feels disgraced.
2954	*a'*: He berates his men.
2966	*b*: He uses the ring to send the Nibelungs fleeing.
	RECITATIVE: THE GODS' SECOND AND THIRD DEMANDS (Bipartite)
2988	*Part 1*: Loge demands the tarnhelm.
3006	*Part 2*: Wotan demands the ring.
	DUET (WOTAN, ALBERICH): THE FATAL CONFLICT (Bipartite: A minor)
	Part 1: Wotan asks:
3023	1. How can you call the ring your own?
3027	2. How did you obtain the gold?
3031	3. Did the gold belong to you?
3035	4. Did the Rhinedaughters give it to you?
	Part 2: Alberich responds:
3040	1. You accuse me of the crime *you* wished to commit?
3047	2. You would have stolen the gold if you could have forged it!
3053	3. How lucky for you that *I* forswore love!
3061	4. Shall my deed benefit you?
3070	5. Beware! if you steal my ring, you sin against all that was, is, and shall be!
3083	*TRANSITION*: WOTAN STEALS THE RING
	SOLO NO. 2 (ALBERICH): THE CURSE (Five-part arch form: B minor)
3117	*Introduction*: Alberich prepares to curse the ring.
3127	*a*: The ring is cursed; it shall bring death to its wearer!
3137	*b*: It shall bring no one happiness!
3141	*c*: Both those who own it and those who do not shall suffer!
3151	*b'*: It shall bring murder rather than gain!
3156	*a'*: The lord of the ring shall be its slave!
3170	*Coda*: Thus the Nibelung blesses his ring!
3180	*Postlude* (Orchestra): Alberich disappears into the ground.

Ex. 10.3

a.

b.

to link together two vocal solos (for Alberich) and a central duet (for Wotan and Alberich). These three musically 'heightened' sections are thus thrown into sharp relief, their effectiveness increased through contrast with their surroundings (Table 10.1).

Each of the three 'set pieces' is tonally closed, in Bb minor, A minor, and B minor respectively. This progression replicates on a lower level the tonal scheme of Episodes 12–14 (Ex. 10.3*a*), and suggests that these three episodes form a large unit dominated by the Nibelungs. On both levels, Bb minor is associated with Alberich's power over his people, and the 'expressive' semitonal descent to A with his downfall at the hands of the gods; but in Episode 14, the rise to B minor represents an expressive semitonal *ascent* from Bb, as Alberich summons his remaining strength and pronounces the curse.

Each of these keys is approached from the E minor of the preceding recitative; E thus functions as a sort of 'trigger tonality' (Ex. 10.3*b*). E minor leads to the dominant of Bb by semitonal motion, as a raised fourth scale degree; it *becomes* the dominant of A minor; and it approaches the dominant of B minor as a normal subdominant. The three dominants involved (F–E–F♯) recall the semitonal neighbouring of V/Bb from Episode 12.

The initial recitative falls into two parts (see Table 10.1). During the first part (mm. 2857–98; 160/1/1–162/4/4), the three protagonists trade insults, in symmetrical alternation: Loge–Alberich–Wotan–Alberich–Loge. Each of Loge's taunts concludes with a mocking variant of his motif (winds and strings), in C and D respectively;

Alberich's rebukes are set to detached string chords, while Wotan's order is supported by broad, sustained harmonies. The tonal level rises to E minor for the second part (mm. 2899–2916; 163/1/1–164/2/1), so that the recitative as a whole ascends 'expressively' C–D–E. The C major promised by the dominant preparation at the end of the Third Transformation has not yet materialized; its local appearance at the beginning of this episode serves only as a point of departure. Alberich's plan to relinquish the hoard but keep the ring is underlined by the ghostly appearance of the Ring, Hoard, and Scheming motifs in low strings.

Although the complete draft of the first recitative differs from the final version only in a few vocal rhythms, it displays more variants in the first solo, Alberich's summoning of the Nibelungs (mm. 2917–87; 164/2/2–167/4/2). Wagner began this passage with a reprise of mm. 2288–95 (133/3/2–133/4/3), the music to which Alberich demonstrated the power of the ring in Episode 12. The complete draft version is written in 4/4 rather than 3/4 metre, and concludes, like its predecessor, on an F minor triad with emphasized fifth; the *Partiturerstschrift* contains the final version. When the Power of the Ring motif reappears at the climax of this solo (mm. 2966 ff.; 166/3/4 ff.), it ends in the complete draft upon the familiar F *major* triad with emphasized *third*, and this doubtless provided the model for Wagner's subsequent alterations. The first appearance of the Hoard motif (mm. 2930 ff.; 164/4/3 ff.) is marked in the complete draft 'hier bloss pizz. in d[en] bassen??' ('here just pizz. in the basses??'), as well as 'od[e]r: Fagott allein' ('or: bassoon alone'). Wagner originally scored it for solo bassoon accompanied by pizzicato basses, then added a second bassoon at the lower octave. At the return of this theme (mm. 2942 ff.; 165/2/6 ff.), the remark 'Tub[a] o[der] Pos[aune]' ('tuba or trombone') in the complete draft was eventually settled in favour of four tubas playing in octaves. Stage directions abound in the draft: 'kuss des ringes', 'Nibelungen mit dem Hort', 'er zeigt den ring', 'die Nibelungen verschwinden'; obviously Wagner mentally choreographed the action as he composed. After a 'false beginning' (mm. 2926–41; 164/3/5–165/2/5), this section unfolds as a clear bar form of 12 + 12 + 22 measures; it brings back the thematic material, the tonality, and the F–Gb–F neighbouring of V/Bb from Episode 12.[5] The moment Alberich once foretold has arrived: the hoard has risen from the silent depths to the light of day!

[5] This entire passage, including the 'false beginning', forms the model for the Prelude to Act I of *Siegfried*.

Ex. 10.4

a. Complete Draft (Version A)

[fo. 30ʳ]
[m. 3061] [Alberich]

lacht? des un – se - lig- sten, angst ver- sehr- ten fluch - fer-ti- ge furchtbar - er that, zu furst -lich- em

b. Complete Draft (Version B)

[fol. 30 ʳ]
[m. 3061]   [Alberich]

lacht?   des un – – se - lig – sten,   angst   ver – sehr – ten   fluch -

fer – ti – ge   furcht - bar - er   that,   zu   fürst - lich - em

The world of the gods has been invaded, visually and musically, by the world of the Nibelungs.

The complete draft differs little from the final version of the second recitative (mm. 2988–3022; 167/4/3–170/1/1), which begins with a varied restatement of Alberich's 'brooding music': he believes he can relinquish the Tarnhelm but still keep the ring. However, the draft of the subsequent Wotan/Alberich duet (mm. 3023–83; 170/1/2–173/2/4) contains much rebarring; for example, Wotan's entire eight-bar segment 'Nüchtern sag' . . . entwandt?' was originally off by two beats. The draft of Alberich's response also displays some rebarring, as well as a recomposed vocal line (Ex. 10.4). The duet's sudden 'explosion' into arioso is triggered by Wotan's demand for the ring. The two protagonists pose four rhetorical questions apiece, each the basis of a discreet musical phrase (Table 10.1); however, Alberich concludes with a fifth remark, warning Wotan that, should the god seize the ring, he would sin against all that ever was, is, or shall be.

Wotan and Alberich now clash physically, to a distorted version of the Spear motif (mm. 3083 ff.; 173/2/4 ff.), here signifying the law which the god is about to violate. As Wotan wrests the ring from

Ex. 10.5

a. Complete Draft

[fo. 31ʳ]
[m. 3151]

b. Partiturerstschrift (Sketch A)

[p. 277]
[m. 3151]

c. Partiturerstschrift (Sketch B)

[p. 277]
[m. 3151]

d. Partiturerstschrift (Final Version)

[p. 277]
[m. 3151]

Alberich, the orchestra shrieks out the Gold motif over a diminished seventh harmony, musically re-creating the moment when Alberich stole the gold (cf. m. 3091 (173/4/1) with m. 704 (50/4/3)). Alberich's cry of despair is underscored by a broken form of the Ring motif and a B♭ minor statement of the 'Weibes Wonne und Werth' melody (mm. 3093 ff.; 173/4/3 ff.). The moment when Wotan puts on the ring marks his moral nadir; he will spend the rest of the tetralogy attempting to atone for this act.[6] While scoring, Wagner revised the passage rhythmically, essentially cutting in half the note-values of the orchestral dotted rhythms (mm. 3099 ff.; 174/1/2 ff.).

The complete draft version of Alberich's Curse (mm. 3117–3203; 174/4/3–178/5/1) is transcribed in the Appendix. While scoring 'Wer ihn besitzt', Wagner elected to insert a measure of preparatory accompaniment (m. 3141; 176/1/1), marking it first into the complete draft. When he came to the instrumentation of 'Ohne Wucher...' (mm. 3151 ff.; 176/3/3 ff.), he decided to expand each of the original two-bar phrases to three bars, marking this in the complete draft (see transcription and Ex. 10.5a). He sketched two different augmentations in the *Partiturerstschrift* (Ex. 10.5b and c) before settling upon yet a third; this final version resulted in a total length of five bars rather than the projected six (Ex. 10.5d). The powerful orchestral Postlude, merely sketched in the complete draft, was enlarged and considerably elaborated while scoring.

The symmetrical formal design of the Curse is shown in Table 10.1, while its tonal structure is displayed in Ex. 10.6. At the background level, this solo is a huge V–i auxiliary cadence in B minor, whose dominant F♯ is neighboured by both G and F (Ex. 10.6a). At a middleground level, F is arpeggiated to suggest V/B♭ minor (Ex. 10.6b): Alberich's original key 'peers through' his new one. The Curse motif itself is an excellent example of a verse-melody which will later be played by the orchestra in order to recall its original words ('Wie durch Fluch er mir gerieth, | verflucht sei dieser Ring!'). The striking harmony of m. 3130 (175/3/2), a C major triad over a pedal F♯ (functionally a conflation of Neapolitan and dominant), was prepared during the Third Transformation through tonal emphasis upon the C–F♯ tritone; it resolves here to V⁹/B minor, but in *Götterdämmerung* will function as a referential sonority, freed from all obligations to resolve.[7] Sections a and a' of the five-part arch are generated by inverting the Ring motif, Sections b and b' by stating

---

[6] Had he immediately returned the ring to the Rhinedaughters, his theft could conceivably have been justified. But by putting it on, Wotan damns himself.

[7] See especially Act II Scene 3, wherein Hagen rallies the Gibichung vassals.

Ex. 10.6

a.

b.

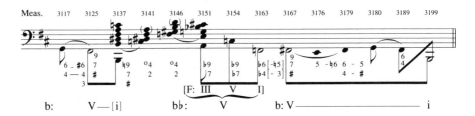

successively the descending seventh chords which, in the original motif, occur simultaneously; Section *c* is based upon the pulsating chords of the Curse's Prelude (a syncopated form of the Nibelungs rhythm). The climax (mm. 3161–3; 177/2/1–3) utilizes the Power of the Ring chords at their original pitch level, while the Postlude (mm. 3180 ff.; 178/1/1 ff.) alters them to suggest C major, the key of the following episode. Alberich leaves the opera to the triple hypermetre which, in Scene 1, had heralded his first appearance.

2. *Episode 15 (mm. 3208–55; 178/5/6–181/2/3)*

This brief episode serves two purposes: it provides welcome relief from the gloom and doom of its predecessor, and it reassembles the rest of the cast in preparation for the ransoming of Freia. The giants approach with their hostage, causing the atmosphere to clear up (although the fortress remains wrapped in mist); Froh, Donner, and Fricka enter; Loge reassures them about the mission's success; and Froh expresses glad feelings over the return of the gods' health and well-being. The prose draft outlines this episode in detail, and its versification caused Wagner few problems.

After a four-bar transition[8] which transforms the previous B minor triad into V^7/C major through the 5–6 technique (mm. 3204–7; 178/5/2–5), the episode falls into two similar halves (25 + 23 bars) which relate formally as AA′ and functionally as antecedent–consequent. Each half contains three distinct components, arranged in an overall | abc | db′c′ | design. Part 1, almost purely orchestral, begins with the Giants rhythm over a big dominant pedal on G; it thus harks back to the second part of the Third Transformation, and suggests that the latter's promise of C major is finally about to be realized. Above this, violins evoke the atmospheric clarification through a rising and falling arch in parallel thirds and sixths (mm. 3208–18; 178/5/6–179/2/2). A reprise of Wellgunde's 'Heia, du Holder!' verse-melody[9] at its original pitch level (mm. 3219–22; 179/2/3–179/3/1) leads to a canon in horns and winds on the Golden Apples motif (mm. 3223–32; 179/3/2–179/4/5). Part 2 replaces the initial violin arch with Alberich's pulsating Resentment chords (mm. 3233–6; 180/1/1–180/2/1), then leads again through 'Heia, du Holder!' (mm. 3237–40; 180/2/2–180/3/1) to a tonicization of the dominant G. At this point Froh, that most minor of minor characters, gets his one chance to shine vocally: he launches into a beautiful cantilena based upon the Apples motif ('Wie liebliche Luft . . .': mm. 3241 ff.; 180/3/2 ff.). His final authentic cadence (mm. 3251–2; 181/1/4–5), the long-awaited resolution to C major, ushers in another canon; Wagner originally based this upon the Apples motif (underscoring the parallelism with the end of Part 1), but wrote out an alternative form in the complete draft drawn from the conclusion of Froh's arioso ('die leidlos ewiger Jugend . . .'). The first canon refers back to the opera's Prelude through its horn timbre and sequential triadic arpeggiations, while the theme of the second already suggests the Rainbow motif which will bring the drama to a close.

3. Episode 16 (3264–455; 181/4/3–192/2/4)

'Finally [the giants] content themselves with as much gold as will cover Freia' reads the second paragraph of the prose sketch. The third informs us that 'the giants obtain the hoard, and also the ring—which Wod. first wanted to keep . . .', while a supplementary note suggests that 'Wodan is momentarily willing to give up Freia for the sake of the ring.' Thus this episode is primarily concerned with

---

[8] This transition is Janus-faced: motivically and textually it looks back to Episode 14 (Ring motif, Wotan's words), while harmonically it points forward to Episode 15.

[9] Wagner probably brought back this verse-melody here because of the verbal association between 'Holder' and 'Holda' (as in 'Freia, die Holda').

the ransoming of Freia, followed by Wotan's refusal to relinquish the ring. The prose draft outlines these events in detail, largely through prose dialogue, and first mentions the giants' staves (*Pfähle*), obviously introduced for the purpose of measuring the hoard. Versification came rather easily; only Wotan's climactic refusal caused some difficulty.

Westernhagen noted that the orchestral cadences which punctuate Fasolt's first address (mm. 3269 and 3273; 182/1/3 and 182/2/1) differ in the complete draft from their final version: in both cases, a $\hat{5}-\hat{6}-\hat{7}-\hat{8}$ melodic pattern was replaced by $\hat{2}-\hat{7}-\hat{5}-\hat{1}$.[10] What Westernhagen did not realize was that Wagner actually scored the original cadences, then wrote out alternative forms in the *Partiturerstschrift*; he ultimately used the second versions, but never crossed out the first. In the complete draft, two bars of the Giants rhythm precede the piling of the hoard, but these were cut to one while scoring (m. 3309; 183/4/1); conversely, one measure of the Nibelungs/Giants combination at Fafner's 'Noch mehr! Noch mehr hieher!' was expanded to two (mm. 3356–7; 186/2/4–5).

Like Episode 6 (the giants' entrance in Scene 2), this episode is controlled by a double tonic: it juxtaposes Eb major and C minor, gradually shifting tonal emphasis from the first key to the second. As suggested earlier, the tonal progression Eb–C recalls that of Scene 1: the renunciation of love in favour of power is about to be repeated. In addition, Eb major has also been linked to Wotan's treaty with the giants. F minor, the giants' original key, is often tonicized as iv/C, while C as a major triad functions locally as V/F; thus, this episode reprises the C–F relationship which opened Episode 6. In addition, G minor is occasionally tonicized as v/C, without any specific associative meaning.

The episode contains four parts: the preparations for measuring the hoard, the actual piling of the hoard, the examination of the hoard for chinks, and Wotan's refusal to surrender the ring. Parts 1–3 are unified thematically through the use of the Treaty, Giants, Nibelungs, Hoard, and Freia motifs, and tonally by the Eb/C oscillation. By contrast, Part 4 uses themes associated with the gold and the ring, and initiates a chain of descending thirds; these significant changes are triggered by Wotan's outburst 'Wie? diesen Ring?'

After a brief transition, during which Fricka's half-cadence in C minor and Fasolt's resolution to Eb establish the basic tonal dichotomy (mm. 3256–64; 181/2/4–181/4/3), the episode begins. Part 1 (mm. 3264–308; 181/4/3–183/3/7) contains two dialogue cycles for Fasolt

[10] *The Forging of the 'Ring'*, 51–2.

and Wotan, during which the orchestra encapsulates the basic power/ love conflict by juxtaposing the Treaty and Freia motifs. Fasolt's first address ('Auf Riesenheim's | ragender Mark...') frames a i–iv$_t$–V progression in C minor[11] with cadences in E♭ major, while Wotan's response ('Bereit liegt die Lösung...') moves from E♭ to a half-cadence in C minor. Fasolt's second address ('Das Weib zu missen...') moves iv$_t$–V in C minor, while Wotan's order ('So stellt das Maass...') tonicizes G minor. Part 1 concludes on a half-cadence in G (v$_t$/C), as the oboe plays a pathetic variant of the goddess's motif.

Part 2, the piling of the hoard (mm. 3309–371; 183/4/1–187/2/5), is structured as a sort of five-part rondo (ABA^{1}B^{1}A^2); the recurrent orchestral refrain is based upon the 'power' themes (Treaty, Hoard, Giants, Nibelungs), while the contrasting sections develop a plaintive form of the Freia motif. Section A presents the Treaty theme in its usual two-part canon, undergirded by the Giants rhythm, and leads from E♭ to a half cadence in G minor (v$_t$/C: m. 3317; 184/1/3). Section B ('Eilt mit dem Werk...') moves from V/G to V/C, preparing for a return of the refrain in C minor. During Section A^1, the Treaty/Giants combination is joined, first by the Nibelungs motif (mm. 3325 ff.; 184/3/1 ff.), then by that of the Hoard (mm. 3339 ff.; 185/2/3 ff.). The significance of this thematic conflict has usually been overlooked: not only does it suggest that the Nibelung hoard is rising yet a second time, but it also depicts musically a fact to which Wagner's Eddaic sources often refer: the strife between the dwarfs and the Giants. In addition, it represents yet another musical 'invasion' of the gods' world by Alberich's underground forces. Section A^1 juxtaposes C minor as tonic with C as V/F minor (the musical 'pun' associated with the Giants in Episode 6). The second episode (B^1: 'Tief in der Brust...') expands F with a i–iv$_t$–V–[i] progression whose expected resolution is interrupted (m. 3356; 186/2/4). At this point Donner, who has but one answer for all things great and small, elects to settle matters with his hammer, disrupting the tonal equilibrium with a violent formal interpolation (mm. 3359–67; 186/3/2–187/2/1). Wotan restores both order and key with a truncated return of the Treaty motif in its original E♭ major (A^2: mm. 3368–71; 197/2/2–5).

Part 3 (mm. 3371–416; 187/2/5–190/1/1) comprises two parallel dramatic cycles. During the first, Fafner peers through the hoard and espies Freia's hair; during the second, Fasolt is struck by his beloved's glance. In each case, a ghostly remnant of the Hoard theme

---

[11] The subscript 't' means that the designated harmonic function has been tonicized; thus i–iv$_t$–V in C minor implies a temporary emphasis upon F minor, the key of the giants.

is interrupted by a theme associated with Freia: Fafner's materialism evokes the Golden Apples motif (at its original D major pitch level), while Fasolt's emotional reaction generates rising sequences upon the goddess's personal motif. Cycle 1 (mm. 3371–90; 187/2/5–188/3/2) cadences upon V/C minor and contains the payment of the Tarnhelm, while Cycle 2 (mm. 3391–3416; 188/3/3–190/1/1) progresses towards G minor and includes Fafner's demand for the ring; however, the tonicized v/C is disrupted by Wotan's violent reaction.

Part 4 (mm. 3417–55; 190/1/2–192/2/4) frames a furious rhythmic development of the Ring motif (mm. 3431–41; 191/1/1–191/3/4) with sections based upon the related 'Rheingold!' and 'Wehe!' verse-melodies. Tonally, it features a remarkable chain of descending thirds: Db–Bb–G–Eb–C–Ab–F. It is almost as if Wotan's refusal to surrender the ring penetrates deep into the earth itself, where it awakens a slumbering subterranean force. Finally (m. 3456: Langsam) the tonal level sinks yet another third to Erda's Db minor, respelled by Wagner as C♯.

4. Episode 17 (mm. 3456–521; 192/3/1–194/4/6)

The Erda episode is obviously a pivotal passage in the *Ring* as a whole. Musically it recalls the *creatio ex nihilo* of the cycle's opening,[12] while textually *and* musically it forecasts the concluding scene of cosmic destruction; reaching out in both directions across the temporal continuum, it simultaneously embraces the beginning and end of the entire drama. Yet this crucial episode invariably provokes questions: Why do the gods ultimately perish even though Wotan heeds Erda's warning and relinquishes the ring? If the gods are ineluctably doomed from the outset, what sense does her warning make at all? Questions such as these go to the very heart of what the *Ring* is all about.

The genesis of this episode is so complex that we must begin outside the *Rheingold* manuscripts.[13] The first paragraph of the 1848 scenario states that Wotan wished to withhold Alberich's ring from the giants, but that 'Wodan yields on the advice of the three women of fate (Norns), who warn him of the downfall of the gods themselves.' This phrase—the origin of the Erda episode—is preceded by a sentence describing how Alberich cursed his ring, that 'it should be

---

[12] We recall from Chapter 6 that the composition of the Erda episode was intimately linked with that of the *Rheingold* Prelude.

[13] For a somewhat more extensive discussion of this episode, including a transcription of the verse draft, see Darcy, '"Alles was ist, endet!"'.

the ruin of all who possess it'. A causal connection is thus implied: if Wotan keeps the ring, the gods are doomed, but if he gives it up, they may somehow be saved.

The Norns' warning to Wotan was, of course, not originally meant to be staged; the audience for *Siegfried's Tod* would learn of it through Alberich's narration to Hagen at the beginning of Act II. As mentioned in Chapter 3, it did find its scenic counterpart in an event intended for the third act: three mermaids with swans' wings warn Siegfried of the curse, and implore him to cast away the ring. Here the causal connection is explicit: if Siegfried does not relinquish the ring, he will die this very day. We have already seen (especially in Chapter 6) the far-reaching results of the dramatic parallelism which Wagner thereby established between the Norns and the Rhinedaughters.

As pointed out in Chapter 3, the prose sketches for Act III of *Der junge Siegfried* show the gradual emergence of the notion of the gods' self-destruction: an earlier entry reads 'Wodan and the Wala: end of the gods', while a later one runs 'Wodan and the Wala—Guilt of the gods, and their necessary downfall'. This marks the first appearance in the *Ring* manuscripts of the as yet unnamed Erda.

The encounter between Wotan and the Wala described in the prose draft of *Der junge Siegfried* contains many features subsequently incorporated into the Erda episode of *Das Rheingold*: the goddess's eerie appearance, rising from the earth amid a darkening atmosphere, illuminated only by a bluish light; her proclamation of wisdom 'ich weiss wie alles war, ich weiss wie alles ist, wie alles sein wird, weiss ich auch' ('I know how everything was, I know how everything is, how everything shall be I also know'), words later transposed almost literally to *Das Rheingold* Scene 4; and finally her mention of the Norns, whose parentage she does not yet claim. The scene culminates in Wotan's announcement that he now wills the end of the gods and yields to the new generation: 'Vergehe das alte, das neue erblühe!' ('Let the old pass away, let the new flourish!'). However, at this stage in the evolution of the *Ring*, Wotan has as yet no intention of burning down Valhalla; in the following scene, he genially yields place to Siegfried without a struggle.

The prose sketch to *Das Rheingold* states that Wotan is 'warned' to relinquish the ring. The prose sketch to *Die Walküre* informs us that Wotan overpowered the Wala and begot Brünnhilde with her. A supplementary jotting in the pocket notebook reveals that the Wala—not the Norns, as in the 1848 scenario—warned Wotan; a second jotting for the first time identifies her as Erda (a name postulated by Jacob Grimm as that of the ancient German earth goddess) and makes the conception of Brünnhilde follow as a direct result of this warning.

In the prose draft of *Das Rheingold*, the outline of the Erda episode appropriates several elements from Act III Scene I of *Der junge Siegfried*: the darkening of the stage, the bluish light, Erda's rising from the earth, her words 'was war, weiss ich, was sein wird weiss ich', and her reference to the Norns, who are now 'three daughters, primally created' ('drei Töchter, urerschaffene'). Finally, Erda warns that the gods' end is slowly approaching ('langsam nahet euch ein ende'), but that it will occur immediately if he does not give up the ring ('doch in jähem sturz ist es da, lässt du den ring nicht los!'). Apparently Wotan can no longer prevent, but only postpone, the end of the gods.

The verse draft contains some interesting changes *vis-à-vis* the prose draft. In the latter, Erda presumably appeared to all the gods ('Erda . . . steigt herauf'); she now appears only—or at least primarily—to Wotan ('von ihm beleuchtet wird Wodan plötzlich Erda sichtbar'). The destruction which threatens Wotan is now described as 'irretrievable dark perdition' ('rettunglos dunklem verderben') and Erda herself as 'the eternal world's primordial Wala' ('der ew'gen welt | Ur-Wala'). Her three primally conceived daughters communicate Erda's knowledge by night; the line 'what I see, they tell' ('was ich sehe, | sagen sie') was later changed to 'what I see, the Norns tell you at night' ('was ich sehe, | sagen dir nächtlich die Nornen'). A passage urging Wotan to heed the Norns' advice was revised in the verse draft, then eliminated altogether in the fair copy, perhaps for reasons of dramatic economy. Erda's threefold exhortation 'höre!' ('Listen!') leads to and highlights her following lines, the climax of the entire episode. This crucial passage originally read: 'A gloomy day dawns for the gods; but your noble race will end in shame if you do not give up the ring!' ('Ein düstrer tag | dämmert den göttern: | in schmach doch endet | dein edles geschlecht, | lässt du den Reif nicht los!'). While setting the episode to music, Wagner substituted these words: 'Everything that is, ends! A gloomy day dawns for the gods: I advise you, shun the ring!' ('Alles was ist, endet! | Ein düstrer Tag | dämmert den Göttern: | dir rath' ich, meide den Ring!'). In neither case can Wotan save himself or the other gods from destruction, only rescue them from a shameful end, from 'irretrievable dark perdition'. Erda's 'Alles was ist, endet!' now predicts not only a *Götteruntergang*, but an all-inclusive *Weltuntergang*.

Having traced the textual genesis of the Erda episode, we are perhaps in a better position to understand its dramatic significance. Rising up unbidden like a voice from Wotan's subconscious, Erda apprises the god of his own mortality; he, along with everything that lives, is fated to pass away. With only a limited time at his disposal—not all eternity, as he had formerly thought—Wotan can save himself from 'irretrievable dark perdition'—from everlasting damnation—only by relinquishing the ring of power and atoning for his past behaviour. This will not spare him physical destruction—which during the course of the tetralogy he learns to accept and ultimately to embrace—but it will afford him spiritual salvation. The process is completed by Brünnhilde who, at the end of the *Ring*, has replaced Siegfried as the gods' redeemer: her self-sacrifice finally releases them from the burden of Alberich's curse. Wotan and the gods *are* redeemed—are purged of their guilt and fear—even as heaven and earth go up in flames.

The complete draft version of Episode 17 is transcribed in the Appendix, beginning at m. 3452; the reader is invited to compare this transcription with the printed score, which differs from the draft in several important respects. While scoring, Wagner rewrote two extended passages, lightly crossing out the originals in the complete draft: mm. 3456–62 ('Langsam' to 'weiche!') and mm. 3470–81 ('Weib?' to 'Erda, mahnt deinen'). He also changed his mind about instrumentation, initially assigning the first appearance of the Erda motif to two horns doubled by bassoon and bass clarinet, later changing this to a pair of Wagner tubas doubled by two bassoons.

Erda's appearance is preceded by the stormy F minor passage which closes Episode 16. At the change to 'Langsam', the bass of the complete draft arpeggiates a descending F♯ minor triad, out of which Erda's theme slowly emerges; this harmony then resolves as sub-dominant to the new tonic C♯ minor. The draft reveals that Wagner originally intended to notate the episode in D♭ minor, a fact which strengthens our interpretation of Erda as an embodiment of Wotan's subconscious. Wagner may have introduced the Erda motif over an F♯ harmony in order to suggest a parallelism with Loge's F♯ appearance in Scene 2, or possibly to reflect the increase in dramatic tension by an 'expressive' rise from F to F♯; in any case, he later changed his mind and began the episode with a second inversion *tonic* triad, shifting emphasis to the descending third relationship F–D♭. In addition, he deleted a second plagally inflected state-ment of Erda's motif and moved directly into the goddess's 'Weiche, Wodan! weiche!'), altering her vocal line so as to exploit the singer's low range and eliminate a premature high e^2.

Erda delivers her introductory warning in a phrase which moves harmonically from the tonic ('Weiche, Wotan! weiche!') to a Nea-politan half-cadence ('weih't dich sein Gewinn'); a D major Neapolitan triad underlines the doom threatening Wotan. The god's question 'Wer bist du mahnendes Weib?' extends the cadential V^7 harmony, and is punctuated by a solemn chord for low brass over a shuddering timpani roll, details already suggested in the draft.

Erda's lengthy reply constitutes the main section of the episode. Originally the phrase 'Wie alles war . . .' began with two tonic statements of her motif followed by two Neapolitan statements, all over a tonic pedal; Wagner later changed the second Neapolitan statement into a vii^{o7} chord resolving back to the tonic. While scoring, he also shifted Erda's 'Wie alles war' forward one and a half bars so that it anticipates, rather than follows, the first tonic chord, and he adjusted the rest of her vocal line rhythmically and melodically, introducing several syncopations. Finally, he telescoped her cadential 'Erda, mahnt deinen Muth' from three bars into two. These changes produced two results: harmonically, the entire phrase is better defined, an initial eight-bar tonic prolongation leading through a two-bar expanded submediant into a plagally tonicized mediant (mm. 3472–82; 193/1/2–193/3/1); and rhythmically, more momentum is generated into the beginning of the next phrase, whose quaver figurations now follow as a natural continuation of this momentum.

The following phrase ('Drei der Töchter . . .') was incorporated without significant change into the final version, once Wagner had settled upon a few vocal details. The Norns' weaving is suggested by a quaver figuration of Erda's motif in the relative major; two statements over this expanded mediant lead to a G♯ dominant pedal at 'was ich sehe', but at 'sagen dir nächtlich die Nornen' the dominant is abandoned in favour of a plagally tonicized submediant. This suggests that the apparent V/C♯ (mm. 3486–7; 193/3/5–193/4/1) should be understood as the unfolded upper third of III (E major), and that the entire phrase moves from III to VI of C♯ minor.

The next phrase ('Doch höchste Gefahr . . .') immediately undermines the stability of A by harmonizing it with a D♯ diminished triad; the subsequent addition of C♯ converts this tonally ambiguous harmony into a half-diminished seventh chord which resolves as $ii^{ø4}_3$ to the structural dominant on G♯. Restless syncopations, a detail only hinted at in the draft, invoke the memory of Alberich's curse and assist in this push to the dominant. The semitone bass resolution A–G♯ is next reiterated as a melodic detail while Erda utters her triple exhortation 'Höre!'; the bass counterpoints this with the ascending semitone Fx–G♯. Such a dramatic arrival at a prolonged and intensified dominant has all the earmarks of a retransition, a dominant preparation heralding a tonal/thematic return. And this, in fact, is what occurs.

The recapitulation (mm. 3498 ff.; 194/1/4 ff.) begins with a tonic statement of Erda's motif over a dominant pedal; the resultant $^6_4$ sonority represents a weakened tonic, not a suspended dominant. Wagner originally *followed* this two-bar pianissimo statement with Erda's new *Weltuntergang* prophecy 'Alles was ist, endet!'; he later moved the vocal line a measure forward, so that it now *overlaps* with the previous motif. This phrase begins as a compressed verbal/musical reprise of 'Wie alles war . . .'; Erda's former expressions 'Wie alles war', 'wie alles wird', 'wie alles sein wird' coalesce into her 'Alles was ist, endet!' In the earlier phrase (mm. 3472 ff.; 193/1/2 ff.), an eight-bar tonic prolongation was followed (in the final version) by a two-bar expanded submediant; in the reprise, two bars of tonic harmony and two bars of submediant lead directly into the musical climax of the episode—a melodic inversion of the Erda theme over a Neapolitan sixth harmony. This inverted theme is usually known as the *Götterdämmerungmotif* (Twilight of the Gods motif) because it accompanies the words 'Ein düstrer Tag | dämmert den Göttern.' However, it might equally well be called the *Weltuntergangmotif* (World Destruction motif): Wagner introduces it immediately after Erda's 'Alles was ist, endet!' as a musical reverberation of those words. Melodic descent and Neapolitan harmony fuse together into a musical metaphor of impending doom and dissolution.

The Neapolitan sixth ultimately resolves to a dominant seventh chord (mm. 3509–10; 194/3/1–2). As Erda begins to disappear, this dominant slides towards its upper neighbour A; Wotan attempts to restrain her by forcing the neighbour to resolve through a German augmented sixth chord back to the dominant. However, Erda gradually slips away from Wotan, and her tonality dissolves, eventually stabilizing (at the beginning of Episode 18) on an E♭ half-cadence (m. 3527; 195/2/4). During the next episode, two reappearances of Erda's motif in E♭ minor accompany Wotan's futile attempt to reach within himself and grasp the full significance of this unexpected revelation (mm. 3527 ff. and 3543 ff.; 195/2/4 ff. and 196/2/1 ff.).

Example 10.7 summarizes the formal/tonal structure of the Erda episode. The harmonic background is quite simple, a threefold move from tonic to dominant of which the first arpeggiation is direct, the second passes through the mediant, and the third moves through a predominant Neapolitan sixth. Perhaps Wagner equated these basic arpeggiations with the fundamental, primordial quality of Erda herself, 'der ew'gen Welt Urwala'; from this viewpoint, the 'less natural' final arpeggiation ($\hat{1}$–$\hat{4}$–$\hat{5}$ in the bass instead of $\hat{1}$–$\hat{3}$–$\hat{5}$) reflects her terrible prophecy. However, the episode lacks harmonic closure: the twice-interrupted dominant refuses to resolve to the

Ex. 10.7

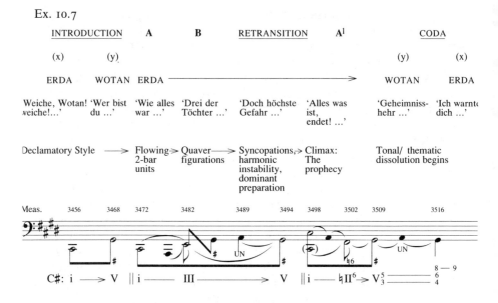

INTRODUCTION	A	B	RETRANSITION	A¹	CODA
(x) (y)					(y) (x)
ERDA WOTAN	ERDA	————————————————————————→			WOTAN ERDA

Weiche, Wotan! 'Wer bist   'Wie alles   'Drei der   'Doch höchste   'Alles was   'Geheimniss-   'Ich warnt
veiche!...'   du ...'   war ...'   Töchter ...'   Gefahr ...'   ist,   hehr ...'   dich ...'
                                                                              endet! ...'

Declamatory Style ——→ Flowing→ Quaver——→ Syncopations,→ Climax: Tonal/ thematic
                       2-bar   figurations harmonic   The   dissolution begins
                       units   instability,   prophecy
                                            dominant
                                            preparation

Meas.   3456   3468   3472   3482   3489   3494   3498   3502 3509   3516

C#: i ——→ V ‖ i —— III ————————————→ V ‖ i — ♮II⁶→ V₃⁵ ——— $^{8-9}_{6}$ $_4$

tonic, just as Erda refuses to satisfy Wotan's desire for further knowledge. Formally, the episode displays a symmetrical structure, an ABA' design flanked by an introduction and coda. This particular ternary form is processive in nature: its sole purpose is to direct the listener's attention to the recapitulation, the moment when Erda delivers her *Weltuntergang* prophecy. The gradual textural progression through the declamatory style of the Introduction, the flowing two-bar units of Section A, the quaver figurations of Section B, the syncopations, harmonic instability, and extended dominant preparation of the Retransition—this progression leads towards, and prepares for, something of monumental importance. That something proves nothing less than a prophecy of cosmic dissolution.

5. *Episode 18 (mm. 3527–666; 195/2/4–203/2/2)*

The third paragraph of the prose sketch concludes: '[Wodan] also gives up [the ring], whereupon Freia is handed over. A dispute immediately breaks out over the ring: one of the giant brothers slays the other. Wodan: "Remember Alberich's curse."' A supplementary note reads: '[Wodan] gives up the ring, Freia returns,' then continues with a parenthetical clause: '[Wodan] reflects upon the benefit which, as ruler, he has gained through the fortress.' The prose draft elaborates this scenario in detail, including a significant expansion of the parenthesis: when Fricka gestures towards the fortress, Wodan hails it and announces his intention to beget a new race. He then commands Donner and Froh (originally just Froh) to build the bridge over the Rhine. While versifying, Wagner decided to delay Wotan's statement of intent concerning Valhalla until *after* Donner and Froh have created the rainbow bridge, which they now do on their own initiative.[14]

The differences between the complete draft and the *Partiturerstschrift* continue to be illuminating. While scoring Donner's 'das Gold wird euch gegeben,' Wagner decided to energize the cadence by adding semiquaver violin figurations (m. 3534; 195/4/3); he first sketched these into the complete draft, using the ends of the staves immediately above the measure in question. The upward-rushing passage which accompanies Freia's release (mm. 3567–8; 197/1/2–3) was also invented (and reworked) while scoring. The fortissimo climax (m. 3569; 197/1/4) features an F–E♭ appoggiatura over a $^6_4$ sonority on E♭, unmistakably recalling the opening of Scene 1; in the complete draft this resolves to a tonic E♭ major triad ($^{6-5}_{4-3}$), whose stability the score subverts by adding a prominent D♭.

Loge's suggestion to Fasolt 'Den Hort lass' ihn raffen' went through three versions in the complete draft, while the giant's 'Zurück! du Frecher!' originally entered two beats earlier (mm. 3598–601; 198/4/2 –199/1/3). The accompaniment to Fafner's 'Müh zum Tausch | vermocht' ich dich Thoren' (m. 3591; 198/1/1) originally featured viola chords and a continuation of the previous Nibelungs rhythm; Wagner eventually struck out both. The orchestral reprise of the Curse motif is preceded in the complete draft by unmeasured tremolo figures, changed to rhythmically distinct triplets while scoring (mm. 3615–16; 200/2/4–200/3/1). Westernhagen has pointed out the alteration and metric displacement of Loge's vocal cadence 'um das Gold, das du vergab'st' (mm. 3638–9; 201/4/2–3),[15] but Wagner made other changes here as well. He first gave the continuation of the Curse theme (mm. 3639 ff.; 201/4/3 ff.) to two clarinets, then doubled these with two bassoons; ultimately he reassigned the idea to trombones alone, thereby linking it through tone colour to the earlier statement of the first portion of this theme (mm. 3618 ff.; 200/3/3 ff.). Finally, Wagner sketched the spacing of the string tremolos at Wotan's 'Erda:

[14] The verse draft reveals that the wording of two passages caused Wagner difficulty: Fafner's response to Fasolt ('Mehr an der Maid als am Gold . . .') and Loge's ironic remark to Wotan ('Was gleicht, Wotan, | wohl deinem Glücke? . . .').

[15] *The Forging of the 'Ring'*, 59.

| zu ihr muss ich hinab!' (mm. 3648 ff.; 202/2/2 ff.) into the complete draft before scoring them.

The episode contains three parts: in the first, Wotan surrenders the ring and obtains Freia's release; in the second, the giants quarrel and Fafner kills Fasolt; while in the third, Wotan broods darkly over the power of Alberich's curse. Tonally, the episode moves from E♭ major/minor to B minor and back; inasmuch as the key of the Curse relates enharmonically to E♭ as ♭VI, this tonal structure is generated by a background 5–♭6–5 neighbouring motion. Thus E♭ major is coloured or tainted by B/C♭, suggesting that the natural world has been contaminated by the curse.

A recitative-like transition (mm. 3522–6; 195/1/1–195/2/3) rises a fifth from the V/C♯ (really V/D♭) which concluded Episode 17; E♭ as dominant is then reinterpreted as a minor tonic at the return of the Erda motif (mm. 3527–8; 195/2/4–195/3/1). This initiates Part 1 (mm. 3527–83; 195/2/4–197/3/8), which is structured as a clear bar form of 16 + 20 + 21 measures. In each Stollen, Wotan's brooding (Erda motif in E♭) is succeeded by energetic music marking his decision to surrender the ring; both times, a progression from i through ♭VI to V is harmonically deflected towards an applied dominant. The Abgesang resolves to the tonic through the aforementioned harmonic reference to Scene 1, almost creating the impression that the opera's original E♭ major has been gloriously restored. Wagner suddenly unleashes his orchestra in a short-lived effusion of passionate lyricism—the sort of music which, though conspicuous by its absence in *Das Rheingold*, will form the basic style of *Die Walküre*.

Part 2 (mm. 3584–615; 197/4/1–200/2/4) begins rather ominously over a pedal E♭ whose tonic status has already been seriously compromised by the previous D♭s; the interplay between two different rhythmic patterns (Giants/Nibelungs) recalls the thematic strife of Episode 16. A transition to B minor is effected through the C major of mm. 3589–90 (197/5/2–3: VI/E♭ = ♮II/B), above which sounds a harmonic distortion of 'Rheingold!' As the giants begin to struggle (mm. 3600 ff.; 199/1/2 ff.), the Ring motif reappears at a transpositional level (e^1–c^1–a–$f♯$) that retrogrades the first four notes of the Curse motif, thus preparing the latter's reappearance at mm. 3618 ff. (200/3/3 ff.) The F♯–G bass oscillation (mm. 3604–5; 199/2/3–199/3/1) soon yields to an F♯/G harmonic clash (mm. 3606–7; 199/3/2–3); this explodes into an E♯^{o7} chord (m. 3608; 200/1/1) when Fafner strikes the fatal blow. The diminished seventh chord finally resolves as vii^{o7}/V to the dominant of B minor (m. 3615; 200/2/4).

Part 3 (mm. 3615–66; 200/2/4–203/2/2) alternates the Curse theme with two contrasting ideas in the manner of a five-part rondo (ABA^{1}CA^2). Wotan broods during Sections A, A^1, and A^2, as the orchestra reprises first the initial two phrases of the Curse ('Wie durch Fluch . . .' / Gab sein Gold . . .'; mm. 3618–26; 200/3/3–200/ 4/6), then the next pair ('Kein Froher . . .' / 'keinem Glücklichen . . .': mm. 3639–43; 201/4/3–202/1/2). During the contrasting sections, Loge and Fricka attempt to reassure Wotan, the first ironically (mm. 3627–39; 20/1/1–201/4/3), the second with genuine concern (mm. 3651–60; 202/2/5–203/1/1). Although neither succeeds in rousing the god from his gloomy thoughts, Fricka at least manages to restore E♭ major, while Loge merely confirms the key of the Curse. The final statement of the Curse motif develops out of the Valhalla and Ring themes (mm. 3660–6; 203/1/1–203/2/2), and cadences a semitone lower than the original, on V^9/B♭ minor; this 'expressive' semitonal depression draws the Curse motif further into the tonal orbit of the governing E♭, and ominously restores Alberich's original associative key.

6. Episode 19 (mm. 3666–712; 203/2/2–208/2/2)

The prose draft describes in more detail than the poem the creation of the rainbow bridge:

At the swing of Donner's hammer, a flash of lightning comes down out of a thundercloud which has quickly formed; from the ground at the foot of the mountain there flares up a coloured flame, to which Froh with outstretched arm points out the way over the valley. There quickly materializes a rainbow bridge, which extends over the Rhine valley to the fortress.

In the verse draft, Donner and Froh are enveloped in clouds, which then part to reveal the bridge. Donner's solo is written out free of alterations, and was carried over without change into the fair copy and 1853 printing; however, it did undergo revision while being set to music:

1853 Printing	*Score*
He da! He da!	Heda! Heda! Hedo!
Zu mir, du Gedüft!	Zu mir, du Gedüft!
ihr Dünste, zu mir!	Ihr Dünste zu mir!
Donner, der Herr,	Donner, der Herr,
ruft euch zu Heer.	ruft euch zu Heer!
Auf des Hammers Schwung	Auf des Hammers Schwung
schwebet herbei:	schwebet herbei!
he da! he da!	Dunstig Gedämpf!
duftig Gedünst!	Schwebend Gedüft!
Donner ruft euch zu Heer!	Donner, der Herr,
	ruft euch zu Heer!
	Heda! Heda! Hedo!

TABLE 10.2 Episode 19: Structural outline

Recitative	6 bars
String Figurations	4 bars
Refrain (Voice): 'Heda! Heda! Hedo!'	2 bars
Quatrain: 'Zu mir, du Gedüft! . . .'	4 bars
Refrain (Horns)	2 bars
Couplet: 'Auf des Hammers Schwung . . .'	2 bars
Refrain (Horns)	2 bars
Quatrain: 'Dunstig Gedämpf! . . .'	4 bars
Refrain (Voice): 'Heda! Heda! Hedo!'	2 bars
String Figurations	4 bars
[Orchestral Development of Refrain, leading to Climax]	[9 bars]
Recitative	6 bars

Obviously Wagner was aiming at greater symmetry: in the revised version, two similar quatrains enclose a couplet, and the whole is framed by a one-line refrain. In fact, Wagner achieved even further symmetry by surrounding the central couplet with an orchestral statement (horns) of the refrain.

The composition of this episode, a recitative–aria structure, did not come all that easily to Wagner. He revised Donner's opening recitative ('Schwüles Gedünst | schwebt in der Luft . . .') once in the complete draft, then a second time while scoring (see transcription in Appendix, beginning at m. 3666, and compare with score). But it is the 'aria' that was changed most radically. Wagner first set his original text, in a rhythmically rather flabby 12/8 metre (see transcription). He then decided to syncopate the rhythm, and indicated this by changing some of the original note-values and barlines (these alterations are not shown in the transcription). Finally he wrote out the revision (with altered text) in ink beneath the original, which he then crossed out. It is interesting to note that the D major horn statement of the refrain (mm. 3686–7; 205/2/2–205/3/1) originated as the vocal setting of a line from the original text.[16]

[16] Certain liberties were taken with the transcription of this portion of the complete draft (Episode 19). Wagner revised the opening recitative ('Schwüles Gedünst . . .'; mm. 3666 ff.; 203/2/2 ff.) by writing over his original version; in the transcription, the two versions (marked [A:] and [B:]) have been separated out and aligned vertically. The draft of the first version of Donner's aria ('Heda! Heda! Hedo!'; mm. 3676 ff.; 204/1/2 ff.) is heavily overwritten and crossed out; the transcription reproduces only the (unrevised) first version, in so far as this can be ascertained. It is unclear whether the snatches of semiquaver figuration included in the transcription were written when the first version was drafted or during the revision. The revised and crossed-out first version is followed (in ink) by the second version; this is transcribed as it appears. In general, my transcription of this episode should be considered provisional, although

Ex. 10.8

a.

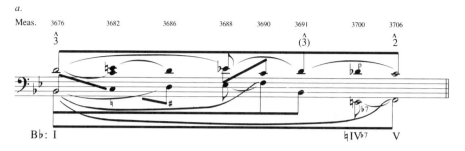

b.

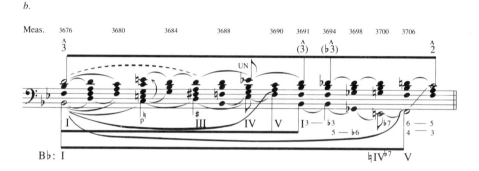

The rigorous symmetrical scheme of the final version is shown in Table 10.2; only the orchestral development of the refrain (a structural interpolation) does not participate in this symmetry. The tonal coherence of the episode is displayed in Ex. 10.8. A detailed explication of these two graphs is probably unnecessary; however, the following supplementary observations should be made.

We have noted, during the course of Scene 4, the gradual interpenetration of the world of the gods by musical elements associated with the Nibelungs. Donner's present task is to 'clear the air' of these alien elements, to transform them in such a way as to render them harmless. His first step, which he accomplishes in his opening recitative, is to change Alberich's Bb minor (mm. 3666 ff.; 203/2/2 ff.) into Bb *major*, which he does at the word 'hell!' ('clear!': m. 3672; 203/4/1). Thus Bb, the tonal symbol of Alberich's power over the

the state of the manuscript at this point makes it unlikely that a 'definitive' transcription will ever be forthcoming.

Nibelungs, now signifies Donner's power over Nature.[17] Donner's cry 'Heda! Heda! Hedo!' is itself a transformation of Alberich's 'Hoho! Hoho!' from Episode 12 (cf. mm. 1987 and 2004; 120/1/4 and 120/4/6). The rising chromatic scale leading to Donner's hammer-stroke (mm. 3702 ff.; 207/1/2 ff.) clearly refers to the similar scales which accompanied Alberich's declarations of power in the same episode (cf. mm. 1984 ff. and 2011 ff.; 120/1/1 ff. and 121/2/1 ff.). Finally, the climax itself develops out of a pre-dominant E^{o7} chord ($\natural iv^{o7}$ or vii^{o7}/V) approached from a G♭ major triad (♭VI); this progression (mm. 3698–3705; 206/4/2–207/3/1) literally reverses the two crucial chords from Alberich's Power of the Ring motif. Donner's successful transmutation of Nibelung elements into ones favourable to the gods ultimately finds its visual manifestation in the spectacle of the rainbow bridge.

7. Episode 20 (mm. 3713–897; 208/3/1–221/6/4)

'(He reflects upon the benefit which, as ruler, he has gained through the fortress.)—Lament of the Rhinedaughters.' Thus concludes one of Wagner's supplementary prose notes. A second jotting runs: 'In conclusion: Wodan—"We gave away the gold—now we need iron."' From these hints, Wagner constructed his magnificent Finale—'The Entrance of the Gods into Valhalla'.

As mentioned during the discussion of Episode 18, the order of events outlined in the prose draft differs a bit at this point from that of the poem. In the former manuscript, Wodan first apostrophizes the fortress: though paid for with 'bad money', it will serve as a stronghold wherein the god will gather to himself a new race. He names it 'Valhalla'. Donner and Froh create the rainbow bridge; in the poem, of course, this event *precedes* Wodan's apostrophe. Fafner gathers his booty and departs. As the gods begin to cross the bridge, they hear the voices of the Rhinedaughters, rising from the depths of the valley. On Wodan's order, Loke bids the sisters cease their complaint and bask in the new-found glory of the gods. The draft contains no hint of Loge's aside about changing back into fire and burning up the gods; it concludes with a prose version of the mermaids' song.

The verse draft of this episode contains several interesting variants. The first concerns Wotan's explication of the name 'Valhalla'; this originated in a marginal notation in the prose draft, and went through at least three versions:

[17] B♮ is, of course, the *dominant* of E♭, the Nature-key. In *Die Walküre*, B♮ will become associated with the love of Siegmund and Sieglinde, suggesting that the power of love is beginning to displace the love of power.

Verse Draft (A)	*Verse Draft (B)*	*Fair Copy*
was bangen gezeugt	Was in mächt'gen bangen	Was, mächtig der Furcht,
und muth gebar,	mein muth mir gebar:	mein Muth mir erfand,
wenn siegend es lebt,	wenn siegend es lebt,	wenn siegend es lebt—
legt so den sinn dir dar!	leg' es den sinn dir dar!	leg' es den Sinn dir dar!

Another variant concerns Loge's monologue 'Ihrem Ende eilen sie zu . . .' Originally, after the gods had begun to cross the rainbow bridge (first Wodan and Fricka, then Froh and Freia, finally Donner), Wagner wrote: 'Loke considers the procession thoughtfully, then goes to join it'; he then completed the draft by versifying the Rhine-daughters' song. Sometime later, Wagner crossed out this sentence and added Loke's new lines in the left margin. He bracketed 'sie aufzuzehren . . . dünkte mich das!' ('to burn up those who once tamed me, instead of foolishly perishing with the blind—even were they the most godlike of gods—that doesn't seem stupid to me!'), as if these words were very important. As suggested in Chapter 3, this probably marks the point when Wagner decided to destroy the gods; he made Loke a fire deity in order to prepare for the final conflagration. This marginal insert was probably entered after completing the verse draft of *Die Walküre*, whose final page also contains a textual addition linking Loke to fire.[18]

The composition draft and the *Partiturerstschrift* display numerous compositional variants. Westernhagen has pointed out that the intervals of Froh's 'beschreitet kühn' (mm. 3730–1; 209/3/3–209/4/1) were enlarged while scoring;[19] Wagner actually copied his original vocal line into the *Partiturerstschrift*, then overwrote it with the revision. The complete draft version of the expanded Valhalla theme (mm. 3733 ff.; 209/4/3 ff.) is again marked for trombones, as in Episode 3, but was eventually reassigned to Wagner tubas. While scoring this theme, Wagner sketched out the harp/violin/wind accompaniment on two blank staves of the complete draft (fo. 37[r], bottom); he then began writing out the six harp parts, but soon decided to notate them on four separate half-sheets and one full sheet cued as supplements ('zu S. 341', etc.).[20] In the complete draft,

[18] Yet another variant concerns the final verse of the Rhinedaughters' song. In the prose draft, Wagner wrote 'und doch in der tiefe nur ist's traulich und treu; was da oben glänzt ist falsch und feig!' Wagner versified the first half of this as 'Traulich und treu | ist's nur in der tiefe' (thus inverting the wording of the prose draft), then continued with 'trugvoll, und falsch, | und feig ist'; crossing out the last two lines, he replaced them with 'falsch und feig | ist was dort oben sich freut!'

[19] *The Forging of the 'Ring'*, 61.

[20] In 1875, Wagner asked the virtuoso harpist Peter Dubez of Prague to arrange the six harp parts, as well as those in *Die Walküre* and the concluding acts of *Siegfried* and *Götterdämmerung*. Wagner's own version of the *Rheingold* harp parts had already been published in the 1872 Schott's edition, and may be studied in the Dover reprint.

Ex. 10.9

a.

b.

a pedal C begins at m. 3770 (212/3/3) and persists until m. 3777 (213/1/1), where it yields to G; while scoring, Wagner advanced the G to m. 3774 (212/4/3), creating a more extensive dominant preparation for the C major Sword motif. The first appearance of this famous arpeggio was originally marked '1^e Tromp[ete] in C', the second '2^e Tr[ompete]', but the 1872 edition of the score (based on Wölfel's copy of Wagner's *Reinschrift*) for some reason assigns *both* statements to the second trumpet. Fricka's query 'Was deutet der Name? . . .' (mm. 3794–7; 213/4/4–214/1/1) was changed once in the complete draft, a second time while scoring.

Westernhagen has noted Wagner's alteration of the Rhinedaughters' vocal harmonies at mm. 3835–6 (217/1/3–4: 'Um dich, du Klares, | wir nun klagen'); Ex. 10.9 offers a slightly more accurate transcription of this process, including some quaver neighbouring motion which Westernhagen does not show (ab^1–g^1–ab^1). The harmonic changes were originally generated by the 5–6 technique: $^{(5)-}_{3-}{}^{6-5}_{\natural2-3}$ in the first bar, $^{(5)-\flat6-}_{3-\flat3-}{}^{5}_{\natural3}$ in the second (Ex. 10.9*a*). Wagner subsequently displaced the neighbouring g^1 so that it became the root of an apparent seventh chord (Ex. 10.9*b*); the resulting suggestion of C major creates a reference back to the second half of Scene 1.

At the conclusion of Loge's advice to the Rhinedaughters ('sonn't euch selig fortan!'), the complete draft launches into a four-bar statement of the Arrogance of Power theme. Wagner scored this in its entirety, then cut the first two bars (the flippant variant of the

TABLE 10.3 Episode 20: Structural outline

Meas.	Section and Content
3713	INTRODUCTION: THE RAINBOW BRIDGE (IV/D♭) As Froh points the way to Valhalla, the Rainbow theme is sequenced through the G♭ triad.
	PART I: WOTAN CONTEMPLATES THE FORTRESS
3733	A: The Splendour of Valhalla (D♭→A♭) The gods contemplate their new home over an extended reprise of Episode 3, Section A' (Valhalla theme).
3763	B: Wotan's Misgivings (V/A♭ minor→V/C minor) Wotan recalls how the fortress was won, over a varied reprise of Episode 3, Section B (Ring motif).
3779	[Interpolation: Wotan's Great Idea (C major)] Wotan has an inspiration how to preserve Valhalla and the gods from harm (Sword motif).
3787	Retransition (C major→V/D♭) Wotan bids Fricka follow him into Valhalla.
	PART II: THE INTERRUPTED PROCESSION
3793	A': The Procession Begins (D♭→F) As Fricka queries Wotan about the name 'Valhalla', the orchestra begins to recapitulate Episode 3, Section A (Valhalla theme).
3807	[Interpolation: Loge's Idea (tonally unstable)]
3823	A' continued: Loge joins the procession (A♭).
3827	[Interpolation: First Verse of the Rhinedaughters' Song (A♭)]
3843	A' continued and developed: Loge mocks the mermaids (D♭).
3858	[Interpolation: Second Verse of the Rhinedaughters' Song (D♭)]
3873	A' continued and concluded (D♭).
3883	CODA: THE GODS CROSS THE RAINBOW BRIDGE (D♭) The Rainbow theme is sequenced through the D♭ triad.

Valhalla motif), so that the vocal cadence elides with the Loge theme (m. 3856; 219/1/2). The opera's orchestral conclusion was originally only eleven bars in length; Wagner expanded it to fifteen by inserting an extra four-bar sequence of the Rainbow motif (mm. 3891–4; 221/5/1–221/6/1) before the final chord.

Structurally Episode 20 functions as a large-scale recapitulation of Episode 3, expanded through extensions and interpolations (Table 10.3). The relationship between these two episodes may best be understood by comparing their interruption structures:

Episode 3: I–III–V ‖ I–IV–V–I
Episode 20: I–IV–V ‖ I–III–V–I

Obviously III and IV have been exchanged. In Episode 20, the first branch of the interruption structure underlies Wotan's reflections, while the second accompanies the procession into Valhalla. The new Introduction (mm. 3713–32; 208/3/1–209/4/2) and Coda (mm. 3883–97; 221/2/3–221/6/4) are both based upon the Rainbow motif; the former's prolonged Gb major deceptively resolves the V/Bb which ended Episode 19 (a hint that the rainbow's promise of hope is illusory), then leads as subdominant preparation into the new tonic Db.

We recall that in Episode 3, Wagner created a Prelude, Scene, and Aria form by interpolating a dominant expansion into a I–V ‖ I–V–I interruption scheme. Because the Aria recapitulates the Prelude's thematic material, this structure could also be considered as an ABA' design: Sections A and B constitute the first branch of the interruption scheme, Section A' the second. Episode 20 begins with a sort of 'reverse recapitulation': it first parallels Section A' (the Aria) of Episode 20 (cf. mm. 3733 ff. (209/4/3 ff.) with mm. 804 ff. (57/1/1 ff.)), but expands it by inserting eight extra bars (mm. 3749–56; 210/4/4–211/2/4). The episode continues by analogy with Section B (the Scene), but expands the length of its prototype by multiplying the sequences on the Ring motif and replacing the Valhalla motif with a recall of Erda's theme (cf. mm. 3763 ff. (212/1/4 ff.) with mm. 791 ff. (56/1/3 ff.)); it gravitates towards a dramatic dominant preparation for C major. At this point (m. 3779; 213/1/3) the first interpolation occurs—the C major passage marking Wotan's 'grand idea', his plan to beget a new race of heroes to help him safeguard Valhalla and regain the ring. Two statements of the new Sword motif frame Wotan's greeting to the fortress ('So grüss' ich die Burg . . .'); the entire passage expands C through a majestic I–vi–V–I progression. As Ex. 10.10 shows, this interpolation can be understood as unfolding the upper third of the dividing dominant Ab; C folds back into V/Db as Wotan invites Fricka to follow him into Valhalla.

The music 'starts over again' on the tonic Db as the procession begins (m. 3793; 213/4/3). Now Episode 20 begins to parallel Section A (the Prelude) of Episode 3 (cf. mm. 769 ff.; 55/1/1 ff.); this 'reverse recapitulation' accounts for the harmonic exchange mentioned above. Four horns present the Valhalla theme in a manner obviously intended to suggest the physical act of walking (piano, 'nicht gebunden'); as Wotan answers Fricka's question about the name 'Valhalla', the theme moves harmonically from I to III$_t$. At this point, the Ab major Coda is expected; instead, Loge interpolates his aside about burning up the gods (mm. 3807–22; 214/3/3–215/4/3). Loge combines material from Section B (sequences on the Ring motif) with his own

Ex. 10.10

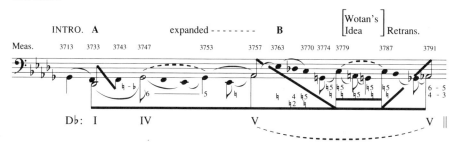

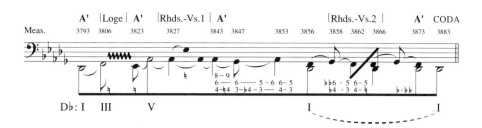

chromatic figurations, in order momentarily to destabilize the tonality (a musical metaphor for 'destroying the gods'). But when, 'assuming a careless manner', he goes to join the others, the music abruptly restabilizes on A♭ (V_t/D♭), and the orchestra presents the 'missing' Coda (cf. mm. 3823 ff. (215/4/4 ff.) with mm. 783 ff. (55/4/3 ff.)).

The tonicized dominant A♭ is prolonged by the first verse of the Rhinedaughters' song (mm. 3827–42; 216/2/1–218/1/2), a symmetrical two-phrase period (8 + 8 bars). The opening f^2–eb^2 ('Rheingold!') and the apparent V^7/C harmony relate this moment back to Scene 1, recalling Woglinde's opening appoggiatura over her referential 'A♭$_4^6$' chord, and simultaneously suggesting the key of the gold. Thus Wagner begins to integrate material from the introductory first scene into the opera's Finale. The entire passage functions as yet another interpolation, a 'voice from the past' that stops the procession cold.

The recapitulation of Episode 3 resumes at m. 3843 (218/1/3 ff.) with further sequential development of the fifth bar of the Valhalla theme over a detonicized dominant; Loge delivers Wotan's message to the mermaids. The resolution to D♭ at m. 3856 (219/1/2) marks the completion of the episode's interruption scheme.

Yet even as the procession resumes, the Rhinedaughters inter-
polate yet another verse of their song, a second two-phrase period
(mm. 3858–73; 219/1/4–220/3/2) whose denunciation of the gods—
the last words of the opera—hangs in the air like an unanswered
accusation. As Ex. 10.10 shows, this verse functions as a large plagal
expansion of the final tonic harmony: G♭ in the bass resolves to
F (m. 3862; 219/3/1), which is then absorbed back into I as its
unfolded upper third (m. 3866; 220/1/2). Locally, however, this F
suggests a half-cadence on V/B♭ minor (m. 3864; 219/3/3), thus
recalling Alberich's baleful key. The striking opening progression
('Rheingold!': m. 3858; 219/1/4) is generated from a $^{\flat\flat6-\hat{5}}_{\flat4-\hat{3}}$ neighbouring of IV; yet the apparent C♭ minor chord suggests enharmoni-
cally the key of Alberich's Curse, while the G♭ major triad recalls the
original pitch level of the rainbow bridge.

The recapitulation concludes in mm. 3873–83 (220/3/2–221/2/3);
further sequences on the Valhalla motif lead to a sonorous rendition
of the Sword arpeggio, now in D♭ major. A final authentic cadence
ushers in the ear-splitting Coda, a sort of gigantic composed-out
fermata over tonic harmony. As the gods in pomp and splendour
cross the bridge to their new home, the curtain falls.

11 *Summary and Conclusion*

> The completion of *Das Rheingold* (a task as difficult as it was important) has restored my sense of self-assurance, as you can see. I have once again realized how much of the work's meaning (given the nature of my poetic intent) is only made clear by the music: I can now no longer bear to look at the poem without music.
>
> (Wagner to August Röckel, 25–6 January 1854)

Our examination of the individual episodes of *Das Rheingold* has revealed that Wagner's formal structures, while certainly 'logical' in the Dahlhausian sense, are also highly architectural. Each episode displays a clear formal/tonal design which grows naturally out of the structure and content of the text. Thus Dahlhaus's 'logical/architectural' dialectic collapses: Wagner's forms are both logical *and* architectural, in equal measure. Dahlhaus is certainly entitled to place the logical aspect in the foreground if he wishes, but by denying the existence of the architectural element he skews his argument in a manner which does justice to neither composer nor music. Furthermore, he employs this false premiss (non-architectural form) as a foundation for constructing an illusory Wagner/Brahms dichotomy, one of the central categories of his grand musicological project.

It remains to address the question of whether the opera as a whole is architectural—that is, whether it displays an overall formal/tonal design. We have already noted that Scene 1 is introductory in nature, and that, in a very general sense, Scenes 2–4 constitute a large ABA′ ternary form supported by a move from D♭ major to its relative minor and back. Table 11.1 reveals the existence of a more complex symmetrical structure, a large five-part arch delineated by the dramatic progression VALHALLA–GIANTS–NIBELUNGS–GIANTS–VALHALLA. The VALHALLA segments are, of course, the related D♭ major episodes (3 and 20), while the NIBELUNGS segment includes the two long episodes of Scene 3 (12 and 13) as well as the equally lengthy Episode 14. Each of the GIANTS segments is tonally closed, in F and E♭ respectively; Loge's F♯ arrival at the centre of the first is mirrored by Erda's C♯ appearance at the midpoint of the second.[1] The first

---

[1] We recall that in the complete draft, Wagner notated the first statement of Erda's motif on F♯, changing it to C♯ while scoring. Originally, then, Loge and Erda both entered on F♯.

TABLE 11.1 Symmetrical macro-structure of *Das Rheingold*

Section	Episode(s)	Key(s)
THE RHINE	1–2	E♭–C
VALHALLA	3	D♭
Freia's Distress	5	E
GIANTS (Loge appears)	6–10	F–D–F♯–D–F
Freia's Distress	11	E
NIBELUNGS	12–14	B♭–A–B
Froh	15	C
GIANTS (Erda appears)	16–18	E♭–C–C♯–E♭
Donner	19	B♭
VALHALLA	20	D♭

GIANTS segment is framed by E minor episodes devoted to Freia's distress, while the second is surrounded by brief vocal solos sung by Freia's brothers. At the background level, then, the formal design of the opera is rigorously symmetrical.

The question of large-scale tonal structure is more complex. It may be helpful first to summarize how Wagner articulates the background levels of the individual episodes. As previously noted, all but three are controlled by a single tonality; of the exception, Episodes 6 and 16 are governed by double tonic complexes (F/D and E♭/C respectively), while Episode 14 features an 'expressive' tonal rise (B♭ to B). Three more episodes (9, 12, and 18) are tonally closed, but are controlled at the background level by linear rather than harmonic means. The majority of the episodes express a single key through the 'classical' tonic/dominant polarity: of these, seven (1, 3, 5, 11, 13, 15, and 20) execute complete I–V–I arpeggiations, while six (2, 7, 8, 10, 17, and 19) conclude on unresolved dominants.[2]

While the tonic/dominant fifth relationship thus prevails at the background levels of a sizeable number of episodes, it is noticeably absent from the background level of the entire opera. D♭ major frames Scenes 2–4 (the story of the gods), but is unsupported by any episode controlled by A♭. We may therefore assume that D♭ is prolonged contrapuntally rather than harmonically.

Example 11.1 offers an interpretation along these lines. At the background level (Ex. 11.1a), a D♭ major triad is expanded by

[2] Episode 4 is something of an anomaly: although controlled linearly at the background level by a single key (D minor), it also effects a transition to the key of the following episode (E minor). Its tonal fluidity is matched by its recitative texture. Of all the episodes, No. 4 is the most transitional in nature, and for that reason does not appear in Table 11.1.

Ex. 11.1

a.

b.

c.

5–6–5 neighbouring motion; the upper neighbour receives bass support, generating a B♭ minor triad. The initial D♭ triad is preceded by its leading tone (an incomplete lower neighbour), while the bass motion from B♭ back to D♭ is filled in by two passing tones (B and C).

At a later level (Ex. 11.1*b*), the upper third of D♭ is unfolded linearly, generating an F major triad; this is also expanded by a chromatic variant of the 5–6–5 motion. The upper third of the initial leading-tone is unfolded (E♭–C), as is that of the later passing tone (C–E♭). The final D♭ major triad is preceded by a chromatic variant of the 6–5 progression.

Example 11.1*c* displays a still later level, containing the tonal progression of the twenty episodes. In Scene 1, the initial E♭ functions as unfolded upper third of the leading-tone C; the latter resolves to D♭ at the beginning of Scene 2. The motion from D♭ to its unfolded

TABLE 11.2 Tonal symbolism in *Das Rheingold*

Key	Dramatic Association
D♭ Major	Valhalla
C♯ minor	Erda
D major*	Freia as goddess of youth, beauty, and love
D minor	Wotan's spear (the will to power)
E♭ major	The Rhine and the natural world
E major*	The potential of the ring
E minor*	Freia's distress
F major/minor	The giants
F♯ major/minor	Loge
G minor*	Mime's woe
G♯/A♭ minor	The tarnhelm
A major*	Alberich's downfall
B♭ major	Donner's power over the storm
B♭ minor	Alberich's power over the Nibelungs
B minor	Alberich's curse
C major	The gold in its natural state
C minor	The renunciation of love

third F is filled in by passing tones (D and E). The chromatic 5–6–5 neighbouring of F generates a move to D major and back; the latter is prolonged by motion to and from its upper third F♯. The final F is neighboured by E, which resolves back to an inner-voice F at the unfolding to B♭. The progression from B♭ back to D♭ is elaborated by the incomplete lower neighbour A and the two C–E♭ unfoldings, the second of which is filled in by Erda's D♭/C♯. The concluding 6–5 resolution generates the final B♭–D♭ move, which itself summarizes the tonal progression of Scenes 3–4.

At this level, then, Bailey's concepts of 'directional' and 'expressive' tonality yield to a more sophisticated notion of linear expansion. But what of 'associative' tonality? It cannot be denied that in *Das Rheingold* Wagner established a rather thoroughgoing system of key symbolism, much of which he would carry over into the main body of the tetralogy. Table 11.2 reveals that every step of the chromatic scale is imbued with semantic meaning; furthermore, only five keys (those marked with an asterisk) shed their initial dramatic associations as the *Ring* proceeds. Yet each key, at whatever level it appears, simultaneously serves a linear and/or harmonic purpose, and is never invoked as a mere tonal 'calling card'.

Our journey through *Das Rheingold* is at an end. Although many facets of the opera have necessarily been left unexamined, it is hoped that the foregoing study will be found useful by readers who wish to investigate other aspects of this endlessly fascinating work. Yet the odyssey of discovery upon which we embarked at the beginning of this book has by no means brought us back to our starting point. The gateway to the 'first day' of the *Ring* lies open and beckoning.

Appendix

Transcriptions from Wagner's Complete Draft

This Appendix contains transcriptions of selected portions of Wagner's Complete Draft (*Gesamtentwurf*) of *Das Rheingold* (WWV 86A Musik II). These transcriptions were made in Bayreuth from Wagner's autograph, and are referred to frequently in the text.

In making these transcriptions, fidelity to the original was balanced against the need for legibility. In the autograph, the textual underlay is often crowded, unhyphenated, and poorly aligned. The transcription reproduces Wagner's capitalizations and punctuation, but aligns syllables with note-heads and hyphenates where necessary. Wagner's stem directions are rather haphazard, and he always stems to the right of a notehead; the transcription preserves the original stem directions, but stems to the right or left according to normal practice. Non-aligned pitches have been properly aligned according to rhythmic placement within the bar. Incomplete rhythms (usually resulting from missing dots or rests) have been reproduced as written, sometimes accompanied by an editorial '*sic*'. All editorial comments and additions, including missing accidentals, are written in square brackets. The symbol [?] indicates an indecipherable notation.

The transcription contains all of Wagner's alterations. Simple changes involving crossed-out notes are reproduced as written. More elaborate changes, involving either crossings-out or overwriting, are represented by multiple vertical layers; successive variants are labelled as [A:], [B:], etc.

Although the entire draft was transcribed in preparation for this study, there could be no question of reproducing it in its entirety. Each portion contained here was selected because it differs significantly from the final version, and/or affords particular insight into the compositional genesis or structure of the passage. Among those sections reproduced in their entirety are:

Scene 1: the Prelude, the Rhinedaughters' first concerted song, and the Postlude

Scene 2: the entrance of Donner and Froh (Episode 7 complete)

Scene 3: the appearance of the giant serpent

Scene 4: Alberich's curse, Erda's warning (Episode 17 complete), and Donner's conjuration of the storm (Episode 19 complete)

Although every effort has been made to ensure accuracy, transcription (like analysis) is necessarily an interpretative process. A 'definitive' reading is probably impossible—one more reason why Wagner's autographs should continue to be the object of scholarly investigation.

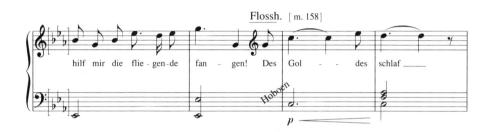

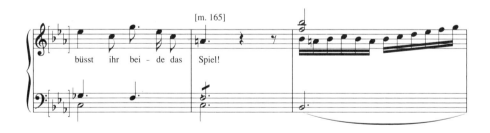

[m. 435]

minn'st?

Treu sind wir, und oh - ne trug dem frei - er, der uns

[Added later]

fängt.

grei - fe nur zu, und grau - se dich nicht, in der fluth entfliehn wir nicht

[m. 441]

8 -

[fo. 4ʳ]

leicht. Wal -la - la!

la la lei - a!

lai - a - la lei!

hei - a! hei - a ha

hei!

cresc. molto —   —   —

[fo. 6 ᵛ]
[m. 716]

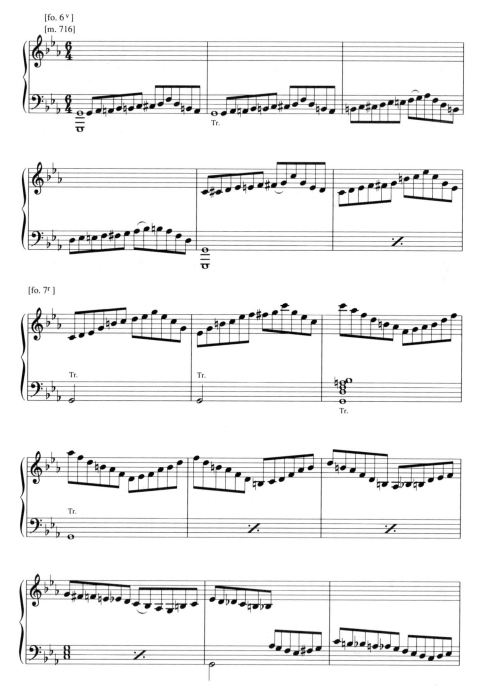

[fo. 7 ʳ]

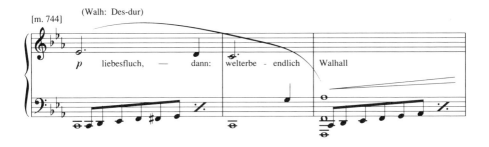

[* This clef indicates
that the repeated
notes are to be read
in tenor clef.]

[* These notes to be read in
treble clef.]

[fo. 25 ᵛ]

[m. 2664]   (langsam u. schneller)

[fo. 37 r]

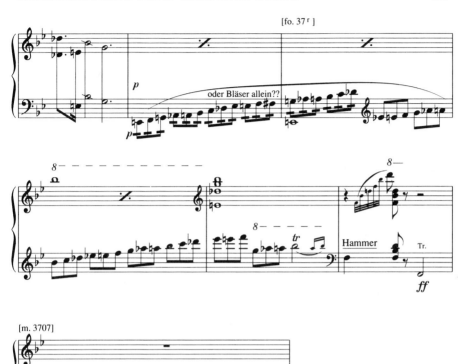

[m. 3707]

Works Cited

I. DOCUMENTARY SOURCES

Documents are cited by WWV catalogue numbers. Terminology follows that of *WWV*. Most manuscripts are housed in the Nationalarchiv der Richard-Wagner-Stiftung, Bayreuth (NA).

a. *Das Rheingold*:

WWV 86A Text Ia	NA (A II g 1). Prose sketch (*Prosaskizze*).
WWV 86A Text Ib	NA (B II a 4). Supplementary prose sketches (*Prosaskizzen*).
WWV 86A Text II	NA (A II g 2). Prose draft (*Prosaentwurf*).
WWV 86A Text III	NA (A II g 3). Verse draft (*Erstschrift des Textbuches*).
WWV 86A Text IV	NA (A II g 4). Fair copy of poem (*Reinschrift des Textbuches*).
WWV 86A Text Va	Pp. 1–20: Musikverlag B. Schott's Söhne, Mainz. Pp. 21–28: NA (A II g 5). Pp. 29–34: lost. Wagner's personal copy of Text VI (*Handexemplar für die Komposition*).
WWV 86A Text Vb	New York, Pierpont Morgan Library. Interleaved copy of Text VI.
WWV 86A Text Vc	Richard-Wagner-Gedenkstätte der Stadt Bayreuth. Copy of Text VI.
WWV 86A Text VI	First (private) printing of *Ring* text (1853), pp. 1–34 (*Erstdruck des Textbuches*).
WWV 86A Text VIIa	First public printing of *Ring* text (Leipzig, 1863), pp. 1–95.
WWV 86A Text VIIb	First independent printing of *Das Rheingold* text (Mainz, 1869).
WWV 86A Text VIIf	*Gesammelte Schriften und Dichtungen*, vol. v (Leipzig, 1872), 257–352.
WWV 86A Musik Ia	NA. Single sketches (*Einzelskizzen*) entered in Text III and Text Va.
WWV 86A Musik Ib	NA (A II a 1). Single sketches (*Einzelskizzen*).
WWV 86A Musik Ic	NA (A II a 5 (*Tristan* sketches!)). Orchestral sketch.
WWV 86A Musik II	NA (A III a 1). Complete draft (*Gesamtentwurf*).

WWV 86A Musik III	NA (A III a 2); New York Public Library (JOC 73-24); Princeton, Scheide Collection. See *WWV* 354–5 for details. Draft of full score (*Partiturerstschrift*).
WWV 86A Musik IV	Lost. Fair copy of full score (*Reinschrift der Partitur*).
WWV 86A Musik Va	Princeton, Scheide Collection. Anonymous copy of Musik IV, Prelude only (*Partitur von fremder Hand*).
WWV 86A Musik Vb	NA. Copy of Musik IV by Friedrich Wölfel (*Partitur von fremder Hand*).
WWV 86A Musik IX	First printing of score (1873) by B. Schott's Söhne, Mainz (*Erstdruck der Partitur*). Repr. by Dover (New York, 1985).
WWV 86A Musik XIb	Critical edition of score, ed. Egon Voss. *Sämtliche Werke*, vol. x.

b. *Die Walküre*:

WWV 86B Text Ia	NA (A II g 1). Prose sketch (*Prosaskizze*).
WWV 86B Text Ib	NA (B II a 4). Supplementary prose sketches (*Prosaskizzen*).
WWV 86B Text II	NA (A II h 1). Prose draft (*Prosaentwurf*).
WWV 86B Text III	NA (A II h 2). Verse draft (*Erstschrift des Textbuches*).

c. *Der junge Siegfried*:

WWV 86C Text I	Private Collection. Photocopy in NA (A II f). Prose sketches (*Prosaskizzen*).
WWV 86C Text II	NA (A II f 1). Prose draft (*Prosaentwurf*).
WWV 86C Text III	Private Collection. Photocopy in NA (A II f). Verse draft (*Erstschrift des Textbuches*).

d. *Siegfried's Tod*:

WWV 86D Text Ia	NA (A II d 2). *Die Nibelungensage (Mythus)*: draft (*Erstschrift*).
WWV 86D Text Ib	NA (A II d 3). *Die Sage von den Nibelungen*: fair copy (*Reinschrift*) of Text Ia. NA (Metal box). Anonymous copy of Text Ia, with pencil corrections and alterations in Wagner's hand.
WWV 86D Text IIa	NA (A II e 1). Prose draft (*Prosaentwurf*) of Acts I–III.
WWV 86D Text IIb	NA (A II e 1). Prose draft (*Prosaentwurf*) of Prologue.

WWV 86D Text III	Private collection. Photocopy in NA (A II e $4^{(1)}$). Verse draft (*Erstschrift des Textbuches*).
WWV 86D Text IV	Stadtbibliothek Winterthur, Switzerland (Fo. no. 201, p. 36). First fair copy of poem (*Zweitschrift des Textbuches*).
WWV 86D Text V	Private collection. Second fair copy of poem (*Drittschrift des Textbuches*).
WWV 86D Text VIa	NA (A II e 2). Revision of Norns scene from Prologue: prose draft (*Prosaentwurf*).
WWV 86D Text VIb	NA (A II e $3^{(1)}$). Verse draft (*Erstschrift des Textbuches*) of Text VIa.
WWV 86D Text VIIIb	NA (B II a 5). Revision of ending: prose sketch (*Prosaskizze*), presumably dating from 1856.
WWV 86D Text VIIIc	Revision of ending: verse draft (*Erstschrift des Textbuches*) and fair copy (*Zweitschrift des Textbuches*), presumably dating from 1871/2. Entered into Wagner's copy of 1853 printing (Text XIIa), p. 159.
WWV 86D Text XIII	First (private) printing of *Ring* text (1853), pp. 121–59 (*Erstdruck des Textbuches*).
WWV 86D Musik Ib–d	Washington, Library of Congress (ML 96. W 56 W 26 Case). One sheet, containing single sketches (*Einzelskizzen*) for the Valkyrie scene (I. 3), a draft (*Entwurf*) of the final song and departure of the Valkyries (I. 3), and a fragmentary draft (*fragmentarischer Entwurf*) of the Prologue. See *WWV* 397 for details.
WWV 86D Musik Ie	Lost. Facsimile published in *L'Illustration* (Paris, 11 Feb. 1933), 167 ff. and *Neue Zeitschrift für Musik* 124, no. 5 (1963), 180–1. Second draft of the Prologue (*Zweiter Entwurf zum Vorspiel*).

II. CATALOGUE AND COLLECTED WORKS

Wagner Werk-Verzeichnis (WWV): Verzeichnis der musikalischen Werke Richard Wagners und ihrer Quellen, ed. John Deathridge, Martin Geck, and Egon Voss (Mainz, 1986).

Richard Wagner, Sämtliche Werke: In Zusammenarbeit mit der Bayerischen Akademie der Schönen Künste, München, gen. eds. Carl Dahlhaus and Egon Voss (planned in 31 vols., Mainz, 1970–).

III. AUTOBIOGRAPHICAL AND COLLECTED WRITINGS

Wagner, Cosima, *Cosima Wagner's Diaries*, ed. Martin Gregor-Dellin and Dietrich Mack, trans. Geoffrey Skelton (2 vols., New York, 1978, 1980).

Wagner, Richard, *Gesammelte Schriften und Dichtungen von Richard Wagner* (10 vols., Leipzig, 1871–83).

—— *Gesammelte Schriften und Dichtungen von Richard Wagner* (10 vols., Leipzig, 1887–8; repr. Hildesheim, 1976).

—— *Richard Wagner's Prose Works*, trans. William Ashton Ellis (8 vols., London, 1892–9).

—— *Mein Leben: Erste authentische Veröffentlichung*, ed. Martin Gregor-Dellin (Munich, 1963).

—— *Das Braune Buch: Tagebuchaufzeichnungen 1865 bis 1882*, ed. Joachim Bergfeld (Zurich, 1975).

—— *The Diary of Richard Wagner 1865–1882: The Brown Book*, trans. George Bird (London, 1980).

—— *My Life*, trans. Andrew Gray, ed. Mary Whittall (Cambridge, 1983).

IV. CORRESPONDENCE

Richard Wagner, Sämtliche Briefe, ed. Gertrude Strobel, Werner Wolf, Hans-Joachim Bauer, and Johannes Forner (Leipzig, 1967–).

Richard Wagners Briefe an Theodor Uhlig, Wilhelm Fischer, Ferdinand Heine (Leipzig, 1888).

Richard Wagner's Letters to August Röckel, trans. Eleanor C. Sellar (Bristol, n.d. [1897]).

Selected Letters of Richard Wagner, trans. and ed. Stewart Spencer and Barry Millington (London, 1987).

Franz Liszt–Richard Wagner Briefwechsel, ed. Hanjo Kesting (Frankfurt, 1988).

V. BOOKS AND ARTICLES

Abbate, Carolyn, 'Opera as Symphony, A Wagnerian Myth', in *Analyzing Opera: Verdi and Wagner*, ed. Carolyn Abbate and Roger Parker (Berkeley and Los Angeles, 1989), 92–124.

—— 'Wagner, "On Modulation", and *Tristan*', *Cambridge Opera Journal*, 1 (1989), 33–58.

—— *Unsung Voices: Opera and Musical Narrative in the Nineteenth Century* (Princeton, NJ, 1991).

——, and Roger Parker, 'Introduction: On Analyzing Opera', in *Analyzing Opera: Verdi and Wagner*, ed. Carolyn Abbate and Roger Parker (Berkeley and Los Angeles, 1989), 1–24.

Bailey, Robert. 'Wagner's Musical Sketches for *Siegfrieds Tod*', in *Studies in Music History: Essays for Oliver Strunk*, ed. Harold Powers (Princeton, NJ, 1968), 459–94.

—— 'The Genesis of *Tristan und Isolde* and a Study of Wagner's Sketches and Drafts for the First Act', Ph.D. diss. (Princeton University, 1969).

—— 'The Structure of the *Ring* and its Evolution', *19th Century Music*, 1 (1977), 48–61.

—— 'The Method of Composition', in *The Wagner Companion*, ed. Peter Burbidge and Richard Sutton (London, 1979), 269–338.

Bailey, Robert, 'An Analytical Study of the Sketches and Drafts', in Richard Wagner, *Prelude and Transformation from 'Tristan und Isolde'*, ed. Robert Bailey (New York, 1985), 113–46.

Brinkmann, Reinhold, '"Drei der Fragen stell' ich mir frei": Zur Wanderer-Szene im I. Akt von Wagners *Siegfried*', in *Jahrbuch des Staatlichen Instituts für Musik-Forschung Preussischer Kulturbesitz* (Berlin, 1972), 120–62.

Brown, Matthew, 'Isolde's Narrative: From *Hauptmotif* to Tonal Model', in *Analyzing Opera: Verdi and Wagner*, ed. Carolyn Abbate and Roger Parker (Berkeley and Los Angeles, 1989), 180–201.

Cooke, Deryck, *An Introduction to 'Der Ring des Nibelungen'* (Decca Records RDN S-1, 1969).

—— *I Saw the World End* (London, 1979).

Coren, Daniel, 'The Texts of Wagner's *Der junge Siegfried* and *Siegfried*', *19th Century Music*, 6 (1982), 17–30.

Dahlhaus, Carl, 'Wagners Begriff der "dichterisch–musikalische Periode"', in *Beiträge zur Geschichte der Musikanschauung im neunzehnten Jahrhundert*, ed. Walter Salmen (Regensburg, 1965), 179–94.

—— *Richard Wagner's Music Dramas*, trans. Mary Whittall (Cambridge, 1979). Originally published as *Die Musikdramen Richard Wagners* (Velber, 1971).

—— *Between Romanticism and Modernism: Four Studies in the Music of the Later Nineteenth Century*, trans. Mary Whittall (Berkeley and Los Angeles, 1980). Originally published as *Zwischen Romantik und Moderne: Vier Studien zur Musikgeschichte des späteren 19. Jahrhunderts* (Munich, 1974).

—— *Nineteenth Century Music*, trans. J. Bradford Robinson (Berkeley and Los Angeles, 1989). Originally published as *Die Musik des 19. Jahrhunderts* (Wiesbaden, 1980).

Darcy, Warren, 'Formal and Rhythmic Problems in Wagner's "Ring" Cycle', D.M.A. diss. (University of Illinois, 1973).

—— 'The Pessimism of the *Ring*', *The Opera Quarterly*, 4/2 (1986), 24–48.

—— '"Alles was ist, endet!" Erda's Prophecy of World Destruction', *Programmheft II ('Das Rheingold') der Bayreuther Festspiele 1988*, 67–92.

—— '*Creatio ex nihilo*: The Genesis, Structure, and Meaning of the *Rheingold* Prelude', *19th Century Music*, 13 (1989), 79–100.

—— 'A Wagnerian *Ursatz*; or, Was Wagner a Background Composer After All?', *Intégral*, 4 (1990), 1–35.

Deathridge, John, 'Wagner's Sketches for the "Ring"', *Musical Times*, 118 (1977), 383–9.

—— 'Cataloguing Wagner', in *The Richard Wagner Centenary in Australia*, ed. Peter Dennison (Adelaide, 1985), 185–99.

——, and Carl Dahlhaus, *The New Grove Wagner* (New York and London, 1984).

Donington, Robert, *Wagner's 'Ring' and its Symbols* (London, 1963, 1969, 1974).

Forte, Allen, 'New Approaches to the Linear Analysis of Music', *Journal of the American Musicological Society*, 41 (1988), 315–48.

Genette, Gérard, *Narrative Discourse: An Essay in Method* (Ithaca, NJ, 1980). Originally published as 'Discours du récit' in *Figures III* (Paris, 1972).

Glass, Frank W., *The Fertilizing Seed: Wagner's Concept of the Poetic Intent* (Ann Arbor, Mich., 1983).

Grey, Thomas, 'Richard Wagner and the Aesthetics of Musical Form in the Mid-19th Century (1840–1860)', Ph.D. diss. (University of California, Berkeley, 1988).

Knapp, J. Merrill, 'The Instrumentation Draft of Wagner's *Das Rheingold*', *Journal of the American Musicological Society*, 30 (1977), 272–95.

Kurth, Ernst, *Romantische Harmonik und ihre Krise in Wagner's 'Tristan und Isolde'* (Berne, 1920).

Lorenz, Alfred, *Das Geheimnis der Form bei Richard Wagner*, i: *Der musikalische Aufbau des Bühnenfestspieles Der Ring des Nibelungen* (Berlin, 1924; repr. Tutzing, 1966).

Magee, Elizabeth, *Richard Wagner and the Nibelungs* (Oxford, 1990).

McCreless, Patrick, *Wagner's 'Siegfried': Its Drama, History, and Music* (Ann Arbor, Mich., 1982).

—— 'Schenker and the Norns', in *Analyzing Opera: Verdi and Wagner*, ed. Carolyn Abbate and Roger Parker (Berkeley and Los Angeles, 1989), 276–97.

Mitchell, William J., 'The *Tristan* Prelude: Techniques and Structure', in *The Music Forum*, i, ed. William J. Mitchell and Felix Salzer (New York, 1967), 163–203.

Newcomb, Anthony, 'The Birth of Music out of the Spirit of Drama: An Essay in Wagnerian Formal Analysis', *19th Century Music*, 5 (1981–2), 38–66.

Newman, Ernest, *The Life of Richard Wagner* (London, 1933–47; repr. Cambridge, 1976).

—— *Wagner Nights* (London, 1949; repr. 1961, 1977). Published in the United States as *The Wagner Operas* (New York, 1949; repr. 1963).

Nitsche, Peter, 'Transponierte Notation bei Wagner', in *Richard Wagner: Werk und Wirkung*, ed. Carl Dahlhaus (*Studien zur Musikgeschichte des 19. Jahrhunderts*, 26; Regensburg, 1971), 221–36.

Porges, Heinrich, *Wagner Rehearsing the Ring*, trans. Robert L. Jacobs (Cambridge, 1983). Originally published as *Die Bühnenproben zu den Bayreuther Festspielen des Jahres 1876* (Chemnitz, 1881–96).

Prince, Gerald, *A Dictionary of Narratology* (Lincoln, Nebr., and London, 1987).

Rimmon-Kenan, Shlomith, *Narrative Fiction: Contemporary Poetics* (London and New York, 1983).

Schenker, Heinrich, 'Organic Structure in Sonata Form', trans. Orin Grossman, in *Readings in Schenkerian Analysis and Other Approaches*, ed. Maury Yeston (New Haven, Conn., 1977), 38–53.

—— *Free Composition*, trans. Ernst Oster (New York, 1979). Originally published as *Der freie Satz*, vol. iii of *Neue musikalische Theorien und Phantasien* (Vienna, 1935).

Strobel, Otto, 'Die Originalpartitur von Richard Wagners *Rheingold*', *Bayreuther Festspielführer* (1928), 47–55.

—— *Richard Wagner: Skizzen und Entwürfe zur Ring-Dichtung: Mit der Dichtung 'Der junge Siegfried'* (Munich, 1930).

—— 'Die Kompositionsskizzen zum *Ring des Nibelungen*: Ein Blick in die Musikwerkstatt Richard Wagners', *Bayreuther Festspielführer* (1930), 114–22.

—— 'Aus Wagners Musikwerkstatt: Betrachtungen über die Kompositions-skizzen zum *Ring des Nibelungen*', *Allgemeine Musikzeitung*, 58 (1931), 463–5, 479–82, 495–8.

Warrack, John, 'Leitmotif', in *The New Grove Dictionary of Music and Musicians*, ed. Stanley Sadie (London, 1980), x. 644–6.

Westernhagen, Curt von, 'Die Kompositions-Skizze zu *Siegfrieds Tod* aus dem Jahre 1850', *Neue Zeitschrift für Musik* 124, no. 5 (1963), 178–82 and musical supplement.

—— *Richard Wagners Dresdener Bibliothek, 1842–1849: Neue Dokumente zur Geschichte seines Schaffens* (Wiesbaden, 1966).

—— *The Forging of the 'Ring'*, trans. Arnold and Mary Whittall (Cambridge, 1976). Originally published as *Die Entstehung des 'Ring'* (Zurich, 1973).

Windell, George C., 'Hegel, Feuerbach, and Wagner's *Ring*', *Central European History*, 9 (1976), 27–57.

Wintle, Christopher, 'The Numinous in *Götterdämmerung*', in *Reading Opera*, ed. Arthur Groos and Roger Parker (Princeton, NJ, 1988), 202–11.

Wolzogen, Hans von, *Thematischer Leitfaden durch die Musik zu Richard Wagner's Festspiel 'Der Ring des Nibelungen'* (Leipzig, 1876).

—— 'Die Motive in Wagner's *Götterdämmerung*', *Musikalisches Wochen-blatt*, 8 (1877), 9 (1878), 10 (1879).

Index

Abbate, Carolyn 49 n., 50, 51 n., 56, 59, 172 n.
Alberich 25–6, 31, 32, 34–42, 48, 60, 87, 97–110, 112–19, 121–3, 125, 150–1, 153, 156, 163–7, 170, 172, 174–9, 181, 183, 185–92, 195, 196–7, 205, 207–8
apples, Freia's (Holda's) 35–6, 43, 140, 143–4, 158

Bailey, Robert 2 n., 9 n., 11, 20, 22, 23, 52–3, 56, 73 n., 100, 218
Bayreuth archives 8–9, 15, 18 n., 21 n., 22 n., 24, 51 n., 220
Beethoven, Ludwig van 108
Symphony No. 9 in D minor 77 n.
Brahms, Johannes 53, 55, 215
Brinkmann, Reinhold 2 n.
Brown, Matthew 55 n.
Brünnhilde (Brünhild, Brünhilde) 8–9, 10 n., 25–30, 32, 35–6, 37 n., 38 n., 87 n., 137 n., 197
Bülow, Hans von 21 n.

compositional process 2–3
Cooke, Deryck 3 n., 32, 49–50, 106 n., 120, 164
Coren, Daniel 39 n.
curse, Alberich's 29, 34, 40, 60, 185, 191–2, 196–7, 199–200, 202, 204, 220

Dahlhaus, Carl 47 n., 53–5, 59, 61, 79, 215
Darcy, Warren 30 n., 55 n., 56 n., 62 n., 68 n., 196 n.
Deathridge, John 2 n., 29 n., 62 n., 63–4, 67, 71, 122–3, 179–80
Donington, Robert 3 n.
Donner (Donnar) 19, 32, 37 n., 42–3, 130 n., 144, 147 n., 192, 195, 203, 205–9, 220
dragon (serpent) 26, 35, 38, 40, 42, 175, 179, 220
Dubez, Peter 209 n.

Eger, Manfred 24 n.
Ellis, William Ashton 9
Erda 13 n., 32, 35, 39, 42, 65, 68–9, 196–202
see also Wala

Fafner 32, 34, 38, 41–3, 130, 140–1, 143–4, 148, 157, 159, 183, 194–6, 203–4, 208
Fasolt 32, 34, 41–2, 140–3, 157, 194–6, 203–4
Feuerbach, Ludwig 28–30
Fischer, Günter 8 n.
Flosshilde (Flosslinde) 42–3, 90–1, 94–5, 97, 99–100, 102–3, 107–9, 114
formal structure 55–8
Bailey and McCreless on 56
Dahlhaus on 57, 61, 215
Lorenz on 56–8, 58–61
Newcomb on 58 n.
Forte, Allen 55 n.
Freia (Freija) 24, 32, 35, 37 n., 39–42, 130, 135, 138–40, 144, 147, 150–2, 183, 193–6, 202–4, 209
Fricka (Frigga, Frikka) 32, 35, 37 n., 39–42, 130–1, 134–41, 144, 150, 155–6, 161, 192, 194, 203, 205, 209–10, 212
Froh (Fro) 37 n., 38 n., 42, 79, 130 n., 144–5, 147 n., 192–3, 203, 205, 208–9, 220

Genette, Gérard 151 n.
giants 26, 34–5, 38, 39–43, 130, 140, 183, 193–5
see also Fafner; Fasolt; Reiffrost; Windfahrer
Glass, Frank W. 46 n., 51 n., 56 n.
gods 26, 34–5, 159, 183, 187, 189, 196–9, 207–8
see also Donner; Erda; Freia; Fricka; Froh; Loge; Wotan
Goethe, Johann Wolfgang, *Faust* 12 n.
Grey, Thomas 58 n.
Grimm, Jacob 42, 197
Gunther 17, 26, 31
Gutrune (Gudrun, Gudrune) 16–17, 32, 38 n.

Hagen 26, 31, 32, 37–8
Hegel, Georg Wilhelm Friedrich 26–7, 29 n.
Herwegh, Georg 63
Hitler, Adolf 23 n.
hoard 34, 39–42, 164–5, 175, 185, 188, 193–5

Jähns, Otto 47 n.

Klindworth, Karl 21 n.
Knapp, J. Merrill 22 n., 73 n., 76 n., 170
Köhler, Louis 21 n.
Kurth, Ernst 53

leitmotifs 45–51
  allied with gesture 45–7, 112–14, 157; as
    foreshadowings 46–8, 120, 136, 141,
    157; as reminiscences 46, 48, 113, 122,
    136; as signs 47–8, 50, 154, 157; as
    symphonic themes 49; formal/referential
    dialectic 49–50
  individual:
    Glorification of Brünnhilde (Love's
    Redemption) 29 n.; Love (Flight) 49 n.;
    Volsungs 30 n.; see also RHEINGOLD
Lippmann, Edmund von 29
Liszt, Franz 9, 11, 21 n., 30, 63
  Piano Sonata in B minor 183 n.
Loge (Loke) 14, 15 n., 20 n., 32, 35, 40–4,
  60, 130, 135, 147–59, 161, 164, 166, 168,
  172, 174–7, 180, 183–4, 187, 192, 203,
  205, 208–13
Lorenz, Alfred 2 n., 49–50, 52, 56–61, 76,
  83, 108, 185
Ludwig II, King of Bavaria 23 n.

McCreless, Patrick 1–2 n., 52, 55–6
Magee, Elizabeth 3 n.
Meyerbeer, Giacomo, Le Prophète 130–1 n.
Mime (Reigin, Eugel) 34, 38, 40–1, 87 n.,
  164–74
Mitchell, William J. 55 n.

Neidhöhle (Gnitaheide, Neidheide) 35, 38 n.
Newcomb, Anthony 58 n.
Newman, Ernest 49, 63
Nibelheim (Nebelheim) 33, 37, 128, 160, 181
Nibelungs 26, 33–5, 37–8, 40–2, 164–5,
  172–3, 185, 188–9
  see also Alberich; Mime
Nitsche, Peter 80 n.
Norns 26, 31, 35–7, 65–6, 86, 196–8, 200

Parker, Roger 49 n.
poetic–musical period 55–60
  Bailey and McCreless on 56
  Dahlhaus on 57, 59
  Grey on 58 n.
  Lorenz on 56–9
  Wagner on 55–6, 59
Porges, Heinrich 17
potion of forgetfulness 27–8

Reiffrost 39, 140

renunciation of love 25, 34, 39–40, 115–19,
  125, 154, 194

RHEINGOLD, DAS, opera by Wagner:
anvils 161–2, 164, 181, 183
associative keys:
  A major/minor 164, 177, 187
  B♭ major 184, 207
  B♭ minor 106, 164, 174, 177–8, 184, 187,
    191, 207, 214
  B minor 184, 187, 191, 204, 214
  C major 88, 155, 213
  C minor 88, 97, 179, 184, 194
  C♯ minor 68–9, 184, 196, 199
  D♭ major 68, 130, 149, 177, 179, 184
  D major 130, 143–4, 157
  D minor 130, 137, 148
  E♭ major 88, 184, 194–5, 204, 207 n.
  E major 137, 156
  F major/minor 130, 140 n., 157, 194
  F♯ major/minor 130, 148–9, 157, 177
  G♯/A♭ minor 168–70, 174, 177–8
associative tonality 52, 60, 130, 140, 149, 184,
  218
  see also associative keys above
break with operatic conventions 1
cast of characters 14
classical tonality 52, 60, 135, 149, 216
compositional history 6–12
  music 11–12
  text 6–11
directional tonality 52, 60, 142, 184, 218
division into episodes 59–61
double-tonic complex 52, 142, 216
expressive tonality 52, 60, 100, 130, 137–8,
  154, 157, 179, 187, 216, 218
formal/tonal structure 59–61
  antecedent-consequent structures 134,
    153–4, 172–3, 193
  arias 131–5, 141–4, 206
  bar forms 83, 100, 104, 108–9, 143–4, 188,
    204
  binary (bipartite) forms 91, 142, 151–3,
    162, 182, 193
  cyclical structures 101–10, 113–14, 116–
    18, 121–3, 155–6, 194–6
  interruption structures 88–90, 134–5,
    139–40, 183, 201–2, 211–13
  recitatives 136–8, 141, 143, 149, 159,
    185–9, 206
  rondo forms 142, 159, 175–8, 195, 204–5
  strophic forms 168, 172–4
  symmetrical patterns 111, 143, 172, 187,
    191–2, 206–7, 215–16
  ternary (tripartite) forms 88, 128–9, 131,
    134, 139, 148, 166–8, 202, 212, 215
  theme and variations 66, 76–86

through-composed structures 136, 146–7, 157, 194, 204
individual episodes:
Prelude 12, 19, 21, 22 n., 23–4, 61, 62–86, 87, 91, 93, 98, 105, 126, 153, 193, 196 n., 220
Ep. 1: 87–112, 114, 126, 216
Transition 112–15
Ep. 2: 60, 87, 112, 115–25, 126, 216
Postlude 87, 120, 125–6
First Transformation 127–8, 134, 138, 174
Ep. 3: 128–9, 130–5, 139, 149, 211–13, 215–16
Ep. 4: 130, 135–8, 141, 143, 216 n.
Ep. 5: 138–40, 216
Ep. 6: 60, 129, 140–4, 157, 184, 194, 216
Ep. 7: 60, 141–2, 144–7, 157, 216, 220
Ep. 8: 130, 147–9, 157, 216
Ep. 9: 149, 150–7, 216
Ep. 10: 157–8, 216
Ep. 11: 158–60, 162, 216
Second Transformation 159, 161–4, 168
Ep. 12: 128, 162, 164–75, 182, 187–8, 208, 215–16
Ep. 13: 60, 175–80, 182, 215–16
Third Transformation 181–4, 193
Ep. 14: 60, 184, 185–92, 193 n., 215–16
Ep. 15: 60, 192–3, 216
Ep. 16: 60, 184, 193–6, 216
Ep. 17: 39, 60, 65–6, 68–70, 86, 196–202, 216, 220
Ep. 18: 60, 202–5, 208, 216
Ep. 19: 205–8, 216, 220
Ep. 20: 128, 208–14, 215–16
influence of poetic rhythm on phraseology 1, 92–6, 98–100, 104–5, 107–11, 118–20
leitmotifs and verse-melodies:
Alberich's Stumbling 103–4, 106, 108, 114, 120 n.
Arrogance of Power 177, 183, 210–11
Curse 191–2, 203–5
Donner 19, 145–6
Dragon 163, 177, 179–80
'dritte so traut, die' (Alberich) 164, 183
Erda/Norns 68–70, 81–2, 93, 199–201, 204, 212
Freia 19, 135, 140, 143, 145, 153–5, 157, 164, 194–6
Froh 145
Giants 19, 135, 139, 141–4, 183, 193–5, 204
Gold 48, 50, 68, 116–17, 120, 154, 157, 164, 191
Golden Apples 143–5, 157, 159, 183, 193, 196
'Heda! heda! hedo!' (Donner) 206
'Heia, du Holder!' (Wellgunde) 104, 114, 157, 193
'Herrliche Wohnung, wonniger Hausrath' (Fricka) 135, 155
Hoard 177, 188, 194–5
Loge 139, 147–9, 153, 158–9, 161, 163, 177, 181–4, 187, 212–13
Magic Fire 148–9
Nature 67, 71–2, 76, 78–80, 84
Nature in Motion 120–1, 123, 126, 128, 153
Nibelungs 161–2, 164, 183, 192, 194–5, 203–4
Power of the Ring 175, 188, 208
Rainbow 79–80, 86, 193, 212
Renunciation of Love 48, 119–20, 122, 127–8, 135–6, 138, 153, 155, 179
Resentment 192–3
'Rheingold! Rheingold!' (the Rhinedaughters) 120, 126, 155, 157, 175, 183, 196, 204, 213
Rhine 83–4, 91, 97, 99–100, 106, 108, 121
Rhinedaughters, see 'Weia! Waga!' below
Ring 122, 127–8, 155, 161–2, 164, 174, 182–3, 188, 191, 193 n., 196, 204–5, 212
'Schein' ich nicht schön dir' (Alberich) 106, 113, 115, 120 n., 174–5
Scheming 188
Spear 136–8, 141–3, 148–9, 189
Sword 30, 48, 210, 212, 214
Tarnhelm 168–70, 174, 177
Toad 177
Treaty with the Giants, see 'Weisst du nicht offen' below
Twilight of the Gods 69–70, 201
Valhalla 19, 47–8, 127–8, 132–4, 142, 148–9, 162, 177, 179, 205, 209–14
'Wehe!' (Alberich) 137, 163–4, 183, 196
'Weia! Waga!' (Woglinde) 71, 91–3, 96–7, 111, 114–15, 117, 121, 154, 157
'Weibes Wonne und Werth' (Loge) 151, 153–4, 156, 163, 191
'Weisst du nicht offen' 184, 194–5
'Wie in den Gliedern' (Alberich) 113–14
lighting effects 87
Loge's narration 42, 120–1, 151–5
love/power dialectic 28–9, 130, 142, 194
manuscript sources (music):
anonymous copy of Prelude 12, 23–4
complete draft (Gesamtentwurf) 11, 19–21, 63, 65–9, 79 n., 91–6, 99–101, 103–8, 111–12, 114, 120–3, 126, 131–2, 138–9, 140–1, 145–6, 147, 151, 153–5, 157–8, 161–3, 168, 179–80, 181–2, 188–91, 193, 194, 199–201, 203–4, 206, 209–11, 220–1
draft of score (Partiturerstschrift) 11–12,

RHEINGOLD (*cont.*):
manuscript sources (music) (*cont.*):
  draft of score (*cont.*):
    21–4, 63, 72–6, 79, 81–2, 98–9, 112,
      122, 128, 132, 139, 141, 146, 157, 168,
      170, 179–80, 182, 188, 191, 194, 203–4,
      209–10
  fair copy of score (*Reinschrift*) 11–12,
      22–3, 73, 112
  orchestral sketch (entrance of Donner and
      Froh) 24, 145
  preliminary sketches 11, 17–19, 64 n.,
      70–2, 76, 82, 91, 132, 135, 141
  Wölfel's copy of score 12, 23–4, 72–3, 210
manuscript sources (text):
  fair copy of poem 10, 15, 91, 127, 135, 144,
      147 n., 150–1, 158, 161, 165–6, 175, 181,
      198, 205, 208–9
  letter to Liszt (20 Nov. 1851) 13, 101,
      115–16
  prose draft 9–10, 13–14, 42–3, 71, 90–1,
      98, 110, 112–13, 117–18, 125, 127, 135,
      138, 140, 144, 147, 150, 155, 158, 161,
      165, 175, 181, 185, 194, 198, 202–3, 205,
      208, 209 n.
  prose sketch (initial) 9–10, 12–13, 31 n.,
      39–40, 101, 110, 112, 115, 125, 127, 130,
      140, 158, 161, 164, 175, 181, 185, 193,
      197, 202
  prose sketches (supplementary) 10, 13,
      41–2, 130, 135, 138, 147, 150, 158, 161,
      164–5, 193, 202, 208
  verse draft 10, 11, 14–15, 17–18, 43, 71,
      90–1, 110, 113, 118, 127, 135, 144,
      147 n., 150–1, 157–8, 161, 165–6, 175,
      181, 185, 198, 203 n., 205, 208–9
narrative techniques 151
overall formal/tonal structure 215–18
parallels with *Götterdämmerung* 31–3, 36–7
printed editions (poem):
  first private printing of *Ring* poem (1853)
      10–11, 15–16, 18, 91, 110, 127, 135, 144,
      166, 175, 181, 205; Wagner's personal
      copy 11, 15–16, 68, other copies 16 n.
  first public printing of *Das Rheingold*
      poem (1869) 16
  first public printing of *Ring* poem (1863)
      11, 16
  Gesammelte Schriften edition of *Ring*
      poem (1872) 11
printed editions (score):
  first printing (1872) 12, 24, 73, 209 n.
  Sämtliche Werke edition 24 n.
title 10, 13, 14 n.
transpositions of brass instruments 24, 73,
      132, 180

Rhinedaughters 31, 34, 36–7, 39–43, 65, 70,
      86, 90–126, 150–1, 154, 156, 197,
      208–10, 213–14, 220
  see also Flosshilde; Wellgunde; Woglinde
Rhinegold 34, 39–42, 48, 50, 60, 87, 101–2,
      115–18, 125, 150, 156, 183
Riemann, Hugo 53–4
Riesenheim 157–8
Rimmon-Kenan, Shlomith 151 n.
ring 34–6, 38, 40–2, 117–18, 125, 150, 175,
      185, 188–91, 193–4, 196–9, 202, 204
Ritter, Emilie 63, 66
Röckel, August 10, 29 n., 33 n.

Sayn-Wittgenstein, Marie 118
Scheide, William A. 24 n.
Scheide Collection (Princeton) 22 n., 23,
      24 n.
Schenker, Heinrich 54, 88 n.
Schenkerian analysis 5, 54–5
  applied divider 89–90, 96, 123, 124 n., 125
  auxiliary cadence 124, 191
  transference of fundamental
      structure 124 n.
Schoenberg, Arnold 53
Schopenhauer, Arthur 29, 33, 63
Schott's publishing house (Mainz) 12, 15–16,
      18
Siegfried 25–32, 34–5, 38–9, 197
Siegfried's Tod, poem by Wagner 25, 36, 197
  ending 9, 10 n., 28–30
  Gesammelte Schriften printing (1871) 8, 16
  Hagen's Watch 9, 37 n.
  manuscript sources: fair copies 8–10, 28;
      musical sketches and draft of Prologue 9,
      65–6, 69; Nietzsche's copy of poem 8;
      prose draft 8, 27–28, 37; verse draft 8,
      37–8
  Prologue: Part 1: Norns scene 10 n., 27,
      37, 44; Part 2: leave-taking scene 27–8
  revisions 8–10, 29–30
  Waltraute scene 10 n.
  see also Wagner: *Nibelungen Mythus*
Sieglinde (Sigelind) 13 n., 35, 48, 207 n.
Siegmund (Sigemund) 13 n., 35, 48, 137 n.,
      151, 207 n.
sketch study 2–3
spear 28, 43, 141, 144
Spezia 'vision' 2 n., 11, 62–4, 66–7, 71
Stabreim 1, 37, 51, 93, 109
Strobel, Otto 9, 21, 24 n., 39 n., 40 n., 41 n.,
      42 n., 43 n., 63–4, 101 n., 102 n., 110 n.,
      115 n., 125 n., 150 n.
sword (Nothung) 28, 48
symphonic web 57

tarnhelm (tarncap) 34, 40–1, 78, 164–5, 170, 175, 177, 189
toad 40, 175
tonality 51–5
  Bailey and McCreless on 52
  Dahlhaus on 53–4
  Lorenz on 52
  Schenkerian analysts on 54–5
  Wagner on 51
  see also RHEINGOLD

Uhlig, Theodor 9–10, 12–13

Valhalla 26, 31, 35, 37, 79, 128, 130–2, 177, 181, 183, 185, 203, 208–9, 212
verse-melody 45
Volsungs 35
  see also Siegfried; Sieglinde; Siegmund

Wagner, Cosima 29 n., 30, 32 n., 62 n.
Wagner, Richard:
  Annals 62–3 n.
  Brown Book 63 n.
  changing attitude towards Siegfried, Wotan, and the Ring 27–31
  concert ending to Gluck's Iphigénie in Aulis 24
  Dresden library 27 n.
  fliegende Holländer, Der 78
  Götterdämmerung 16, 27, 37, 170, 191, 209; Norns scene 31, 65; parallels with Das Rheingold 31–3, 36–7; Siegfried's Funeral Procession 30, 48; see also Siegfried's Tod
  junge Siegfried, Der 28, 165; fair copies 9, 10; musical sketches 9; prose draft 9, 39, 197; prose sketches 9, 38–9, 197; revision 10, 28–9; verse draft 9
  Lohengrin 1, 28, 36, 93 n.
  Meistersinger von Nürnberg, Die 131
  Mittheilung an meine Freunde, Eine 9
  Nibelungen Mythus, Der, prose scenario by Wagner 37–8, 196–7; anonymous copy 8; draft (Die Nibelungensage) 7–8, 25–7, 33–6; fair copy (Die Sage von den Nibelungen) 7–8, 35 n.; Gesammelte Schriften edition (1871) 8
  on modulation 51
  Oper und Drama 9, 13, 45–7, 51, 55–8, 59, 130
  Red Pocket-Book 62–3 n.
  Ring des Nibelungen, Der: conflicting versions of text 16–17; evolution of text 6–11, 25–31; Feuerbachian and Schopenhauerian endings 29–30; title 10
  Siegfried 16, 34, 39, 87 n., 130, 188 n., 209
  Über die Anwendung der Musik auf das Drama 50–1
  Walküre, Die 16, 29, 35, 151, 204, 207 n.; fair copy of poem 10; prose draft 10, 43; prose sketches (initial) 10, 13, 39–41, 197; prose sketches (supplementary) 10, 13, 197–8; verse draft 10, 209
  Zukunftsmusik 51
  see also Rheingold; Siegfried's Tod
Wala 28, 39, 42, 197–8
  see also Erda
Warrack, John 47 n.
Weber, Carl Maria von 47 n.
Wellgunde 42–3, 90, 102–6, 119
Wesendonck, Mathilde 16 n., 20
Westernhagen, Curt von 20, 27 n., 63–4, 67, 71–2, 100 n., 122–3, 140, 154, 166, 179–80, 184, 194, 203, 209–10
Windell, George C. 29 n.
Windfahrer 39, 140
Wintle, Christopher 48 n., 55 n.
Woglinde (Bronnlinde, Woghilde) 17, 42–3, 66, 68 n., 77, 90, 93, 96, 100, 102–3, 108, 118–19, 122, 125
Wölfel, Friedrich 12
Wolzogen, Hans von 29 n., 47–9, 52
Wotan (Wodan) 8, 13 n., 14, 15 n., 16, 28, 30, 34–6, 37 n., 38–43, 47, 60, 68–9, 130–44, 146, 149–51, 153, 156–8, 160–1, 164–6, 172, 180, 183, 187–91, 193–205, 208–9, 212–13

Ymir 33